THE ROUTLEDGE ATLAS OF
BRITISH HISTORY

4th edition

Martin Gilbert

Routledge
Taylor & Francis Group

LONDON AND NEW YORK

First published 1968 as *Atlas of British History*
by Weidenfeld and Nicolson Ltd
Second edition published 1993

Third edition published 2003 by Routledge
Fourth edition published 2007 by Routledge
2 Park Square, Milton Park, Abingdon, Oxon, OX14 4RN

Simultaneously published in the USA and Canada
by Routledge
270 Madison Avenue, New York, NY 10016

Routledge is an imprint of the Taylor & Francis Group, an informa business

© 2007 Martin Gilbert

Typeset in Sabon by
Keystroke, 28 High Street, Tettenhall, Wolverhampton
Printed and bound in Great Britain by
Bell & Bain Ltd, Glasgow

British Library Cataloguing in Publication Data
A catalogue record for this book is available from the British Library

Library of Congress Cataloging in Publication Data
A catalog record for this book has been requested

ISBN 978–0–415–39550–2 (hbk)
ISBN 978–0–415–39551–9 (pbk)

Preface

The maps in this atlas are intended to provide a visual introduction to British history. I have used the word 'British' in its widest sense, including when relevant England, Scotland, Ireland and Wales, the changing overseas empire, the wars and treaties in which Britain engaged, the alliances in time of peace, the growth of industry and trade, and, on five of the maps, famine and plague.

The story of the British Isles forms the central theme. I have included maps to illustrate economic, social and political problems as well as territorial and military ones. I hope this atlas will help to show that there is more to British history than Hastings and Crécy, Blenheim and Waterloo, Passchendaele and Dunkirk, all of which moments of glory I have tried to put in their wider, and no less important, contexts.

For the maps covering the period before the Norman Conquest the sources are often conflicting on specific details. I have therefore drawn these maps on the basis of probability. In many instances precise knowledge of early frontiers is lacking. I have tried nevertheless to give a clear if also, of necessity, an approximate picture.

As British history advances from wattle huts to timber mansions, and thence on to steel and concrete, so too do the number and variety of facts available to the historian. This is reflected in the maps themselves. I have tried to avoid too complex or too cluttered a page; but a map cannot always satisfy all the demands made upon it, and only the reader can judge where clarity of design and sufficiency of information have been successfully combined.

I am under an obligation of gratitude to those historians and colleagues who kindly scrutinised my draft maps at an early stage, and who made many suggestions for their scope and improvement; in particular Dr J. M. Wallace-Hadrill, Dr Roger Highfield, Mr Ralph Davies, Mr T. F. R. G. Braun, Dr C. C. Davies and Miss Barbara Malament. When the maps were more completed, they were checked by Mr Adrian Scheps, Mr Edmund Ranallo, Mrs Elizabeth Goold, Mr Tony Lawdham and Mrs Jean Kelly, to all of whom my thanks are due.

Twenty-five years have passed since the first edition of this atlas. Within a year of its publication, violence in Northern Ireland re-emerged at the centre of the political stage: I have drawn three new maps to reflect this. The evolution of the European Community has led to growing British participation in Europe, culminating in the Maastricht Treaty of February 1992 and the Edinburgh Summit of December 1992, both of which are a part of the new maps. The Falkland Islands and Persian Gulf wars are included, as are the natural and man-made disasters of the past forty years. Also mapped are many of the problems and challenges of the 1990s, among them asylum, charity, homelessness, unemployment trade, education, religious diversity, and ethnic minorities. Britain's oil and gas resources are a new feature, as is the most recent phase of the reduction of British overseas possessions, her dwindling military and naval commitments world wide, and her new overseas responsibilities.

The first 118 maps were produced for this atlas by Arthur Banks and his team of cartographers, including Terry Bicknell. The new maps in this edition were produced by Tim Aspden and Robert Bradbrook; I have been helped considerably in the task of compiling them by Abe Eisenstat and Kay Thomson. For their help in providing material for this volume, I would also like to thank the Information Officer, Private Secretary's Office, Buckingham Palace; the Board of Deputies of British Jews, Central Information Desk; the Building Societies Association Press Office; the Lesotho High Commission; the Race Relations Commission; the Refugee Arrivals Project, London Airport; and the Royal Ulster Constabulary Press Office, Belfast.

24 June 1993

MARTIN GILBERT
Merton College, Oxford

Note to the Fourth Edition

Since the publication of the Third Edition in 2002, I have created sixteen new maps, spanning four years of British history. Their topics represent the main focal points of that short but intense period. Maps 169 and 170 cover the London suicide bombings of 7 July 2005. Four maps, maps 158 to 161, detail British exports and imports both to Europe and beyond. Maps 162 and 163 focus on British arms sales abroad, a growing facet of the national economy.

The question of immigration and new citizenship is addressed in five maps, maps 164 to 168. Map 171 follows two predecessors in the previous edition in setting out the details of British Government spending, in this map for the fiscal year 2005–6. Map 172 shows the home towns of British soldiers killed in southern Iraq between March 2003 and May 2006. Map 173 touches on the question of food miles and carbon emissions, an aspect of the global warming; and does so by showing the country of origin of some of the fresh fruit and vegetables brought thousands of miles by air to the British table.

I am grateful for information on the new maps to the Prime Minister's Office; the Home Office and its Statistical Bulletin; the Defence Export Services Organisation (DESA) website; the Campaign Against Arms Trade (CAAT); *The Times*; the *Sunday Times*; the *Daily Telegraph*; the *Guardian* and its website; Waitrose Holloway Road; and Richard Johnson of the *Guardian*.

My main debt is to Tim Aspden, the cartographer, who for two decades has created maps for my books and atlases, thus enabling me to fulfil the instruction I was given by one of my early teachers, to 'make history visible'.

Maps

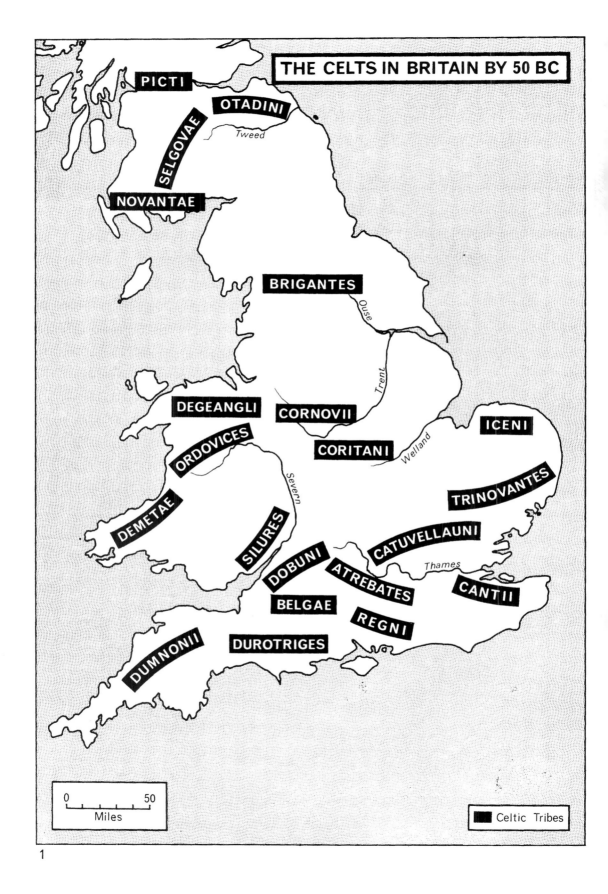

THE CELTS IN BRITAIN BY 50 BC

PICTI

OTADINI

Tweed

SELGOVAE

NOVANTAE

BRIGANTES

Ouse

Trent

DEGEANGLI

CORNOVII

ICENI

ORDOVICES

CORITANI

Welland

Severn

TRINOVANTES

DEMETAE

SILURES

CATUVELLAUNI

DOBUNI

Thames

ATREBATES

CANTII

BELGAE

REGNI

DUMNONII

DUROTRIGES

0   50
Miles

■ Celtic Tribes

1

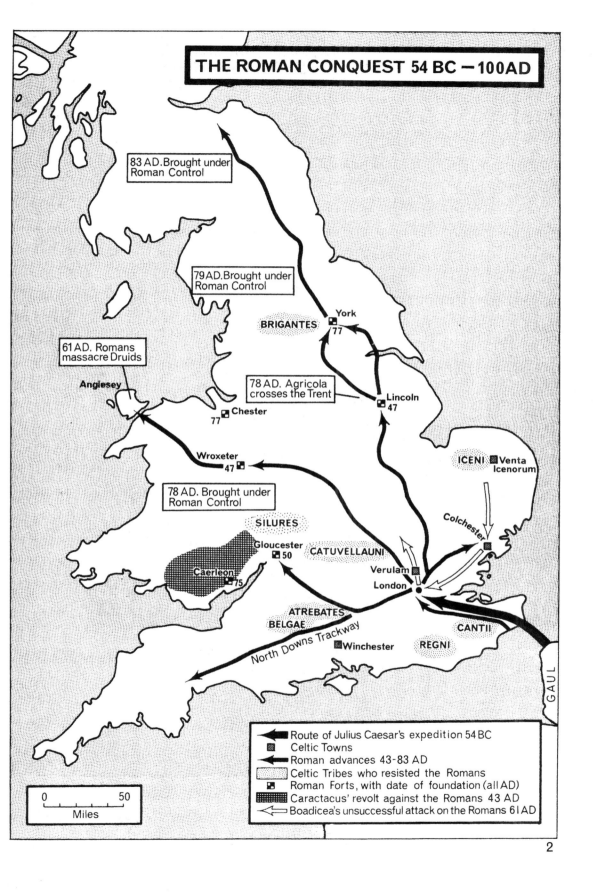

THE ROMAN CONQUEST 54 BC – 100 AD

83 AD. Brought under Roman Control

79 AD. Brought under Roman Control

BRIGANTES

York 77

61 AD. Romans massacre Druids

Anglesey

78 AD. Agricola crosses the Trent

Lincoln 47

Chester 77

Wroxeter 47

ICENI Venta Icenorum

78 AD. Brought under Roman Control

SILURES

Gloucester 50

CATUVELLAUNI

Colchester

Caerleon 75

Verulam

London

ATREBATES

BELGAE

North Downs Trackway

Winchester

CANTII

REGNI

GAUL

0   50
Miles

Route of Julius Caesar's expedition 54 BC
Celtic Towns
Roman advances 43-83 AD
Celtic Tribes who resisted the Romans
Roman Forts, with date of foundation (all AD)
Caractacus' revolt against the Romans 43 AD
Boadicea's unsuccessful attack on the Romans 61 AD

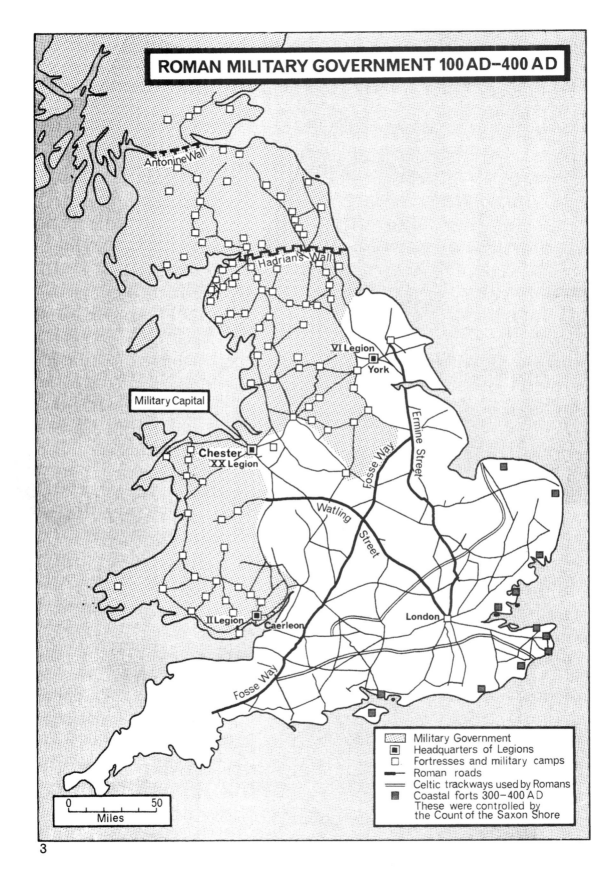

ROMAN MILITARY GOVERNMENT 100 AD–400 AD

Antonine Wall

Hadrian's Wall

VI Legion
York

Military Capital

Chester
XX Legion

Ermine Street

Fosse Way

Watling Street

II Legion
Caerleon

London

Fosse Way

Military Government
Headquarters of Legions
Fortresses and military camps
Roman roads
Celtic trackways used by Romans
Coastal forts 300–400 A D
These were controlled by
the Count of the Saxon Shore

0   50
Miles

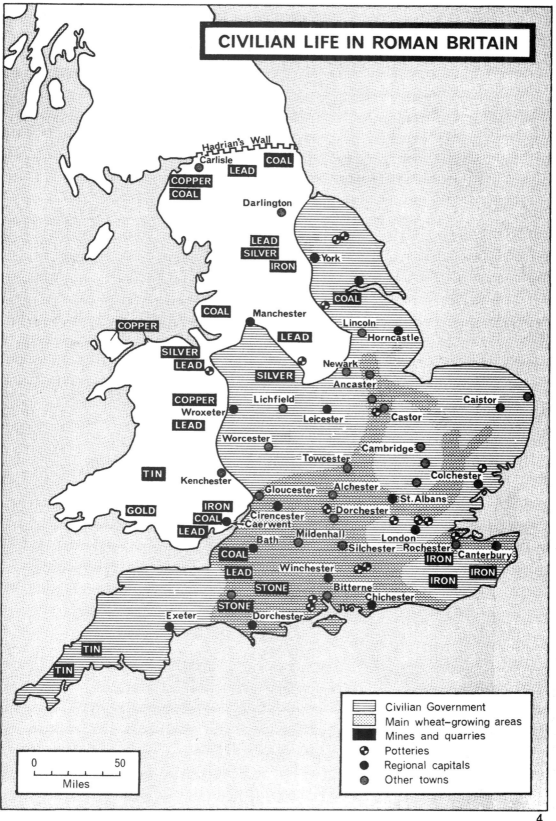

CIVILIAN LIFE IN ROMAN BRITAIN

Hadrian's Wall

Carlisle
COAL
LEAD

COPPER
COAL

Darlington

LEAD
SILVER
IRON

York

COAL

COAL

Manchester

LEAD

Lincoln

Horncastle

COPPER

SILVER
LEAD

SILVER

Newark

Ancaster

COPPER
LEAD

Lichfield

Leicester

Castor

Caistor

Wroxeter

Worcester

Cambridge

TIN

Kenchester

Towcester

Colchester

GOLD

IRON
COAL
LEAD

Gloucester

Alchester

St. Albans

Cirencester
Caerwent

Dorchester

COAL

Bath

Mildenhall

London

Rochester

LEAD

Silchester

IRON

Canterbury

STONE

Winchester

Bitterne

IRON

IRON

STONE

Dorchester

Chichester

Exeter

TIN

TIN

	Civilian Government
	Main wheat-growing areas
	Mines and quarries
	Potteries
	Regional capitals
	Other towns

0   50
Miles

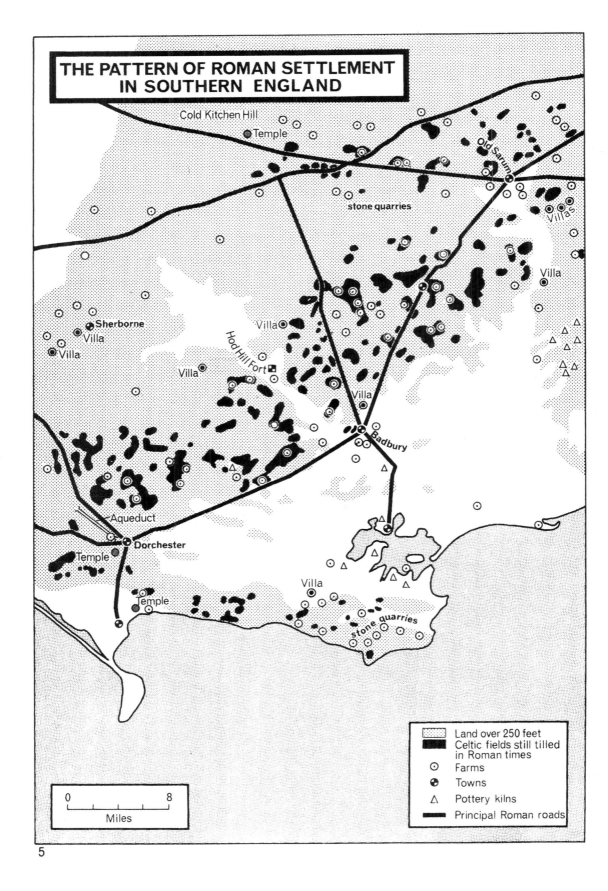

THE PATTERN OF ROMAN SETTLEMENT IN SOUTHERN ENGLAND

Cold Kitchen Hill

Temple

Old Sarum

stone quarries

Villas

Villa

Sherborne
Villa

Villa

Villa

Hod Hill Fort

Villa

Villa

Badbury

Aqueduct

Dorchester

Temple

Villa

Temple

stone quarries

Land over 250 feet
Celtic fields still tilled in Roman times
⊙ Farms
⊕ Towns
△ Pottery kilns
━ Principal Roman roads

0   8
Miles

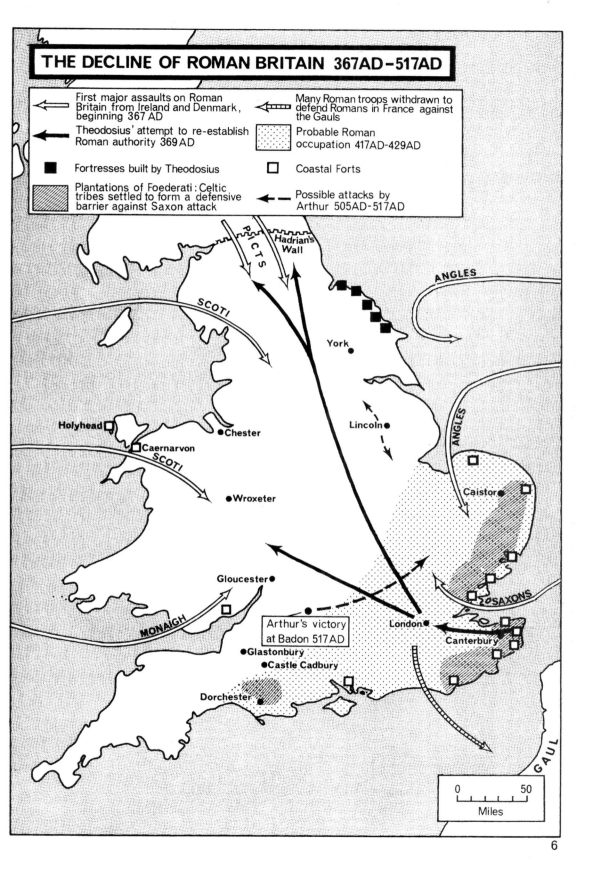

THE DECLINE OF ROMAN BRITAIN 367AD–517AD

First major assaults on Roman Britain from Ireland and Denmark, beginning 367 AD

Theodosius' attempt to re-establish Roman authority 369 AD

Fortresses built by Theodosius

Plantations of Foederati: Celtic tribes settled to form a defensive barrier against Saxon attack

Many Roman troops withdrawn to defend Romans in France against the Gauls

Probable Roman occupation 417AD–429AD

Coastal Forts

Possible attacks by Arthur 505AD–517AD

PICTS

Hadrian's Wall

ANGLES

SCOTI

York

ANGLES

Holyhead

Chester

Lincoln

Caernarvon

SCOTI

Caistor

Wroxeter

Gloucester

SAXONS

MONAIGH

Arthur's victory at Badon 517AD

London

Canterbury

Glastonbury

Castle Cadbury

Dorchester

GAUL

0   50
Miles

6

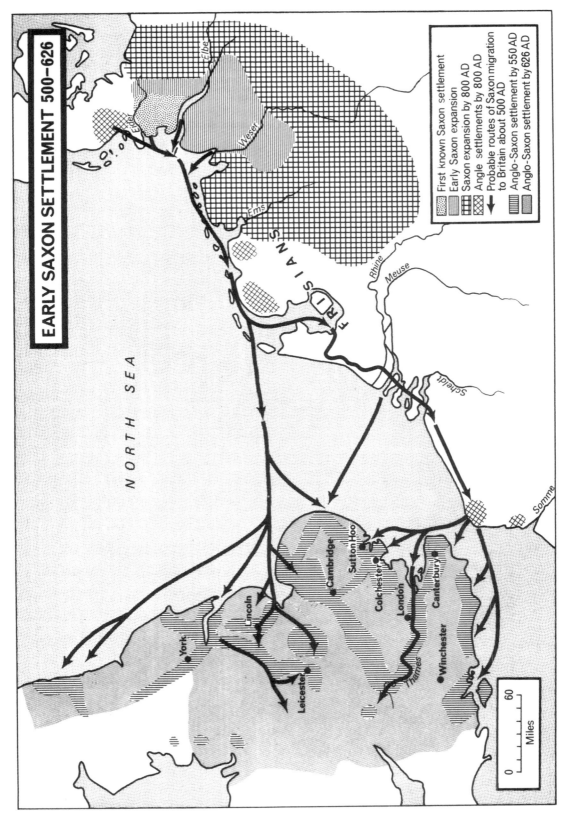

EARLY SAXON SETTLEMENT 500–626

Legend:
- First known Saxon settlement
- Early Saxon expansion
- Saxon expansion by 800 AD
- Angle settlements by 800 AD
- Probable routes of Saxon migration to Britain about 500 AD
- Anglo-Saxon settlement by 550 AD
- Anglo-Saxon settlement by 626 AD

NORTH SEA

FRISIANS

Elbe
Weser
Ems
Rhine
Meuse
Scheldt
Somme
Thames

Exeter

York
Lincoln
Leicester
Cambridge
Sutton Hoo
Colchester
London
Canterbury
Winchester

0   60
Miles

SAXON KINGDOMS AND BRETWALDASHIPS 630-829

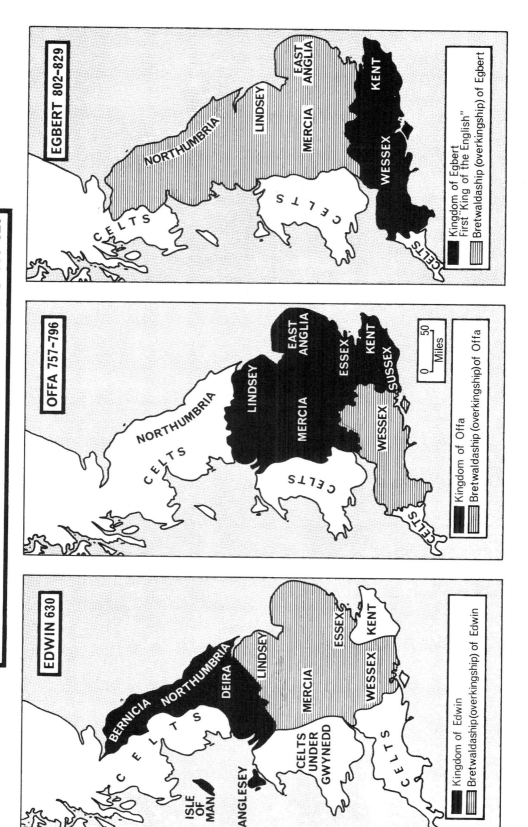

EDWIN 630

BERNICIA
NORTHUMBRIA
DEIRA
LINDSEY
MERCIA
ESSEX
KENT
WESSEX
CELTS
CELTS UNDER GWYNEDD
CELTS
ISLE OF MAN
ANGLESEY

Kingdom of Edwin
Bretwaldaship (overkingship) of Edwin

OFFA 757-796

NORTHUMBRIA
CELTS
LINDSEY
EAST ANGLIA
MERCIA
ESSEX
KENT
WESSEX
SUSSEX
CELTS
CELTS

0 50 Miles

Kingdom of Offa
Bretwaldaship (overkingship) of Offa

EGBERT 802-829

NORTHUMBRIA
CELTS
LINDSEY
EAST ANGLIA
MERCIA
KENT
WESSEX
CELTS
CELTS

Kingdom of Egbert First King of the English"
Bretwaldaship (overkingship) of Egbert

8

THE CHURCH 700–850

† Abercorn
Coldingham
Lindisfarne
† Melrose

L I N D I S F A R N E

WHITHORN

† Coquet Island

† Whithorn

Hexham †
HEXHAM

† Tynemouth
† Jarrow
Monkwearmouth

Hartlepool

† Gainford
Gilling
Lastingham †
Hackness†

Sockburn †
Whitby

Y O R K

† Ripon
York

Barrow †
Syddensis Civitas
(site not known)

LINDSEY

LICHFIELD

Elmham

Repton †
Lichfield
† Breedon
Peterborough †
Leicester
† Oundle
Ely

ELMHAM

Dunwich
† Bury St.
Edmunds

HEREFORD

Worcester

† Brixworth
LEICESTER

DUNWICH

Hereford

W O R C E S T E R

DORCHESTER

LONDON

† Malmesbury
Abingdon
Dorchester
Barking
London

ROCH
ESTER

Reculver

Minster

WINCHESTER

† Woking

Canterbury
CANTER
BURY

Dover
Folkestone
Lyminge

Glastonbury †
Sherborne

† Tisbury
Winchester
Nursling †

SELSEY

Selsey

SHERBORNE
Exeter †

Wimborne †

† Religious houses founded by 850

⊕ Double houses where monks and
nuns lived under the rule of an
abbess

— Approximate diocesan boundaries

● Diocesan seats

▨ Archbishoprics

0 — — — 50
Miles

9

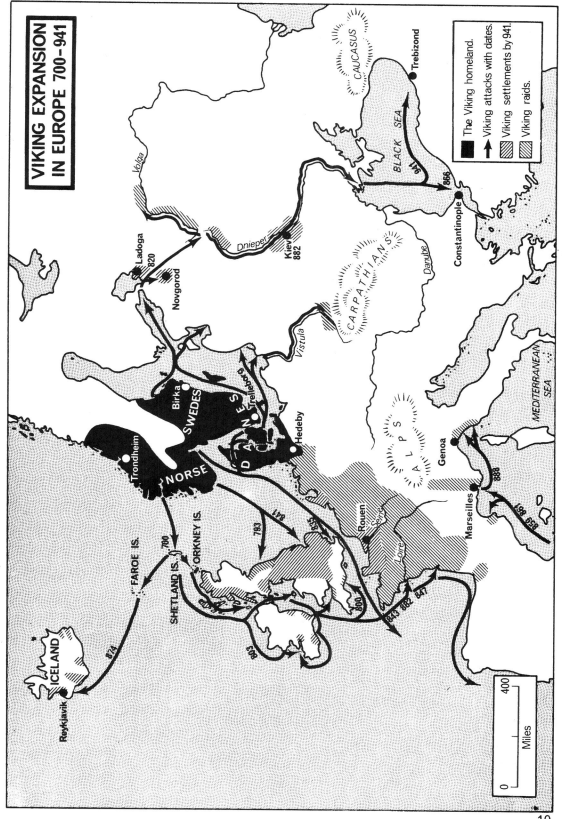

VIKING EXPANSION IN EUROPE 700–941

Key:
- The Viking homeland.
- ↑ Viking attacks with dates.
- Viking settlements by 941.
- Viking raids.

CAUCASUS

Trebizond

BLACK SEA

941

866

Constantinople

Volga

Ladoga
820

Novgorod

Dnieper

Kiev
882

Danube

CARPATHIANS

Vistula

NORSE

SWEDES

Birka

DANES

Trelleborg

Hedeby

ALPS

Genoa

Rouen
Seine

Marseilles

888

859

860

Trondheim

700

FAROE IS.

SHETLAND IS.

ORKNEY IS.

793

Loire

833 883 847

860

859

789

865

ICELAND

Reykjavik

874

0   400
Miles

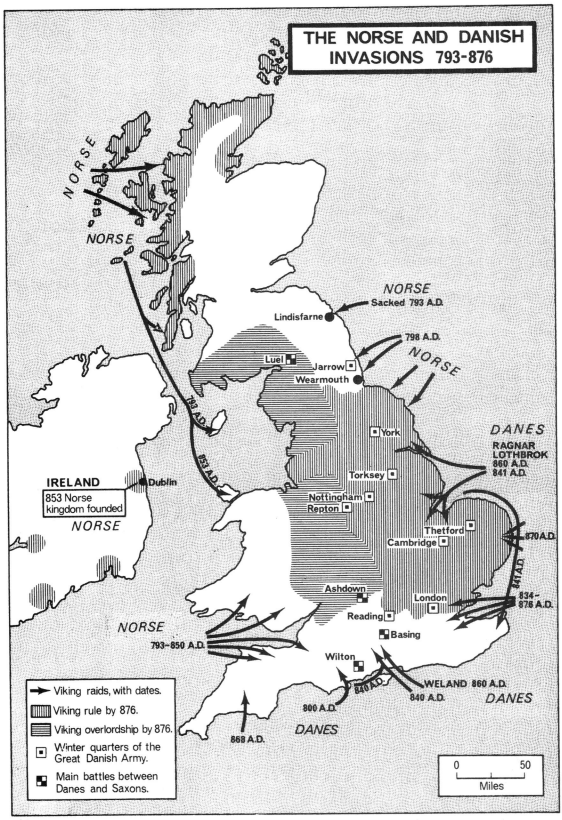

THE NORSE AND DANISH INVASIONS 793-876

NORSE

NORSE

NORSE
Sacked 793 A.D.
Lindisfarne

798 A.D.

NORSE

Luel

Jarrow
Wearmouth

York

DANES

RAGNAR
LOTHBROK
860 A.D.
841 A.D.

Torksey

IRELAND
853 Norse
kingdom founded
Dublin

Nottingham
Repton

NORSE

Thetford
Cambridge

870 A.D.

847 A.D.

834–
876 A.D.

Ashdown
London

Reading

Basing

WELAND 860 A.D.
840 A.D.

DANES

NORSE
793–850 A.D.

Wilton

840 A.D.

800 A.D.

Viking raids, with dates.

Viking rule by 876.

Viking overlordship by 876.

Winter quarters of the Great Danish Army.

Main battles between Danes and Saxons.

868 A.D.

DANES

0   50
Miles

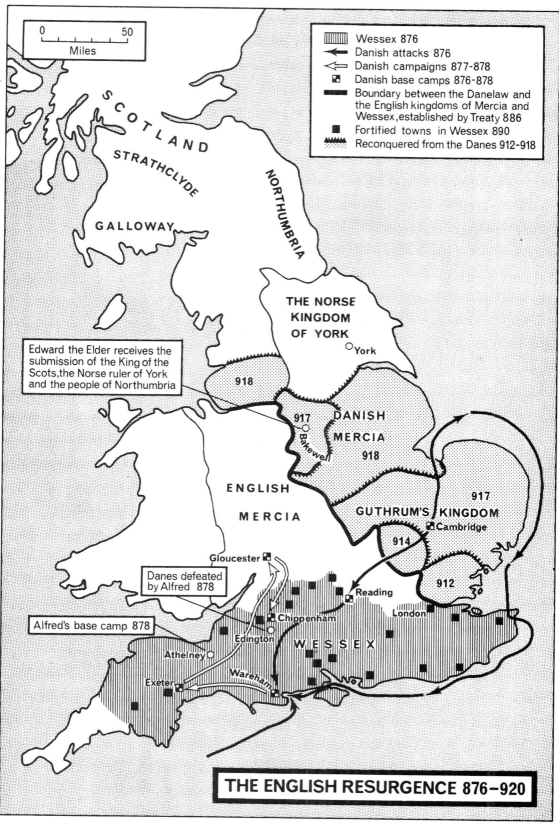

SCOTLAND

STRATHCLYDE

GALLOWAY

NORTHUMBRIA

THE NORSE
KINGDOM
OF YORK

○ York

Edward the Elder receives the
submission of the King of the
Scots, the Norse ruler of York
and the people of Northumbria

918

917
○ Bakewell

DANISH

MERCIA

918

ENGLISH

MERCIA

GUTHRUM'S KINGDOM

917

▢ Cambridge

914

Gloucester ▢

Danes defeated
by Alfred 878

912

Reading

London

Alfred's base camp 878

Chippenham

Edington

WESSEX

Athelney ○

Exeter ▢

Wareham

Legend

▥	Wessex 876
←	Danish attacks 876
⇐	Danish campaigns 877-878
▣	Danish base camps 876-878
━	Boundary between the Danelaw and the English kingdoms of Mercia and Wessex, established by Treaty 886
■	Fortified towns in Wessex 890
⣿	Reconquered from the Danes 912-918

Miles
0   50

THE ENGLISH RESURGENCE 876–920

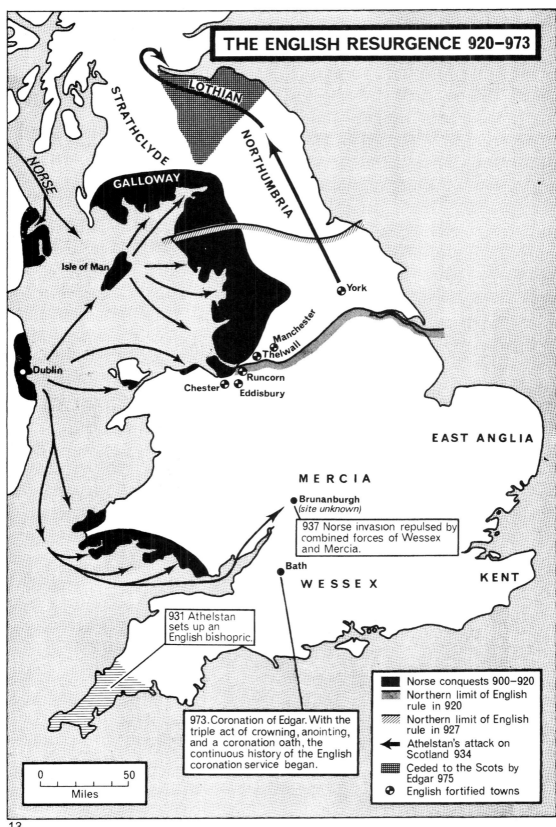

THE ENGLISH RESURGENCE 920–973

STRATHCLYDE

NORSE

LOTHIAN

GALLOWAY

NORTHUMBRIA

Isle of Man

York

Dublin

Manchester

Thelwall

Chester

Runcorn

Eddisbury

EAST ANGLIA

MERCIA

Brunanburgh
(site unknown)

937 Norse invasion repulsed by
combined forces of Wessex
and Mercia.

Bath

KENT

WESSEX

931 Athelstan
sets up an
English bishopric.

973. Coronation of Edgar. With the
triple act of crowning, anointing,
and a coronation oath, the
continuous history of the English
coronation service began.

Norse conquests 900–920

Northern limit of English
rule in 920

Northern limit of English
rule in 927

Athelstan's attack on
Scotland 934

Ceded to the Scots by
Edgar 975

English fortified towns

0   50
Miles

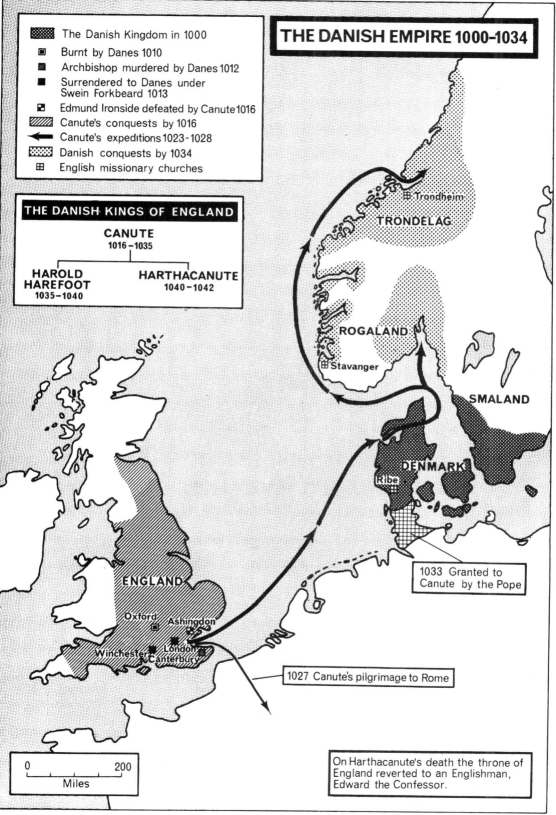

THE DANISH EMPIRE 1000–1034

Legend

- The Danish Kingdom in 1000
- Burnt by Danes 1010
- Archbishop murdered by Danes 1012
- Surrendered to Danes under Swein Forkbeard 1013
- Edmund Ironside defeated by Canute 1016
- Canute's conquests by 1016
- Canute's expeditions 1023-1028
- Danish conquests by 1034
- English missionary churches

THE DANISH KINGS OF ENGLAND

CANUTE
1016–1035

HAROLD HAREFOOT
1035–1040

HARTHACANUTE
1040–1042

Trondheim

TRONDELAG

ROGALAND

Stavanger

SMALAND

DENMARK

Ribe

1033 Granted to Canute by the Pope

ENGLAND

Oxford   Ashingdon

Winchester   London
Canterbury

1027 Canute's pilgrimage to Rome

On Harthacanute's death the throne of England reverted to an Englishman, Edward the Confessor.

0 _____ 200
Miles

BISHOPRICS AND MONASTERIES 1000-1066

ST. CUTHBERT'S SEE

Chester-le-Street
Carlisle
Durham

Y O R K
York

Barton-on-Humber

Lincoln

LICHFIELD
Lichfield

North Elmham
St Benet of Hulme
E L M H A M

D O R C H E S T E R

Ramsey
Ely
Bury St.Edmunds

HEREFORD
Worcester
Hereford

WORCESTER

Westbury on Trym
Abingdon
Dorchester

LONDON
London

CANTERBURY

RAMSBURY
Ramsbury

Rochester
Canterbury

Wells
WINCHESTER
Winchester

WELLS

SELSEY
Selsey
Sompting

Dover

CREDITON
Exeter
Crediton

Sherborne

SHERBORNE

ROCHESTER

ST. GERMANS

1058 joins with Ramsbury

1027 Sees join

Boundaries of the bishoprics
✤ Cathedral minsters
⊕ Cathedral monasteries
◉ Monasteries

0   50
Miles

15

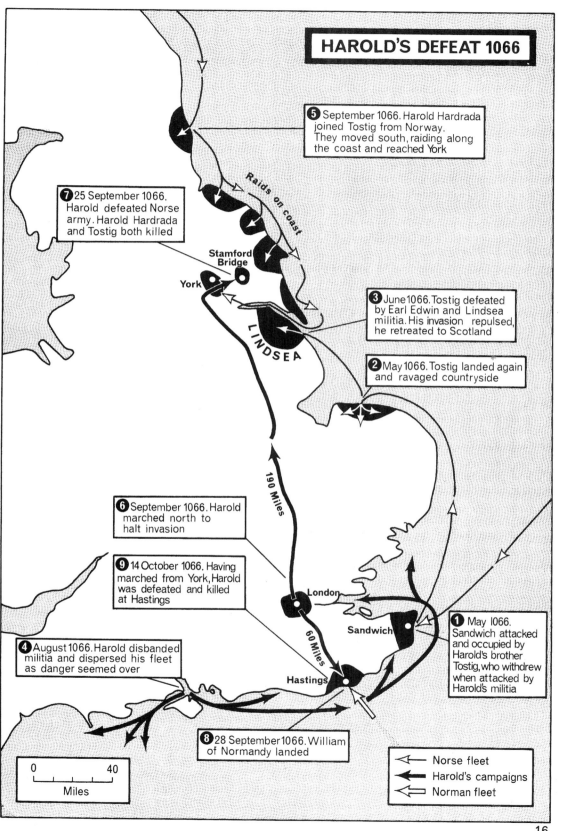

HAROLD'S DEFEAT 1066

5 September 1066. Harold Hardrada joined Tostig from Norway. They moved south, raiding along the coast and reached York

Raids on coast

7 25 September 1066. Harold defeated Norse army. Harold Hardrada and Tostig both killed

Stamford Bridge

York

LINDSEA

3 June 1066. Tostig defeated by Earl Edwin and Lindsea militia. His invasion repulsed, he retreated to Scotland

2 May 1066. Tostig landed again and ravaged countryside

190 Miles

6 September 1066. Harold marched north to halt invasion

9 14 October 1066. Having marched from York, Harold was defeated and killed at Hastings

London

Sandwich

1 May 1066. Sandwich attacked and occupied by Harold's brother Tostig, who withdrew when attacked by Harold's militia

60 Miles

4 August 1066. Harold disbanded militia and dispersed his fleet as danger seemed over

Hastings

8 28 September 1066. William of Normandy landed

0 — 40
Miles

⇐ Norse fleet
← Harold's campaigns
⇐ Norman fleet

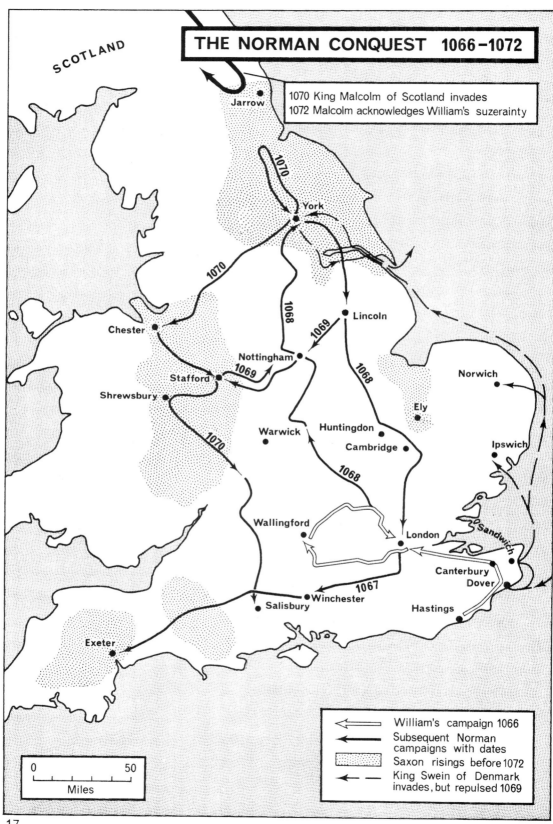

THE NORMAN CONQUEST 1066-1072

SCOTLAND

1070 King Malcolm of Scotland invades
1072 Malcolm acknowledges William's suzerainty

Jarrow

1070

York

1070

1068

Chester

1069

Lincoln

Nottingham

1069

Stafford

Shrewsbury

1068

Norwich

1070

Warwick

Ely

Huntingdon

Ipswich

Cambridge

1068

Wallingford

London

Sandwich

1068

Canterbury

Dover

1067

Winchester

Salisbury

Hastings

Exeter

William's campaign 1066
Subsequent Norman campaigns with dates
Saxon risings before 1072
King Swein of Denmark invades, but repulsed 1069

0   50
Miles

17

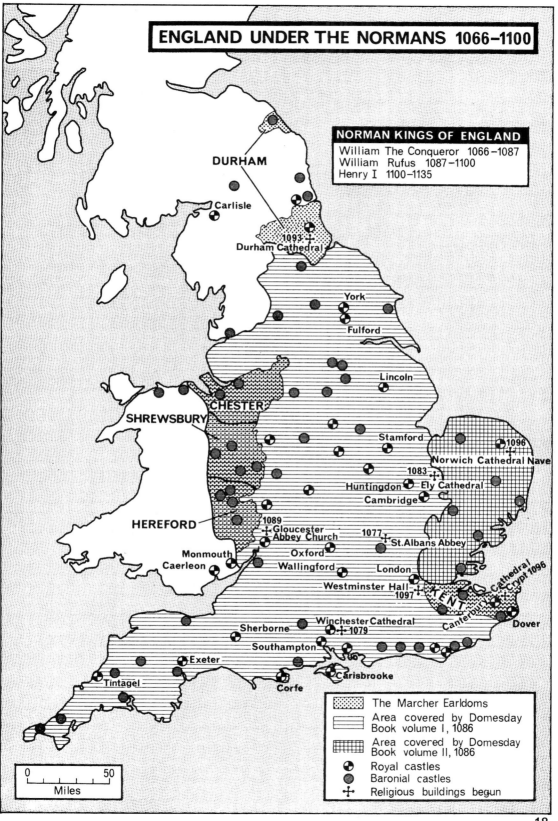

ENGLAND UNDER THE NORMANS 1066–1100

NORMAN KINGS OF ENGLAND
William The Conqueror 1066–1087
William Rufus 1087–1100
Henry I 1100–1135

DURHAM

Carlisle

1093
Durham Cathedral

York

Fulford

Lincoln

CHESTER

SHREWSBURY

Stamford

1096
Norwich Cathedral Nave

1083
Huntingdon   Ely Cathedral

Cambridge

HEREFORD

1089
Gloucester
Abbey Church

1077
St. Albans Abbey

Oxford

Monmouth
Caerleon

Wallingford

London

Westminster Hall
1097

KENT

Canterbury Cathedral
Crypt 1096

Winchester Cathedral
1079

Sherborne

Dover

Southampton

Exeter

Carisbrooke

Tintagel

Corfe

The Marcher Earldoms

Area covered by Domesday
Book volume I, 1086

Area covered by Domesday
Book volume II, 1086

Royal castles

Baronial castles

Religious buildings begun

0   50
Miles

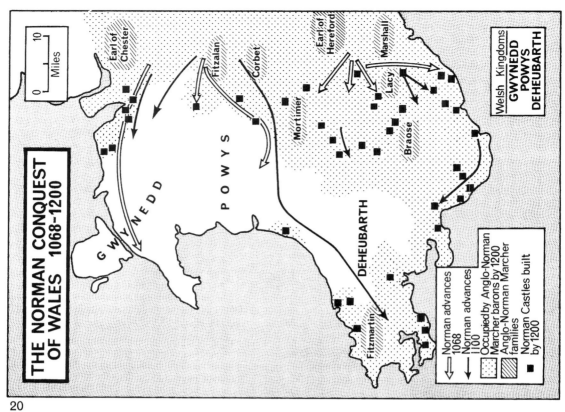

THE NORMAN CONQUEST OF WALES 1068–1200

Welsh Kingdoms
GWYNEDD
POWYS
DEHEUBARTH

Earl of Chester

Fitzalan

Corbet

Earl of Hereford

Marshall

Lacy

Mortimer

Braose

Fitzmartin

GWYNEDD

POWYS

DEHEUBARTH

0 — 10 Miles

Norman advances 1068
Norman advances 1100
Occupied by Anglo-Norman Marcher barons by 1200
Anglo-Norman Marcher families
Norman Castles built by 1200

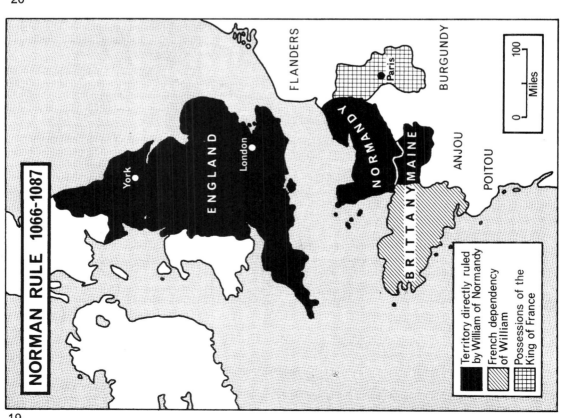

NORMAN RULE 1066–1087

FLANDERS

BURGUNDY

Paris

ENGLAND

York

London

NORMANDY

MAINE

ANJOU

POITOU

BRITTANY

0 — 100 Miles

Territory directly ruled by William of Normandy
French dependency of William
Possessions of the King of France

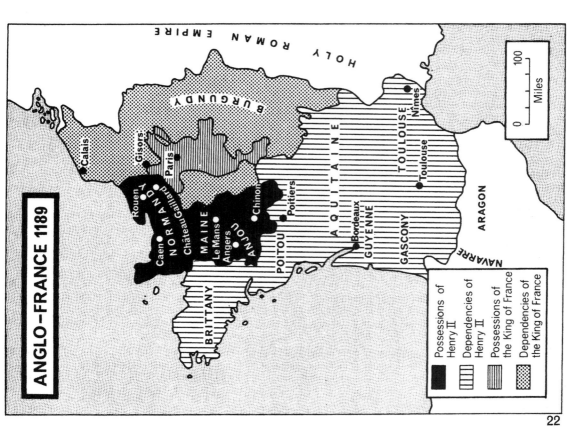

ANGLO–FRANCE 1189

HOLY ROMAN EMPIRE

BURGUNDY

Calais
Gisors
Rouen
NORMANDY
Château Gaillard
Paris
Caen
Le Mans
MAINE
Angers
ANJOU
Chinon
BRITTANY
POITOU
Poitiers
AQUITAINE
Bordeaux
GUYENNE
GASCONY
TOULOUSE
Toulouse
Nîmes
ARAGON
NAVARRE

	Possessions of Henry II
	Dependencies of Henry II
	Possessions of the King of France
	Dependencies of the King of France

0   100
Miles

22

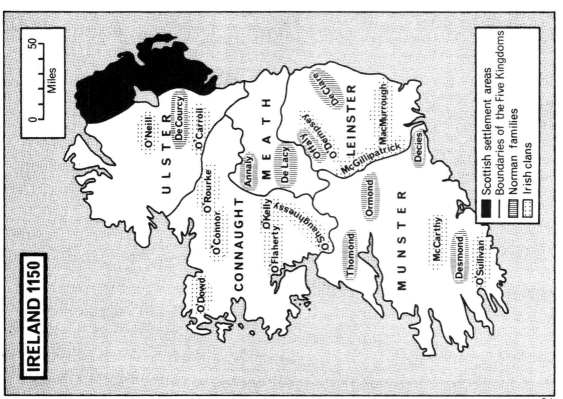

IRELAND 1150

0   50
Miles

ULSTER
O'Neill
De Courcy
O'Carroll
O'Rourke
O'Connor
CONNAUGHT
O'Dowd
O'Flaherty
O'Kelly
O'Shaughnessy
Annaly
MEATH
De Lacy
O'Tail
O'Dempsey
De Clare
LEINSTER
MacMurrough
McGillipatrick
Decies
Thomond
Ormond
MUNSTER
McCarthy
Desmond
O'Sullivan

	Scottish settlement areas
	Boundaries of the Five Kingdoms
	Norman families
	Irish clans

21

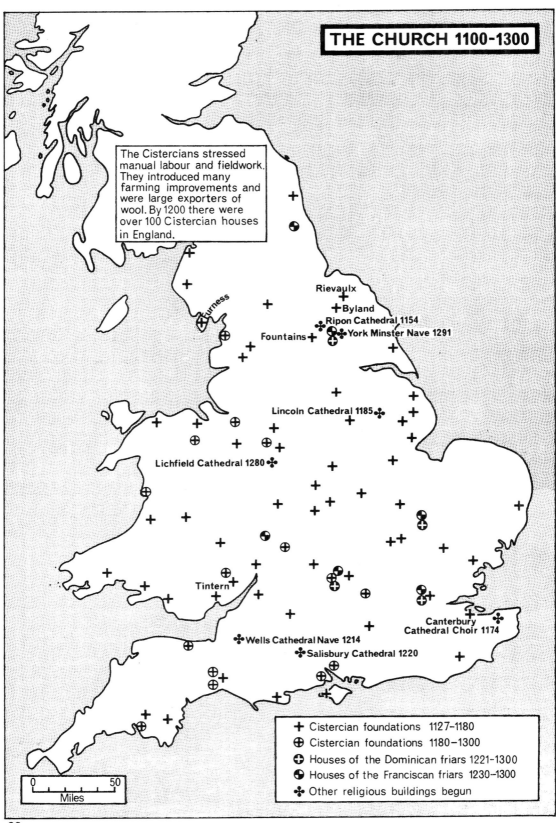

THE CHURCH 1100-1300

The Cistercians stressed manual labour and fieldwork. They introduced many farming improvements and were large exporters of wool. By 1200 there were over 100 Cistercian houses in England.

Furness

Rievaulx
Byland
Ripon Cathedral 1154
York Minster Nave 1291
Fountains

Lincoln Cathedral 1185

Lichfield Cathedral 1280

Tintern

Canterbury
Cathedral Choir 1174

Wells Cathedral Nave 1214
Salisbury Cathedral 1220

✚ Cistercian foundations 1127–1180
⊕ Cistercian foundations 1180–1300
⊕ Houses of the Dominican friars 1221–1300
⊖ Houses of the Franciscan friars 1230–1300
✤ Other religious buildings begun

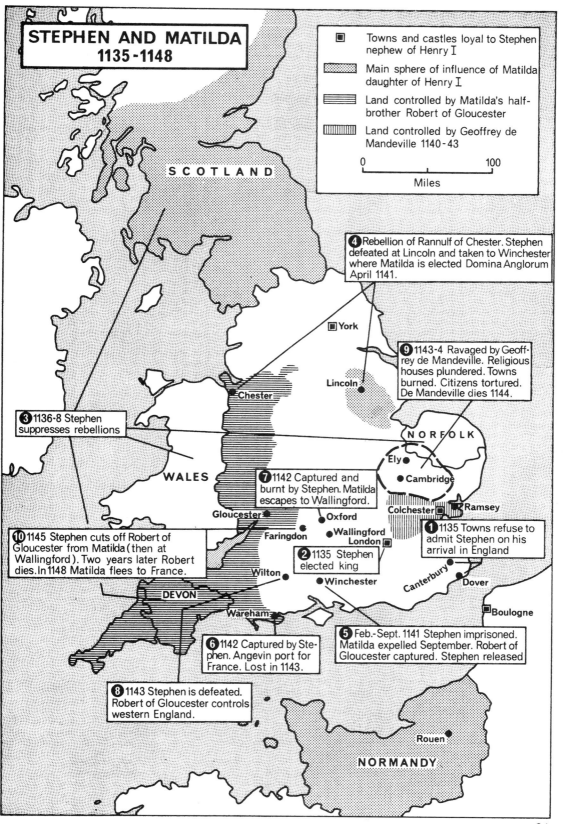

STEPHEN AND MATILDA
1135-1148

Legend:

◧ Towns and castles loyal to Stephen nephew of Henry I

▨ Main sphere of influence of Matilda daughter of Henry I

▤ Land controlled by Matilda's half-brother Robert of Gloucester

▥ Land controlled by Geoffrey de Mandeville 1140-43

0 — 100 Miles

SCOTLAND

❹ Rebellion of Rannulf of Chester. Stephen defeated at Lincoln and taken to Winchester where Matilda is elected Domina Anglorum April 1141.

❾ 1143-4 Ravaged by Geoffrey de Mandeville. Religious houses plundered. Towns burned. Citizens tortured. De Mandeville dies 1144.

◧ York

Lincoln

❸ 1136-8 Stephen suppresses rebellions

Chester

NORFOLK

Ely ●

● Cambridge

WALES

❼ 1142 Captured and burnt by Stephen. Matilda escapes to Wallingford.

Colchester ◧ ◧ Ramsey

Gloucester ◧

● Oxford

Faringdon ● Wallingford
London ◧

❶ 1135 Towns refuse to admit Stephen on his arrival in England

❿ 1145 Stephen cuts off Robert of Gloucester from Matilda (then at Wallingford). Two years later Robert dies. In 1148 Matilda flees to France.

❷ 1135 Stephen elected king

Wilton ●

● Winchester

Canterbury ● Dover

DEVON

Wareham ●

◧ Boulogne

❻ 1142 Captured by Stephen. Angevin port for France. Lost in 1143.

❺ Feb.-Sept. 1141 Stephen imprisoned. Matilda expelled September. Robert of Gloucester captured. Stephen released

❽ 1143 Stephen is defeated. Robert of Gloucester controls western England.

Rouen ●

NORMANDY

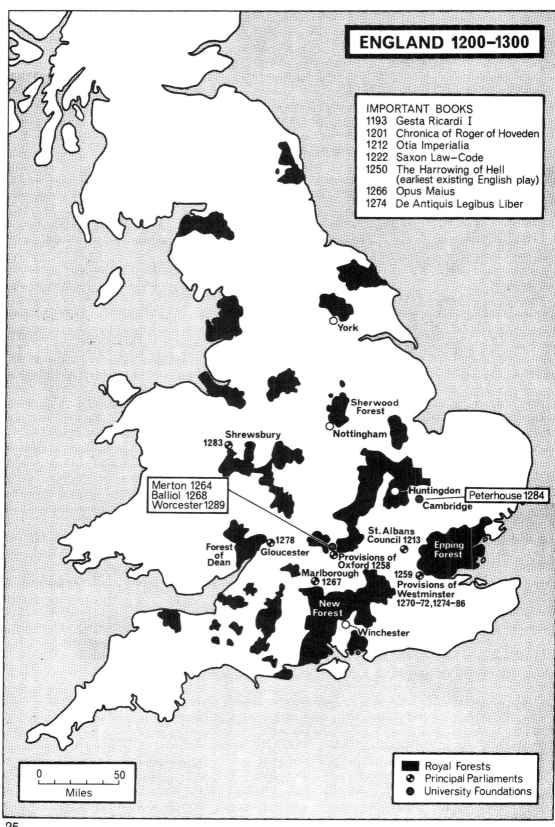

ENGLAND 1200–1300

IMPORTANT BOOKS
1193 Gesta Ricardi I
1201 Chronica of Roger of Hoveden
1212 Otia Imperialia
1222 Saxon Law–Code
1250 The Harrowing of Hell
(earliest existing English play)
1266 Opus Maius
1274 De Antiquis Legibus Liber

York

Sherwood
Forest

Nottingham

Shrewsbury
1283

Merton 1264
Balliol 1268
Worcester 1289

Huntingdon

Peterhouse 1284

Cambridge

St. Albans
Council 1213

Epping
Forest

1278
Gloucester

Forest
of
Dean

Provisions of
Oxford 1258

Marlborough
1267

1259
Provisions of
Westminster
1270–72, 1274–86

New
Forest

Winchester

0   50
Miles

■ Royal Forests
⊕ Principal Parliaments
● University Foundations

THE ECONOMY 1200–1300

1245 Papal money-raiser expelled from England by king, clergy and barons
1274 Anglo-Flanders Commercial Treaty
1275 King to receive duty on wool
1280 German merchants in England form a Hansa
1290 Expulsion of the Jews from England
1299 Act to repress bad coinage passed

York
blues
Beverley

Lincoln scarlets
Lincoln

Nottingham

Stamfords
Norwich
Leicester
Stamford
Somersham
Coventry
Huntingdon
Ramsey
Northampton
Bury St.Edmunds
Worcester
Cambridge
Ipswich
Warwick
Sudbury
Bedford
Gloucester
russets
Colchester
russets
Chepstow
russets
Oxford
Wallingford
London
Bristol
Marlborough
Sandwich
Devizes
Canterbury
russets
Hythe
Wilton
Winchester
Romney
Rye
Salisbury
Winchelsea
Hastings
Dover

Cloth producing areas with names of cloth
Towns with weavers guilds by 1200
The Cinque Ports: special liberties granted 1278
The liberties of Chepstow, Ramsey and Somersham
Towns with Jewish settlements where Jewish loans were recorded 1190–1290

0   50
Miles

26

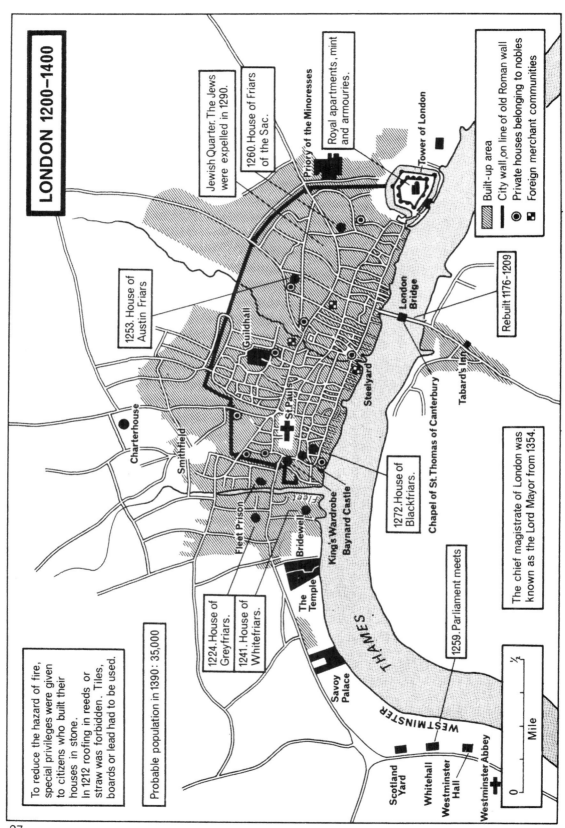

LONDON 1200-1400

To reduce the hazard of fire, special privileges were given to citizens who built their houses in stone.
In 1212 roofing in reeds or straw was forbidden. Tiles, boards or lead had to be used.

Probable population in 1390: 35,000

1224. House of Greyfriars.

1241. House of Whitefriars.

The Temple

Savoy Palace

Scotland Yard

Whitehall

Westminster Hall

Westminster Abbey

WESTMINSTER

THAMES

0   Mile   ½

1259. Parliament meets

The chief magistrate of London was known as the Lord Mayor from 1354.

1272. House of Blackfriars.

Chapel of St.Thomas of Canterbury

Rebuilt 1176-1209

London Bridge

Tabard's Inn

Steelyard

St.Paul's

Guildhall

King's Wardrobe
Baynard Castle

Bridewell

Fleet Prison

Fleet

Charterhouse

Smithfield

1253. House of Austin Friars

Jewish Quarter. The Jews were expelled in 1290.

1260. House of Friars of the Sac.

Priory of the Minoresses

Royal apartments, mint and armouries.

Tower of London

Built-up area

City wall, on line of old Roman wall

Private houses belonging to nobles

Foreign merchant communities

27

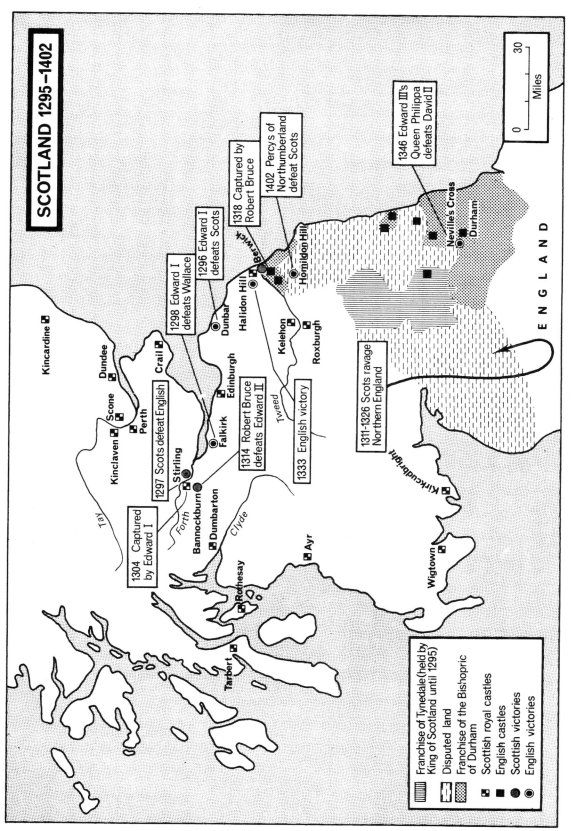

SCOTLAND 1295–1402

Kincardine

Dundee

Scone

Kinclaven

Perth

Tay

1297 Scots defeat English

Stirling

Crail

Falkirk

Edinburgh

1304 Captured by Edward I

Forth

Bannockburn

Dumbarton

Clyde

Rothesay

Ayr

Tarbert

Wigtown

Kirkcudbright

1298 Edward I defeats Wallace

1296 Edward I defeats Scots

1318 Captured by Robert Bruce

1402 Percys of Northumberland defeat Scots

Berwick

Dunbar

Halidon Hill

Kelehon

Roxburgh

Tweed

1314 Robert Bruce defeats Edward II

1333 English victory

1311-1326 Scots ravage Northern England

Homildon Hill

1346 Edward III's Queen Philippa defeats David II

Nevilles Cross

Durham

ENGLAND

0   30
Miles

Franchise of Tynedale (held by King of Scotland until 1295)

Disputed land

Franchise of the Bishopric of Durham

Scottish royal castles

English castles

Scottish victories

English victories

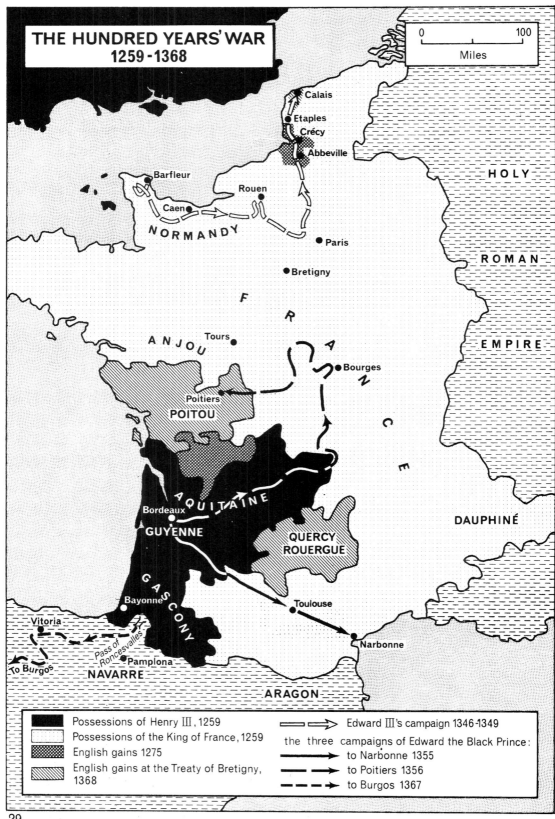

THE HUNDRED YEARS' WAR
1259-1368

0   100

Miles

Calais

Etaples

Crécy

Abbeville

HOLY

Barfleur

Rouen

ROMAN

Caen

N O R M A N D Y

Paris

Bretigny

F
R

EMPIRE

A N J O U

Tours

A
N

Bourges

Poitiers

C

POITOU

E

DAUPHINÉ

A Q U I T A I N E

Bordeaux

GUYENNE

QUERCY
ROUERGUE

G
A
S
C
O
N
Y

Bayonne

Toulouse

Vitoria

Pass of
Roncesvalles

Narbonne

To Burgos

Pamplona

NAVARRE

ARAGON

▰ Possessions of Henry III, 1259	⟹ Edward III's campaign 1346-1349
⠂ Possessions of the King of France, 1259	the three campaigns of Edward the Black Prince:
▨ English gains 1275	→ to Narbonne 1355
▧ English gains at the Treaty of Bretigny, 1368	— → to Poitiers 1356
	- → to Burgos 1367

29

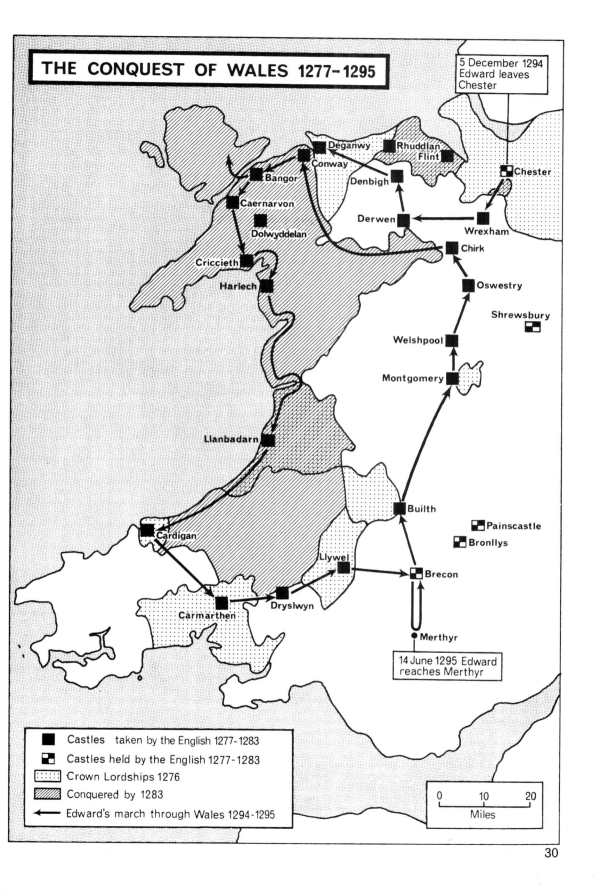

THE CONQUEST OF WALES 1277-1295

5 December 1294
Edward leaves
Chester

Deganwy
Conway
Rhuddlan
Flint
Chester
Bangor
Denbigh
Caernarvon
Derwen
Dolwyddelan
Wrexham
Criccieth
Chirk
Harlech
Oswestry
Shrewsbury
Welshpool
Montgomery
Llanbadarn
Builth
Painscastle
Cardigan
Bronllys
Llywel
Brecon
Carmarthen
Dryslwyn
Merthyr

14 June 1295 Edward
reaches Merthyr

■ Castles   taken by the English 1277-1283
◧ Castles held by the English 1277-1283
⠿ Crown Lordships 1276
▨ Conquered by 1283
→ Edward's march through Wales 1294-1295

0   10   20
Miles

30

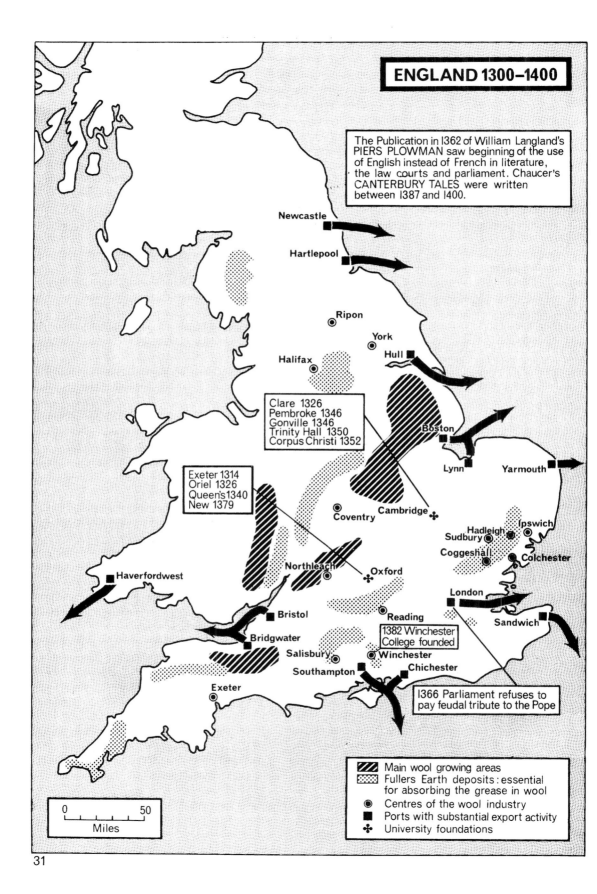

ENGLAND 1300–1400

The Publication in 1362 of William Langland's PIERS PLOWMAN saw beginning of the use of English instead of French in literature, the law courts and parliament. Chaucer's CANTERBURY TALES were written between 1387 and 1400.

Newcastle

Hartlepool

Ripon

York

Hull

Halifax

Clare 1326
Pembroke 1346
Gonville 1346
Trinity Hall 1350
Corpus Christi 1352

Boston

Lynn

Yarmouth

Exeter 1314
Oriel 1326
Queen's 1340
New 1379

Coventry

Cambridge

Ipswich

Hadleigh

Sudbury

Coggeshall

Colchester

Haverfordwest

Northleach

Oxford

London

Sandwich

Bristol

Reading

Bridgwater

1382 Winchester
College founded

Salisbury

Winchester

Southampton

Chichester

Exeter

1366 Parliament refuses to
pay feudal tribute to the Pope

///// Main wool growing areas

::::: Fullers Earth deposits: essential
for absorbing the grease in wool

◉ Centres of the wool industry

■ Ports with substantial export activity

✤ University foundations

0   50
Miles

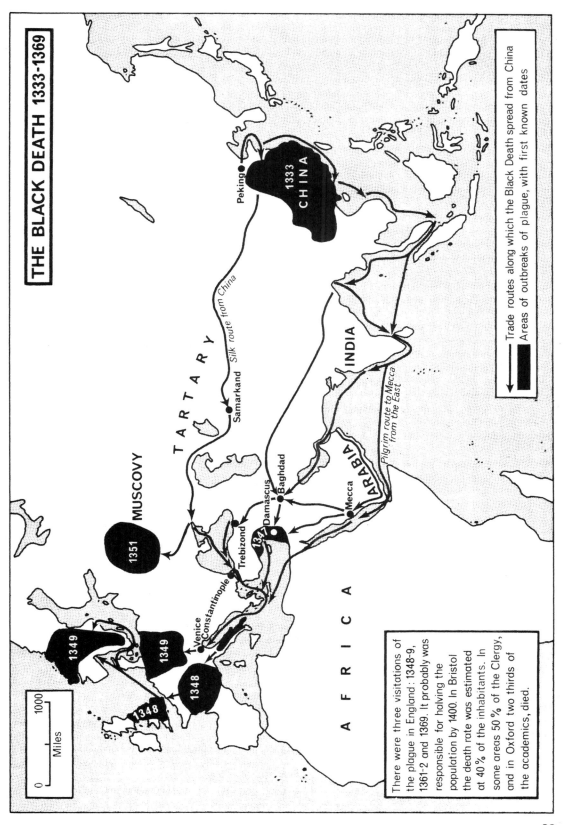

THE BLACK DEATH 1333-1369

1333 CHINA

Peking

Samarkand · Silk route from China

T A R T A R Y

INDIA

ARABIA

Pilgrim route to Mecca from the East

Baghdad

Mecca

Damascus

1347

MUSCOVY

1351

Trebizond

Constantinople

Venice

A F R I C A

1349

1349

1348

1348

1000

Miles

0

→ Trade routes along which the Black Death spread from China

■ Areas of outbreaks of plague, with first known dates

There were three visitations of the plague in England : 1348-9, 1361-2 and 1369. It probably was responsible for halving the population by 1400. In Bristol the death rate was estimated at 40% of the inhabitants. In some areas 50% of the Clergy, and in Oxford two thirds of the academics, died.

32

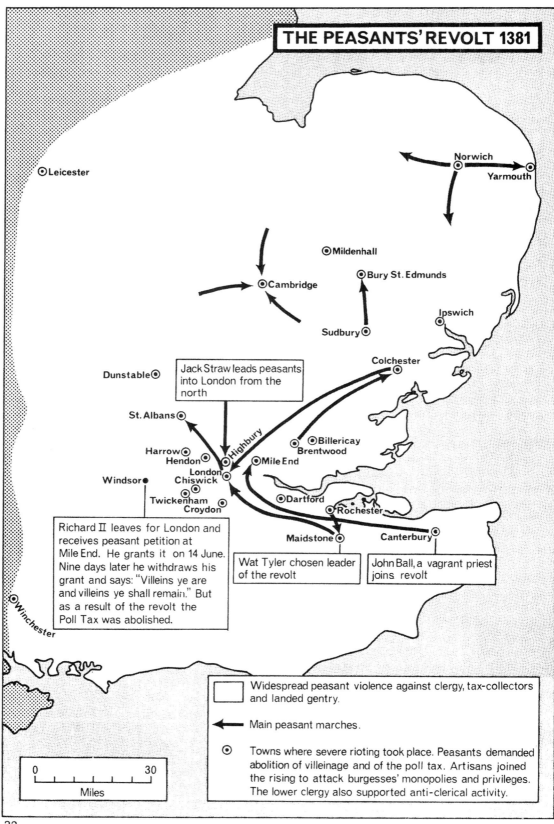

THE PEASANTS' REVOLT 1381

Leicester

Norwich

Yarmouth

Mildenhall

Bury St. Edmunds

Cambridge

Sudbury

Ipswich

Colchester

Jack Straw leads peasants into London from the north

Dunstable

St. Albans

Highbury

Billericay

Brentwood

Harrow

Hendon

Mile End

London

Chiswick

Windsor

Twickenham

Croydon

Dartford

Rochester

Richard II leaves for London and receives peasant petition at Mile End. He grants it on 14 June. Nine days later he withdraws his grant and says: "Villeins ye are and villeins ye shall remain." But as a result of the revolt the Poll Tax was abolished.

Winchester

Maidstone

Canterbury

Wat Tyler chosen leader of the revolt

John Ball, a vagrant priest joins revolt

Widespread peasant violence against clergy, tax-collectors and landed gentry.

Main peasant marches.

Towns where severe rioting took place. Peasants demanded abolition of villeinage and of the poll tax. Artisans joined the rising to attack burgesses' monopolies and privileges. The lower clergy also supported anti-clerical activity.

0   30

Miles

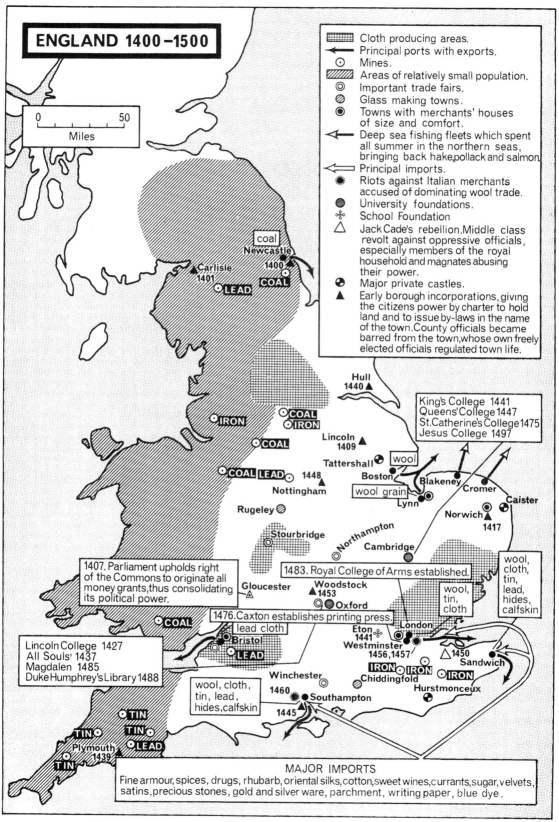

ENGLAND 1400–1500

0 ─────── 50
Miles

Legend:

▦	Cloth producing areas.
←	Principal ports with exports.
⊙	Mines.
◎	Areas of relatively small population.
◎	Important trade fairs.
◉	Glass making towns.
◉	Towns with merchants' houses of size and comfort.
⇐	Deep sea fishing fleets which spent all summer in the northern seas, bringing back hake, pollack and salmon.
⇐	Principal imports.
✳	Riots against Italian merchants accused of dominating wool trade.
⊖	University foundations.
⚭	School Foundation
△	Jack Cade's rebellion. Middle class revolt against oppressive officials, especially members of the royal household and magnates abusing their power.
◑	Major private castles.
▲	Early borough incorporations, giving the citizens power by charter to hold land and to issue by-laws in the name of the town. County officials became barred from the town, whose own freely elected officials regulated town life.

coal
Newcastle
1400
COAL

Carlisle
1401
⊙**LEAD**

⊙**IRON**   ⊙**COAL**
⊙**IRON**

⊙**COAL**

Lincoln
1409 ▲

Hull
1440 ▲

King's College 1441
Queens' College 1447
St. Catherine's College 1475
Jesus College 1497

⊙**COAL** **LEAD**⊙   1448 ▲
Nottingham

Tattershall ◑   wool

Boston
Blakeney   **Cromer**
wool grain
Lynn   **Caister**

Norwich ◉ ▲
1417

Rugeley ◉

Stourbridge ◎

Northampton ◎   **Cambridge**

1483. Royal College of Arms established.

1407. Parliament upholds right of the Commons to originate all money grants, thus consolidating its political power.

Gloucester △

Woodstock ▲
1453
◎ ◉ **Oxford**

wool, tin, cloth

wool, cloth, tin, lead, hides, calfskin

1476. Caxton establishes printing press.

⊙**COAL**

lead cloth
Bristol ◎
⊙**LEAD**

Eton ⚭
1441
Westminster
1456, 1457
London
△ 1450
Sandwich

IRON⊙ ⊙**IRON**
Chiddingfold ⊙**IRON**
Hurstmonceux ◑

Lincoln College 1427
All Souls' 1437
Magdalen 1485
Duke Humphrey's Library 1488

Winchester ◎
1460 ✳
Southampton ◉
1445 ▲

wool, cloth, tin, lead, hides, calfskin

⊙**TIN**

⊙**TIN**   ⊙**TIN**
⊙**LEAD**

Plymouth
1439 ▲
⊙**TIN**

MAJOR IMPORTS
Fine armour, spices, drugs, rhubarb, oriental silks, cotton, sweet wines, currants, sugar, velvets, satins, precious stones, gold and silver ware, parchment, writing paper, blue dye.

34

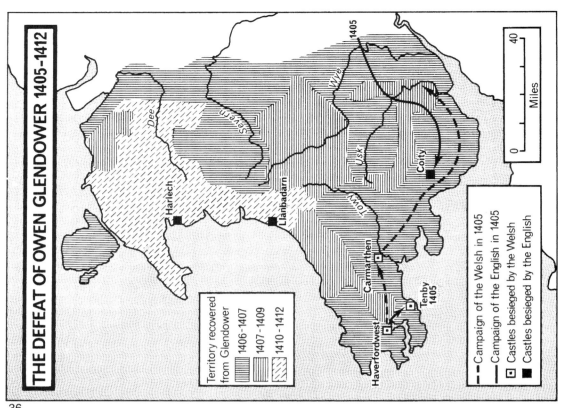

THE DEFEAT OF OWEN GLENDOWER 1405-1412

Territory recovered from Glendower
- 1406-1407
- 1407-1409
- 1410-1412

- - - Campaign of the Welsh in 1405
——— Campaign of the English in 1405
☐ Castles besieged by the Welsh
■ Castles besieged by the English

Harlech
Llanbadarn
Dee
Severn
Wye
Usk
Towy
Coity
Carmarthen
Tenby 1405
Haverfordwest
1405

0   40
Miles

36

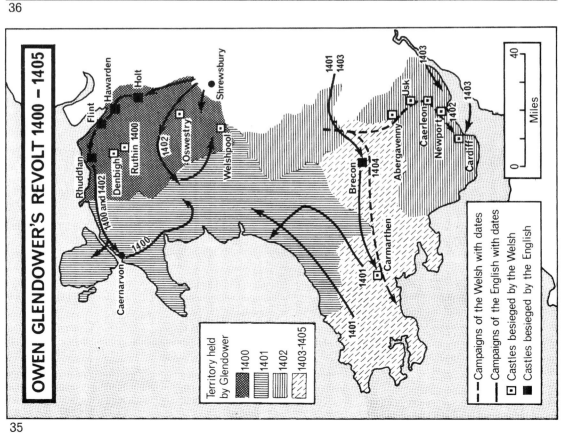

OWEN GLENDOWER'S REVOLT 1400 – 1405

Territory held by Glendower
- 1400
- 1401
- 1402
- 1403-1405

- - - Campaigns of the Welsh with dates
——— Campaigns of the English with dates
☐ Castles besieged by the Welsh
■ Castles besieged by the English

Flint
Hawarden
Holt
Rhuddlan
1400 and 1402
1400
Caernarvon
Denbigh
Ruthin 1400
Oswestry
1402
Welshpool
Shrewsbury
1401
1401
1403
Brecon
1404
Carmarthen
Abergavenny
Usk
Caerleon
Newport
1402
Cardiff
1403
1403
1401
1403

0   40
Miles

35

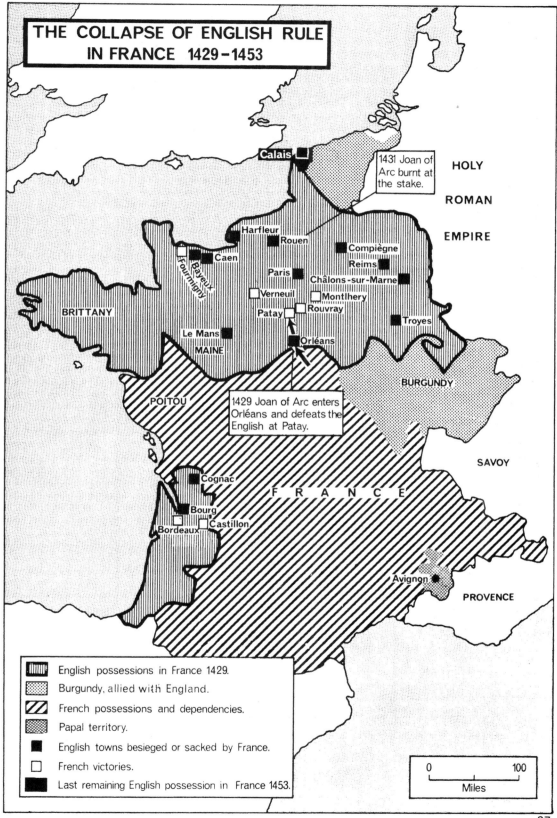

THE COLLAPSE OF ENGLISH RULE
IN FRANCE 1429–1453

1431 Joan of Arc burnt at the stake.

HOLY

ROMAN

EMPIRE

Calais

Harfleur
Rouen
Compiègne
Reims
Bayeux
Caen
Fourmigny
Paris
Châlons-sur-Marne
Verneuil
Montlhery
Patay
Rouvray
Troyes
BRITTANY
Le Mans
MAINE
Orléans

1429 Joan of Arc enters Orléans and defeats the English at Patay.

BURGUNDY

POITOU

SAVOY

F R A N C E

Cognac

Bourg
Castillon
Bordeaux

Avignon

PROVENCE

English possessions in France 1429.

Burgundy, allied with England.

French possessions and dependencies.

Papal territory.

English towns besieged or sacked by France.

French victories.

Last remaining English possession in France 1453.

0   100
Miles

37

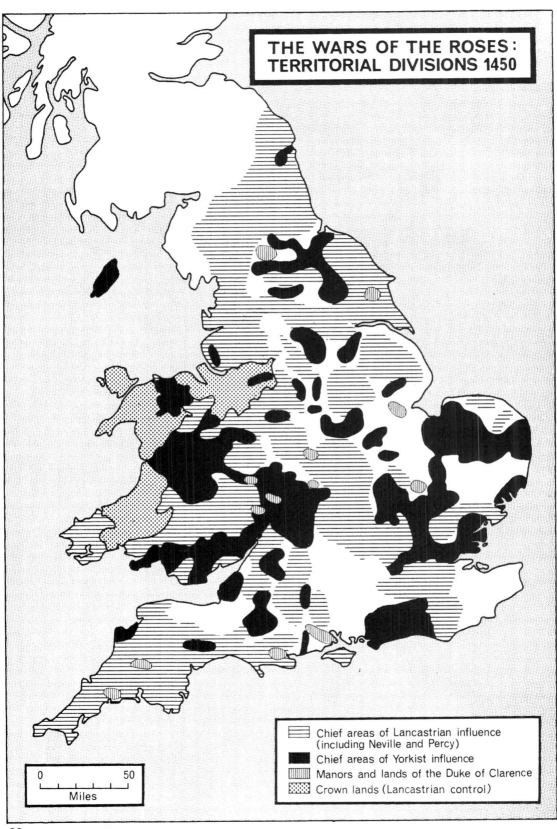

THE WARS OF THE ROSES: TERRITORIAL DIVISIONS 1450

Chief areas of Lancastrian influence (including Neville and Percy)

Chief areas of Yorkist influence

Manors and lands of the Duke of Clarence

Crown lands (Lancastrian control)

0 — 50

Miles

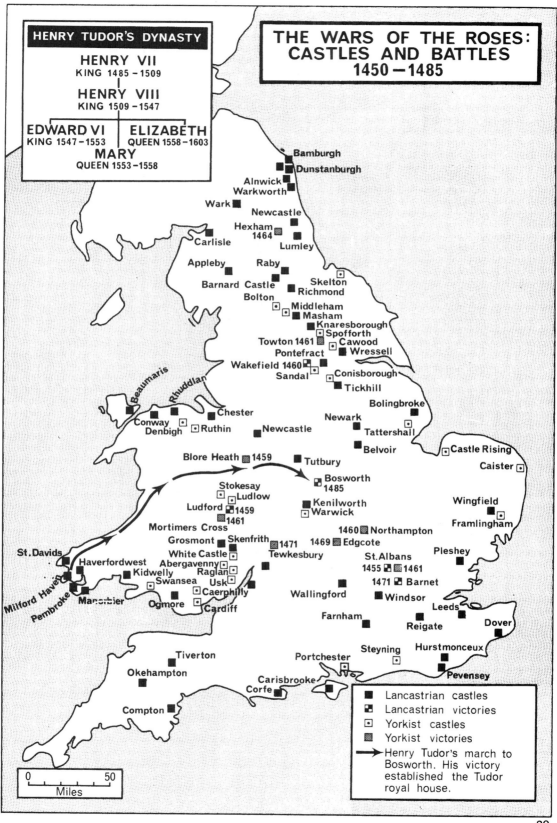

THE WARS OF THE ROSES: CASTLES AND BATTLES 1450–1485

HENRY TUDOR'S DYNASTY

HENRY VII
KING 1485–1509

HENRY VIII
KING 1509–1547

EDWARD VI
KING 1547–1553

ELIZABETH
QUEEN 1558–1603

MARY
QUEEN 1553–1558

Bamburgh
Dunstanburgh
Alnwick
Warkworth
Wark
Newcastle
Hexham 1464
Lumley
Carlisle
Appleby
Raby
Barnard Castle
Skelton
Richmond
Bolton
Middleham
Masham
Knaresborough
Spofforth
Towton 1461
Cawood
Pontefract
Wressell
Wakefield 1460
Sandal
Conisborough
Tickhill
Bolingbroke
Beaumaris
Rhuddlan
Chester
Newark
Conway
Denbigh
Ruthin
Newcastle
Tattershall
Belvoir
Castle Rising
Blore Heath 1459
Tutbury
Caister
Bosworth 1485
Stokesay
Ludlow
Ludford 1459 1461
Kenilworth
Warwick
Wingfield
Mortimers Cross
Grosmont
Skenfrith 1471
1460 Northampton
1469 Edgcote
Framlingham
White Castle
Tewkesbury
St.David's
Abergavenny
Raglan
St.Albans 1455 1461
Pleshey
Haverfordwest
Kidwelly
Swansea
Usk
1471 Barnet
Milford Haven
Manorbier
Pembroke
Caerphilly
Ogmore
Cardiff
Wallingford
Windsor
Leeds
Farnham
Reigate
Dover
Tiverton
Steyning
Hurstmonceux
Okehampton
Portchester
Carisbrooke
Corfe
Pevensey
Compton

0   50
Miles

■ Lancastrian castles
▣ Lancastrian victories
◻ Yorkist castles
▨ Yorkist victories
→ Henry Tudor's march to Bosworth. His victory established the Tudor royal house.

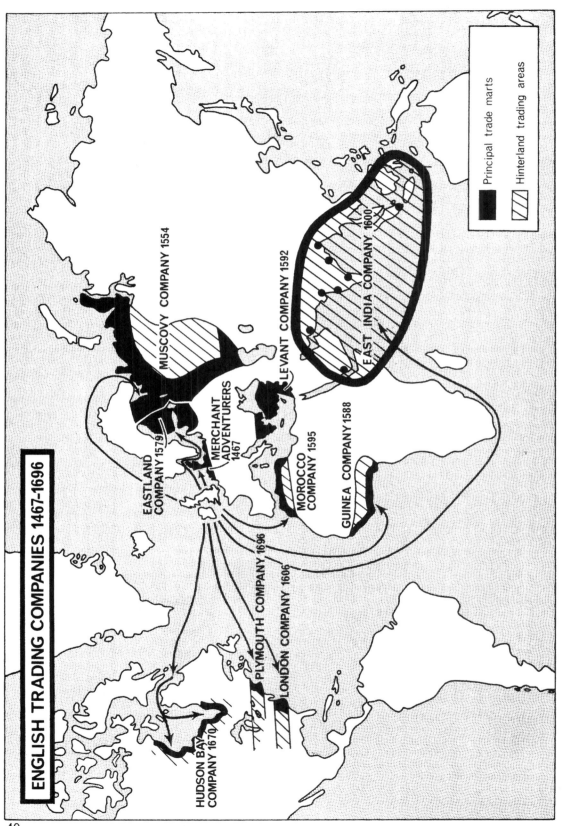

ENGLISH TRADING COMPANIES 1467-1696

MUSCOVY COMPANY 1554

LEVANT COMPANY 1592

EAST INDIA COMPANY 1600

MERCHANT ADVENTURERS 1467

EASTLAND COMPANY 1579

MOROCCO COMPANY 1595

GUINEA COMPANY 1588

PLYMOUTH COMPANY 1696

LONDON COMPANY 1606

HUDSON BAY COMPANY 1670

Principal trade marts

Hinterland trading areas

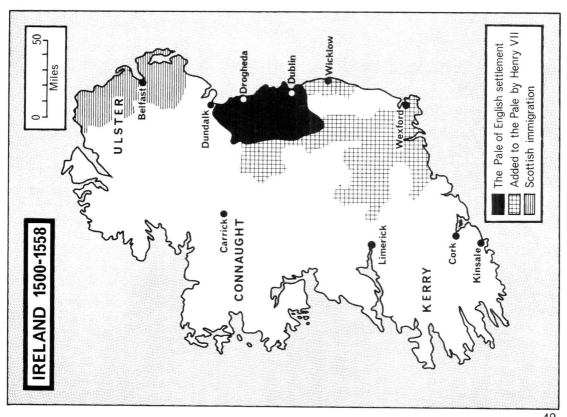

IRELAND 1500-1558

ULSTER

Belfast

Dundalk

Drogheda

Dublin

Wicklow

Wexford

Carrick

CONNAUGHT

Limerick

KERRY

Cork

Kinsale

0 50
Miles

The Pale of English settlement
Added to the Pale by Henry VII
Scottish immigration

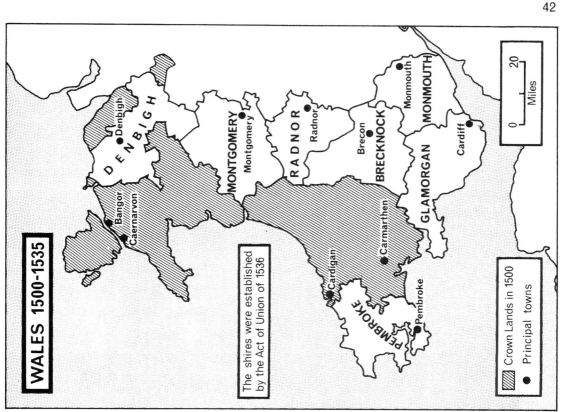

WALES 1500-1535

DENBIGH
Denbigh

Bangor
Caernarvon

MONTGOMERY
Montgomery

RADNOR
Radnor

Brecon

BRECKNOCK

Monmouth

MONMOUTH

Cardigan

Carmarthen

GLAMORGAN

Cardiff

PEMBROKE
Pembroke

The shires were established
by the Act of Union of 1536

Crown Lands in 1500
Principal towns

0 20
Miles

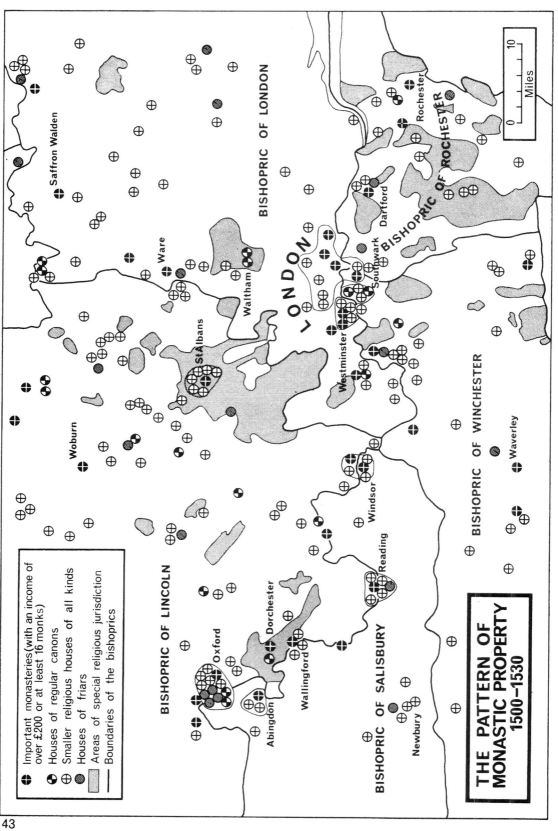

THE PATTERN OF
MONASTIC PROPERTY
1500–1530

Important monasteries (with an income of
over £200 or at least 16 monks)

Houses of regular canons

Smaller religious houses of all kinds

Houses of friars

Areas of special religious jurisdiction

Boundaries of the bishoprics

BISHOPRIC OF LONDON

BISHOPRIC OF ROCHESTER

BISHOPRIC OF WINCHESTER

BISHOPRIC OF LINCOLN

BISHOPRIC OF SALISBURY

LONDON

Saffron Walden

Ware

Waltham

St Albans

Woburn

Westminster

Southwark

Rochester

Dartford

Waverley

Windsor

Reading

Oxford

Dorchester

Wallingford

Abingdon

Newbury

Miles

10

0

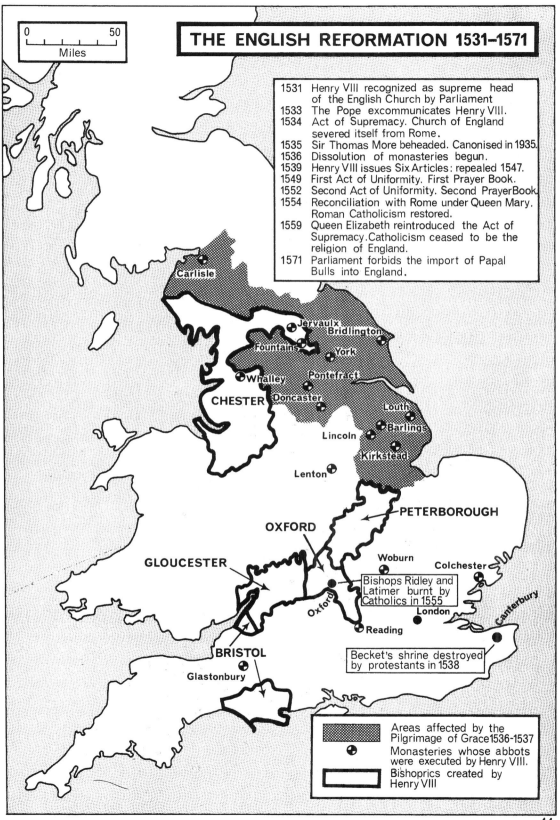

THE ENGLISH REFORMATION 1531–1571

1531 Henry VIII recognized as supreme head of the English Church by Parliament
1533 The Pope excommunicates Henry VIII.
1534 Act of Supremacy. Church of England severed itself from Rome.
1535 Sir Thomas More beheaded. Canonised in 1935.
1536 Dissolution of monasteries begun.
1539 Henry VIII issues Six Articles: repealed 1547.
1549 First Act of Uniformity. First Prayer Book.
1552 Second Act of Uniformity. Second Prayer Book.
1554 Reconciliation with Rome under Queen Mary. Roman Catholicism restored.
1559 Queen Elizabeth reintroduced the Act of Supremacy. Catholicism ceased to be the religion of England.
1571 Parliament forbids the import of Papal Bulls into England.

Carlisle

Jervaulx
Bridlington
Fountains
York
Whalley
Pontefract
CHESTER
Doncaster
Louth
Barlings
Lincoln
Kirkstead
Lenton

PETERBOROUGH

OXFORD

GLOUCESTER

Woburn
Colchester

Bishops Ridley and Latimer burnt by Catholics in 1555

Oxford
London
Canterbury

Reading

BRISTOL

Becket's shrine destroyed by protestants in 1538

Glastonbury

Areas affected by the Pilgrimage of Grace 1536-1537
Monasteries whose abbots were executed by Henry VIII.
Bishoprics created by Henry VIII

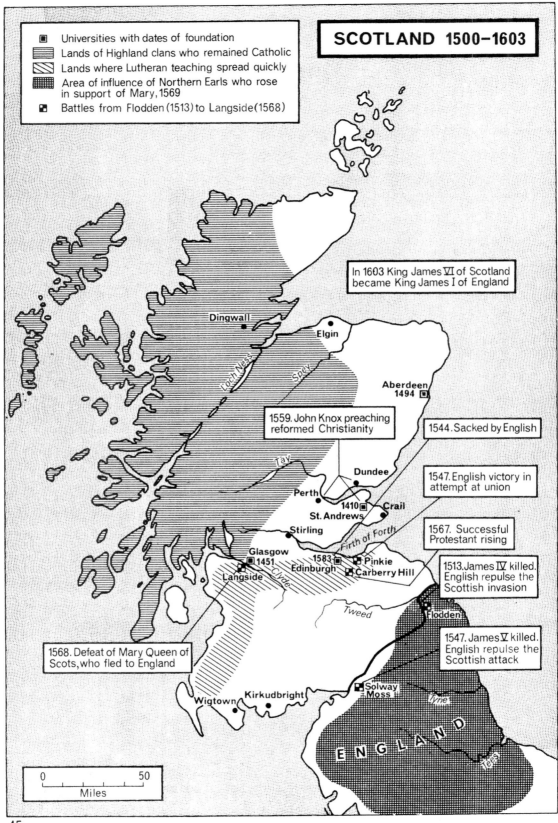

SCOTLAND 1500–1603

Legend:
- Universities with dates of foundation
- Lands of Highland clans who remained Catholic
- Lands where Lutheran teaching spread quickly
- Area of influence of Northern Earls who rose in support of Mary, 1569
- Battles from Flodden (1513) to Langside (1568)

In 1603 King James VI of Scotland became King James I of England

1559. John Knox preaching reformed Christianity

1544. Sacked by English

1547. English victory in attempt at union

1567. Successful Protestant rising

1513. James IV killed. English repulse the Scottish invasion

1547. James V killed. English repulse the Scottish attack

1568. Defeat of Mary Queen of Scots, who fled to England

Dingwall
Elgin
Aberdeen 1494
Dundee
Perth
1410 St. Andrews   Crail
Stirling
Glasgow
1451
Langside   1583
Edinburgh   Pinkie
Carberry Hill
Kirkudbright   Solway Moss
Wigtown
Flodden

Loch Ness
Spey
Tay
Firth of Forth
Clyde
Tweed
Tyne
Tees

ENGLAND

0   50
Miles

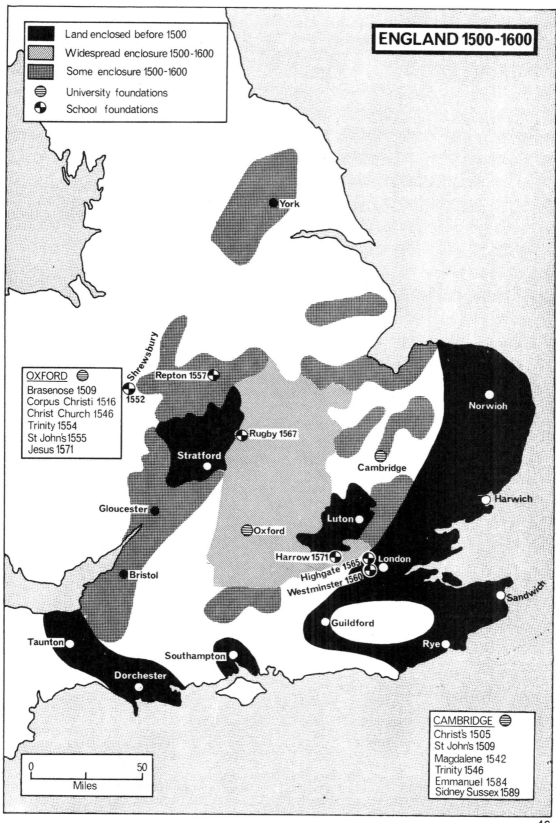

ENGLAND 1500-1600

Land enclosed before 1500
Widespread enclosure 1500-1600
Some enclosure 1500-1600
University foundations
School foundations

OXFORD
Brasenose 1509
Corpus Christi 1516
Christ Church 1546
Trinity 1554
St John's 1555
Jesus 1571

CAMBRIDGE
Christ's 1505
St John's 1509
Magdalene 1542
Trinity 1546
Emmanuel 1584
Sidney Sussex 1589

York
Shrewsbury
1552
Repton 1557
Norwioh
Rugby 1567
Stratford
Cambridge
Harwich
Gloucester
Luton
Harrow 1571
Highgate 1565
London
Bristol
Westminster 1560
Sandwich
Taunton
Guildford
Southampton
Rye
Dorchester

0   50
Miles

46

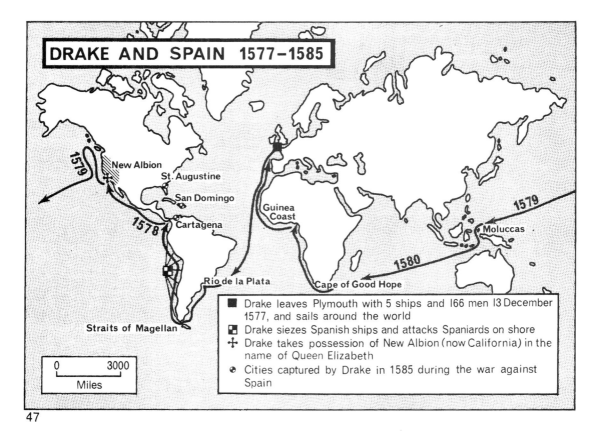

DRAKE AND SPAIN 1577–1585

1579

New Albion

St. Augustine

San Domingo

1578 Cartagena

Guinea Coast

Rio de la Plata

Straits of Magellan

Cape of Good Hope

1579

Moluccas

1580

■ Drake leaves Plymouth with 5 ships and 166 men 13 December 1577, and sails around the world

▣ Drake siezes Spanish ships and attacks Spaniards on shore

✛ Drake takes possession of New Albion (now California) in the name of Queen Elizabeth

● Cities captured by Drake in 1585 during the war against Spain

0 —— 3000
Miles

47

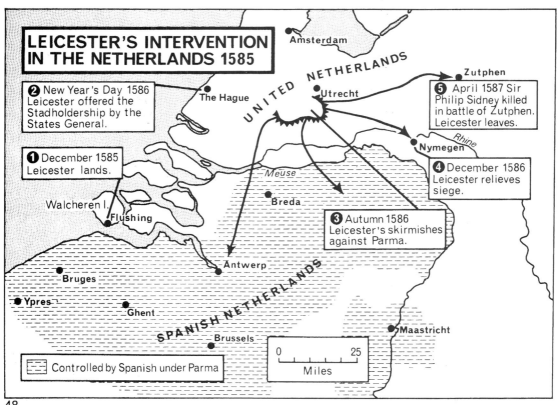

LEICESTER'S INTERVENTION IN THE NETHERLANDS 1585

Amsterdam

UNITED NETHERLANDS

Zutphen

2 New Year's Day 1586 Leicester offered the Stadholdership by the States General.

The Hague

Utrecht

5 April 1587 Sir Philip Sidney killed in battle of Zutphen. Leicester leaves.

Rhine

Nymegen

1 December 1585 Leicester lands.

Meuse

4 December 1586 Leicester relieves siege.

Walcheren I.

Flushing

Breda

3 Autumn 1586 Leicester's skirmishes against Parma.

Antwerp

Bruges

SPANISH NETHERLANDS

Ypres

Ghent

Maastricht

Brussels

0 —— 25
Miles

▦ Controlled by Spanish under Parma

48

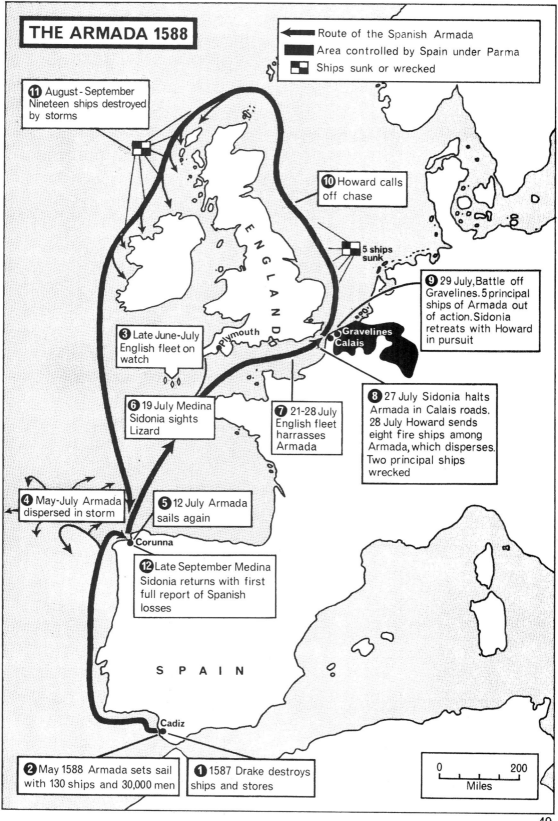

THE ARMADA 1588

← Route of the Spanish Armada
■ Area controlled by Spain under Parma
▨ Ships sunk or wrecked

11 August - September Nineteen ships destroyed by storms

10 Howard calls off chase

3 Late June-July English fleet on watch

6 19 July Medina Sidonia sights Lizard

7 21-28 July English fleet harrasses Armada

5 ships sunk

9 29 July, Battle off Gravelines. 5 principal ships of Armada out of action. Sidonia retreats with Howard in pursuit

8 27 July Sidonia halts Armada in Calais roads. 28 July Howard sends eight fire ships among Armada, which disperses. Two principal ships wrecked

4 May-July Armada dispersed in storm

5 12 July Armada sails again

12 Late September Medina Sidonia returns with first full report of Spanish losses

Plymouth

Gravelines
Calais

E N G L A N D

Corunna

S P A I N

Cadiz

2 May 1588 Armada sets sail with 130 ships and 30,000 men

1 1587 Drake destroys ships and stores

0   200
Miles

49

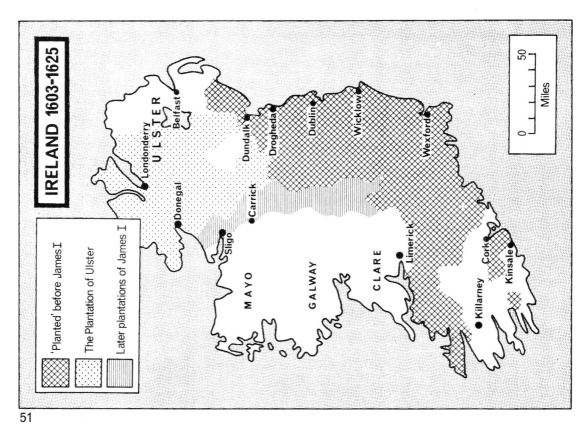

IRELAND 1603-1625

ULSTER

Londonderry
Belfast
Donegal
Sligo
Carrick
Dundalk
Drogheda
Dublin
Wicklow
Wexford
Limerick
Cork
Kinsale
Killarney

MAYO
GALWAY
CLARE

'Planted' before James I
The Plantation of Ulster
Later plantations of James I

0   50
Miles

51

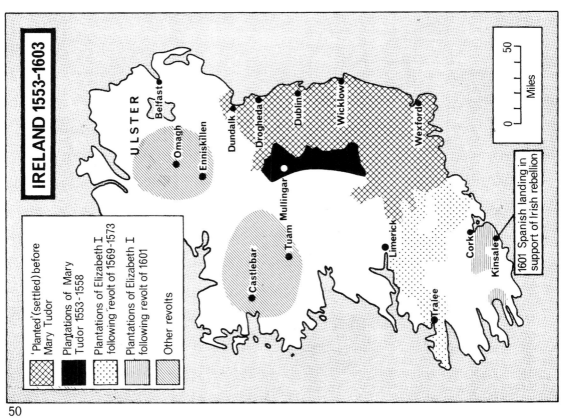

IRELAND 1553-1603

ULSTER

Belfast
Omagh
Enniskillen
Dundalk
Drogheda
Dublin
Wicklow
Wexford
Castlebar
Tuam
Mullingar
Limerick
Tralee
Cork
Kinsale

'Planted' (settled) before Mary Tudor
Plantations of Mary Tudor 1553-1558
Plantations of Elizabeth I following revolt of 1569-1573
Plantations of Elizabeth I following revolt of 1601
Other revolts

1601 Spanish landing in support of Irish rebellion

0   50
Miles

50

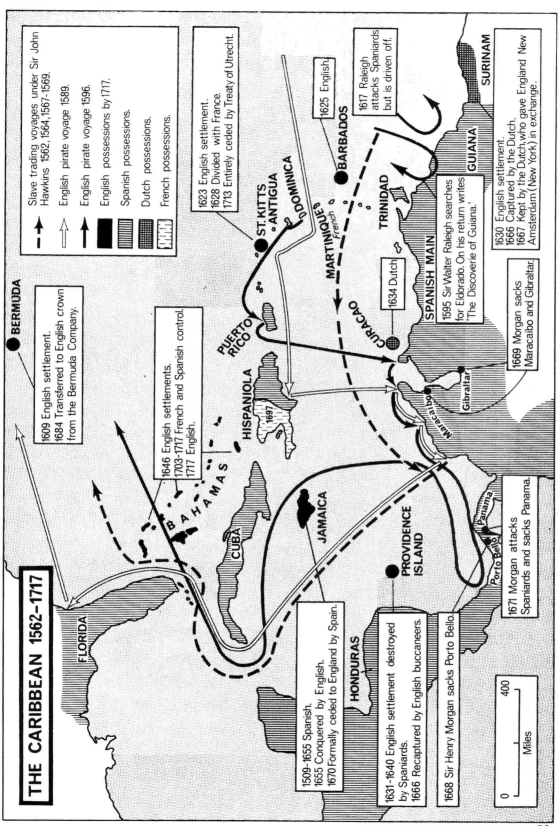

THE CARIBBEAN 1562–1717

Slave trading voyages under Sir John Hawkins 1562, 1564, 1567-1569.

English pirate voyage 1589.

English pirate voyage 1596.

English possessions by 1717.

Spanish possessions.

Dutch possessions.

French possessions.

1623 English settlement.
1628 Divided with France.
1713 Entirely ceded by Treaty of Utrecht.

1625 English.

1617 Raleigh attacks Spaniards but is driven off.

SURINAM

BARBADOS

1595 Sir Walter Raleigh searches for Eldorado. On his return writes 'The Discoverie of Guiana.'

1630 English settlement.
1666 Captured by the Dutch.
1667 Kept by the Dutch, who gave England New Amsterdam (New York) in exchange.

GUIANA

TRINIDAD

ST. KITTS
ANTIGUA
DOMINICA
MARTINIQUE French

1634 Dutch

CURAÇAO

SPANISH MAIN

1669 Morgan sacks Maracaibo and Gibraltar.

BERMUDA

1609 English settlement.
1684 Transferred to English crown from the Bermuda Company.

PUERTO RICO

Maracaibo

Gibraltar

1646 English settlements.
1703-1717 French and Spanish control.
1717 English.

HISPANIOLA
1697

BAHAMAS

CUBA

JAMAICA

PROVIDENCE ISLAND

Panama

Porto Bello

FLORIDA

1509-1655 Spanish.
1655 Conquered by English.
1670 Formally ceded to England by Spain.

1631-1640 English settlement destroyed by Spaniards.
1666 Recaptured by English buccaneers.

1668 Sir Henry Morgan sacks Porto Bello.

1671 Morgan attacks Spaniards and sacks Panama.

HONDURAS

0   400
Miles

52

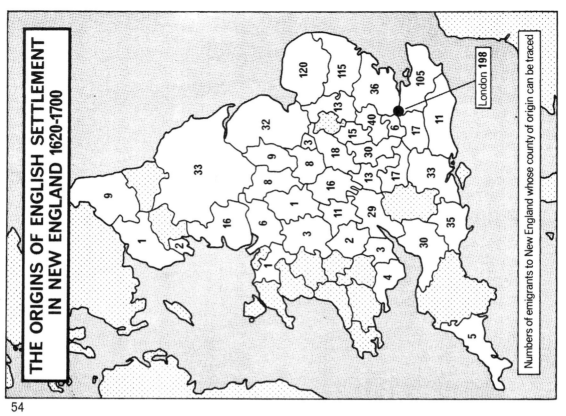

THE ORIGINS OF ENGLISH SETTLEMENT IN NEW ENGLAND 1620-1700

London 198

Numbers of emigrants to New England whose county of origin can be traced

54

THE ORIGINS OF ENGLISH SETTLEMENT IN VIRGINIA 1607-1700

0 50
Miles

London 179

Numbers of emigrants to Virginia whose county of origin can be traced

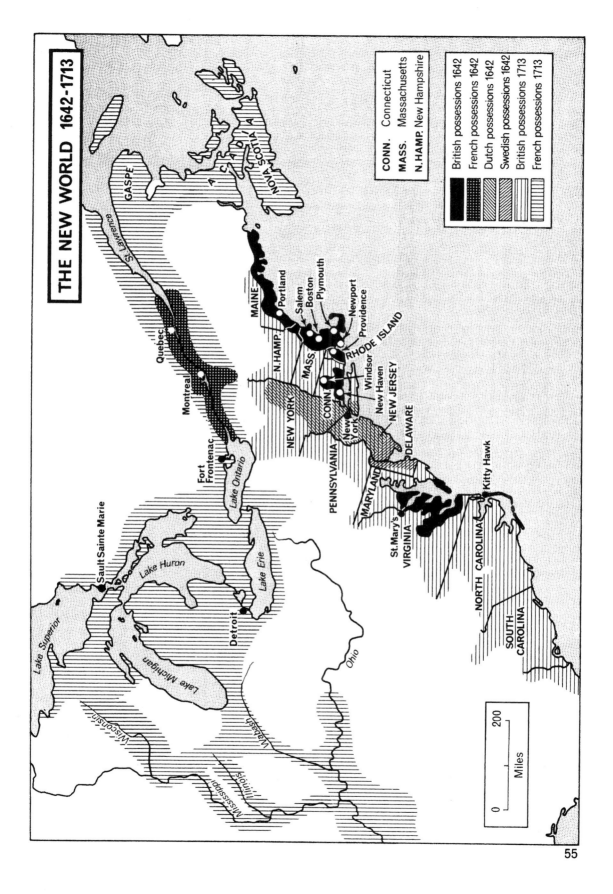

THE NEW WORLD 1642-1713

CONN.	Connecticut
MASS.	Massachusetts
N. HAMP.	New Hampshire

British possessions 1642
French possessions 1642
Dutch possessions 1642
Swedish possessions 1642
British possessions 1713
French possessions 1713

GASPE

NOVA SCOTIA

St. Lawrence

Quebec

Montreal

Fort Frontenac

Lake Ontario

Sault Sainte Marie

Lake Superior

Lake Michigan

Lake Huron

Lake Erie

Detroit

Ohio

Wabash

Illinois

Wisconsin

Mississippi

MAINE

Portland
Salem
Boston
Plymouth
Newport
Providence

N. HAMP.

MASS.

RHODE ISLAND

Windsor

CONN.

New Haven

New York

NEW YORK

NEW JERSEY

DELAWARE

PENNSYLVANIA

MARYLAND

St. Mary's

VIRGINIA

Kitty Hawk

NORTH CAROLINA

SOUTH CAROLINA

0   200

Miles

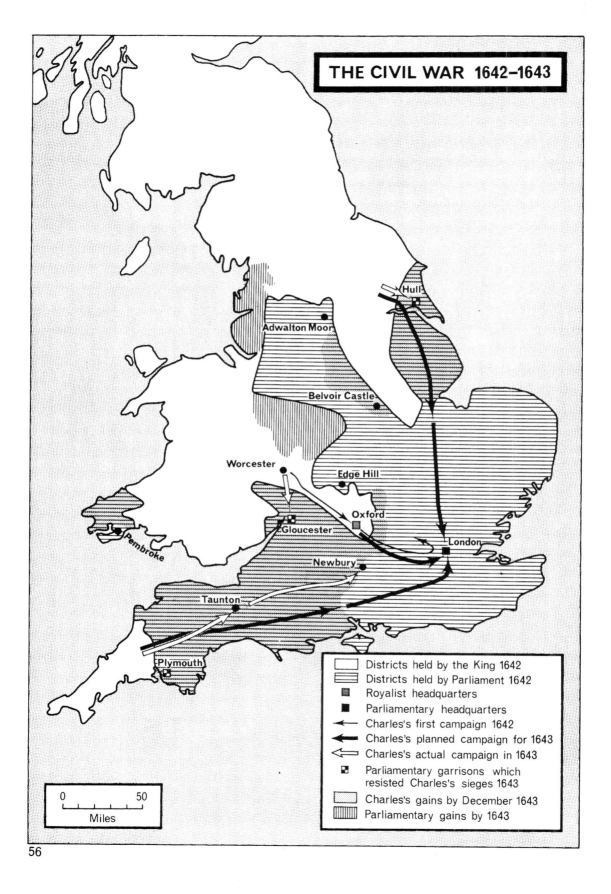

THE CIVIL WAR 1642–1643

Hull

Adwalton Moor

Belvoir Castle

Worcester

Edge Hill

Oxford

Gloucester

Pembroke

Newbury

London

Taunton

Plymouth

Districts held by the King 1642

Districts held by Parliament 1642

Royalist headquarters

Parliamentary headquarters

Charles's first campaign 1642

Charles's planned campaign for 1643

Charles's actual campaign in 1643

Parliamentary garrisons which resisted Charles's sieges 1643

Charles's gains by December 1643

Parliamentary gains by 1643

0   50

Miles

THE CIVIL WAR 1644–1646

In May 1646 King Charles surrendered to the Scottish Army at Newark. In February 1647 the Scots sold the King to Parliament for £400,000. He was beheaded on 30 January 1649.

Carlisle

Marston Moor

Hull

Preston
Bolton
Liverpool
Stockport
Sandal Castle
Hulme
Nantwich
Newark
Belvoir Castle
Shrewsbury
Ashby
Lichfield
Naseby
Holmby House
Banbury
Cropredy Bridge
Gloucester
Oxford
Donnington Castle
Bridgewater
Taunton
Lyme Regis
Corfe Castle
Plymouth

⬚ The Eastern Association: main recruiting ground for Parliamentary Army 1643
← Campaign of Prince Rupert to Marston Moor.
← Parliamentary advances to Marston Moor, where the Royalists were defeated 2 July 1644
▤ Area controlled by Parliament in December 1644.
▦ Area gained by Parliament by December 1645.
▪ Districts held by the King in May 1646.
☐ Area gained by Parliament by December 1646.

0   50
Miles

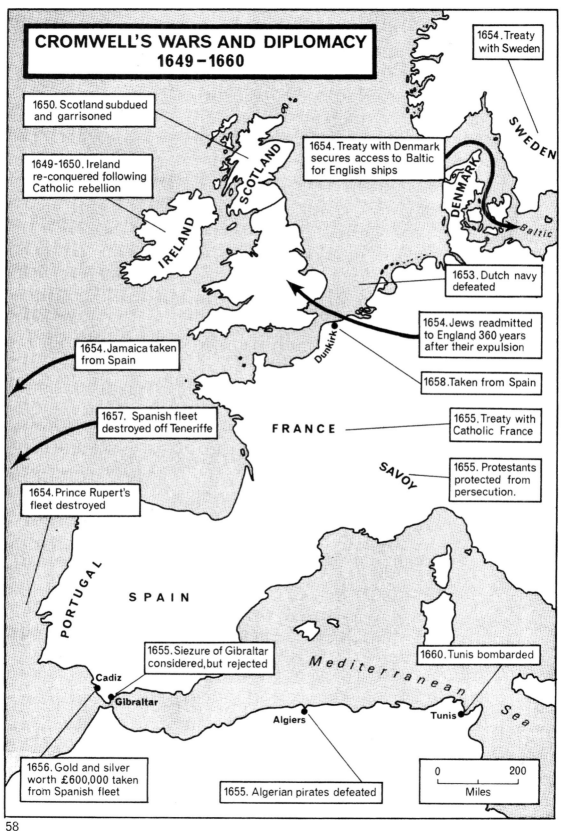

CROMWELL'S WARS AND DIPLOMACY 1649–1660

1654. Treaty with Sweden

1650. Scotland subdued and garrisoned

1654. Treaty with Denmark secures access to Baltic for English ships

1649-1650. Ireland re-conquered following Catholic rebellion

SWEDEN

DENMARK

Baltic

SCOTLAND

IRELAND

1653. Dutch navy defeated

1654. Jamaica taken from Spain

1654. Jews readmitted to England 360 years after their expulsion

Dunkirk

1658. Taken from Spain

1657. Spanish fleet destroyed off Teneriffe

FRANCE

1655. Treaty with Catholic France

SAVOY

1655. Protestants protected from persecution.

1654. Prince Rupert's fleet destroyed

PORTUGAL

SPAIN

1655. Siezure of Gibraltar considered, but rejected

Mediterranean Sea

1660. Tunis bombarded

Cadiz

Gibraltar

Algiers

Tunis

1656. Gold and silver worth £600,000 taken from Spanish fleet

1655. Algerian pirates defeated

0   200
Miles

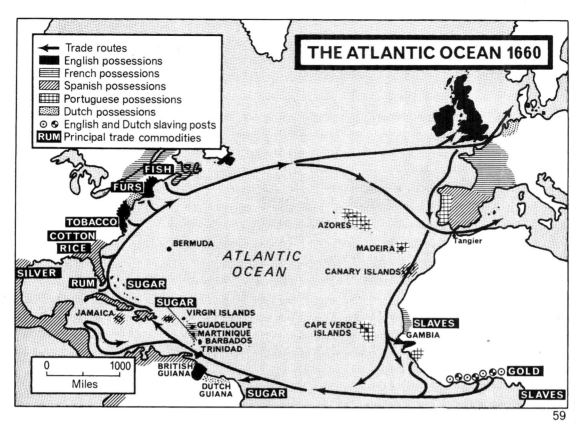

THE ATLANTIC OCEAN 1660

Legend:
- → Trade routes
- ■ English possessions
- French possessions
- Spanish possessions
- Portuguese possessions
- Dutch possessions
- ⊙ ⊛ English and Dutch slaving posts
- **RUM** Principal trade commodities

FISH
FURS
TOBACCO
COTTON
RICE
SILVER
RUM
SUGAR
SUGAR
JAMAICA
VIRGIN ISLANDS
GUADELOUPE
MARTINIQUE
BARBADOS
TRINIDAD
BERMUDA
BRITISH GUIANA
DUTCH GUIANA
SUGAR
AZORES
MADEIRA
Tangier
CANARY ISLANDS
CAPE VERDE ISLANDS
SLAVES
GAMBIA
GOLD
SLAVES

ATLANTIC OCEAN

0   1000
Miles

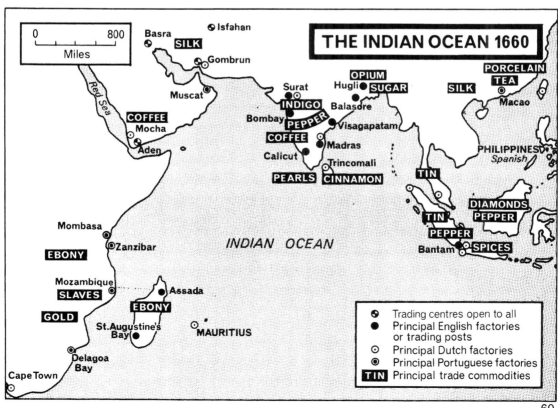

THE INDIAN OCEAN 1660

0   800
Miles

Basra
⊛ Isfahan
SILK
Gombrun
Muscat
COFFEE
Mocha
Aden
Red Sea
Surat
INDIGO
Bombay
PEPPER
COFFEE
Calicut
PEARLS
Hugli
Balasore
Visagapatam
Madras
Trincomali
CINNAMON
OPIUM
SUGAR
SILK
PORCELAIN
TEA
Macao
PHILIPPINES *Spanish*
TIN
DIAMONDS
PEPPER
TIN
PEPPER
Bantam
SPICES
Mombasa
⊚ Zanzibar
EBONY
Mozambique
SLAVES
GOLD
Assada
EBONY
St. Augustine's Bay
⊙ MAURITIUS
Delagoa Bay
Cape Town

INDIAN OCEAN

Legend:
- ⊛ Trading centres open to all
- ● Principal English factories or trading posts
- ⊙ Principal Dutch factories
- ⊚ Principal Portuguese factories
- **TIN** Principal trade commodities

THE THREE DUTCH WARS

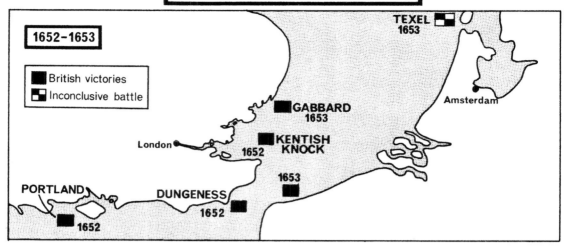

1652–1653

- ■ British victories
- ▨ Inconclusive battle

TEXEL 1653

Amsterdam

GABBARD 1653

KENTISH KNOCK 1652

London

PORTLAND 1652

DUNGENESS 1652

1653

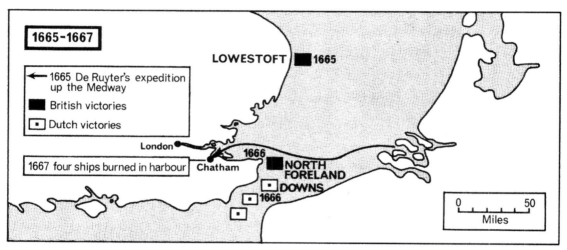

1665–1667

- ← 1665 De Ruyter's expedition up the Medway
- ■ British victories
- ▣ Dutch victories

LOWESTOFT ■ 1665

London

1667 four ships burned in harbour

Chatham 1666

NORTH FORELAND DOWNS

▣ 1666

▣

0   50
Miles

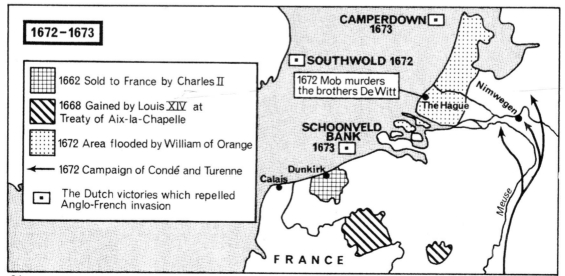

1672–1673

- ▦ 1662 Sold to France by Charles II
- ▨ 1668 Gained by Louis XIV at Treaty of Aix-la-Chapelle
- ⣿ 1672 Area flooded by William of Orange
- ← 1672 Campaign of Condé and Turenne
- ▣ The Dutch victories which repelled Anglo-French invasion

CAMPERDOWN ▣ 1673

▣ SOUTHWOLD 1672

1672 Mob murders the brothers De Witt

The Hague

Nimwegen

SCHOONVELD BANK 1673 ▣

Dunkirk

Calais

Meuse

FRANCE

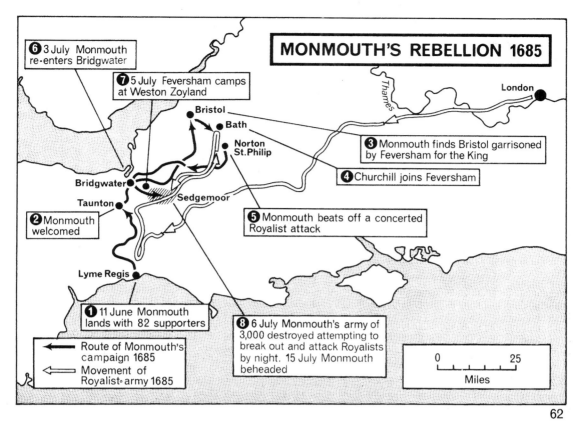

MONMOUTH'S REBELLION 1685

6 3 July Monmouth re-enters Bridgwater

7 5 July Feversham camps at Weston Zoyland

3 Monmouth finds Bristol garrisoned by Feversham for the King

4 Churchill joins Feversham

2 Monmouth welcomed

5 Monmouth beats off a concerted Royalist attack

1 11 June Monmouth lands with 82 supporters

8 6 July Monmouth's army of 3,000 destroyed attempting to break out and attack Royalists by night. 15 July Monmouth beheaded

Bristol
Bath
Norton St.Philip
Bridgwater
Sedgemoor
Taunton
Lyme Regis
London
Thames

→ Route of Monmouth's campaign 1685
⇐ Movement of Royalist army 1685

0   25
Miles

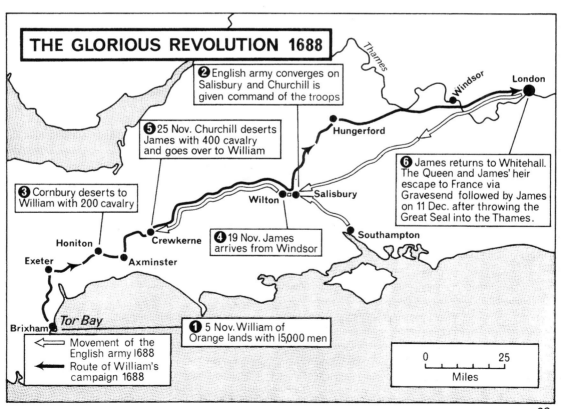

THE GLORIOUS REVOLUTION 1688

2 English army converges on Salisbury and Churchill is given command of the troops

5 25 Nov. Churchill deserts James with 400 cavalry and goes over to William

3 Cornbury deserts to William with 200 cavalry

6 James returns to Whitehall. The Queen and James' heir escape to France via Gravesend followed by James on 11 Dec. after throwing the Great Seal into the Thames.

4 19 Nov. James arrives from Windsor

1 5 Nov. William of Orange lands with 15,000 men

Thames
Windsor
London
Hungerford
Wilton
Salisbury
Southampton
Honiton
Crewkerne
Exeter
Axminster
Brixham
Tor Bay

⇐ Movement of the English army 1688
← Route of William's campaign 1688

0   25
Miles

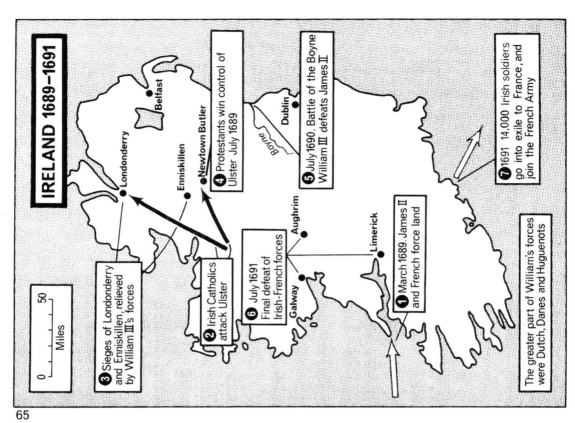

IRELAND 1689–1691

❸ Sieges of Londonderry and Enniskillen, relieved by William III's forces

Londonderry

Belfast

Enniskillen

❷ Irish Catholics attack Ulster

Newtown Butler

❹ Protestants win control of Ulster July 1689

Boyne

Dublin

❺ July 1690. Battle of the Boyne William III defeats James II

❻ July 1691 Final defeat of Irish-French forces

Aughrim

Galway

Limerick

❶ March 1689. James II and French force land

❼ 1691 14,000 Irish soldiers go into exile to France, and join the French Army

The greater part of William's forces were Dutch, Danes and Huguenots

Miles
0   50

65

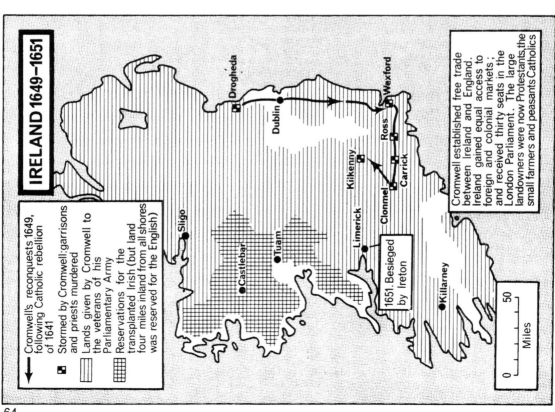

IRELAND 1649–1651

→ Cromwell's reconquests 1649, following Catholic rebellion of 1641

■ Stormed by Cromwell: garrisons and priests murdered

▨ Lands given by Cromwell to the veterans of his Parliamentary Army

▦ Reservations for the transplanted Irish (but land four miles inland from all shores was reserved for the English)

Sligo

Castlebar

Tuam

Killarney

Limerick

Clonmel

Kilkenny

Carrick

Ross

Wexford

Dublin

Drogheda

1651. Besieged by Ireton

Cromwell established free trade between Ireland and England. Ireland gained equal access to foreign and colonial markets; and received thirty seats in the London Parliament. The large landowners were now Protestants, the small farmers and peasants Catholics

Miles
0   50

64

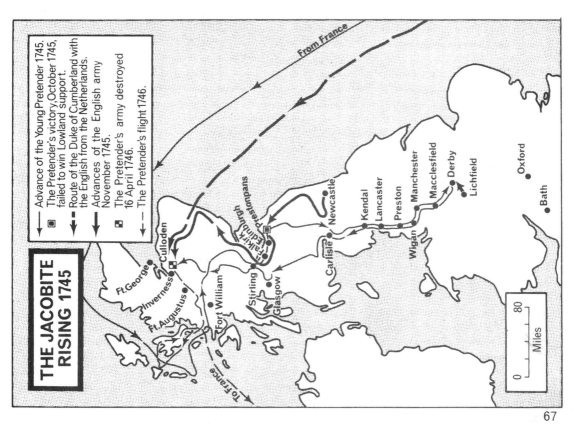

THE JACOBITE RISING 1745

From France

To France

Legend:
- Advance of the Young Pretender 1745.
- The Pretender's victory, October 1745, failed to win Lowland support.
- Route of the Duke of Cumberland with the English from the Netherlands.
- Advances of the English army November 1745.
- The Pretender's army destroyed 16 April 1746.
- The Pretender's flight 1746.

Ft.George, Culloden, Inverness, Ft.Augustus, Fort William, Stirling, Glasgow, Falkirk, Edinburgh, Prestonpans, Carlisle, Newcastle, Kendal, Lancaster, Preston, Wigan, Manchester, Macclesfield, Derby, Lichfield, Oxford, Bath

0 — 80 Miles

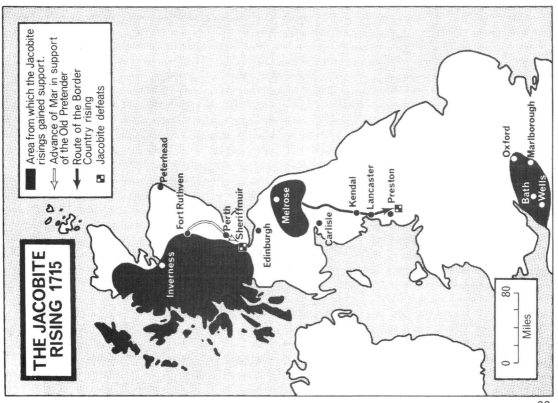

THE JACOBITE RISING 1715

Legend:
- Area from which the Jacobite risings gained support.
- Advance of Mar in support of the Old Pretender
- Route of the Border Country rising
- Jacobite defeats

Peterhead, Inverness, Fort Ruthven, Perth, Sheriffmuir, Edinburgh, Melrose, Carlisle, Kendal, Lancaster, Preston, Oxford, Bath, Marlborough, Wells

0 — 80 Miles

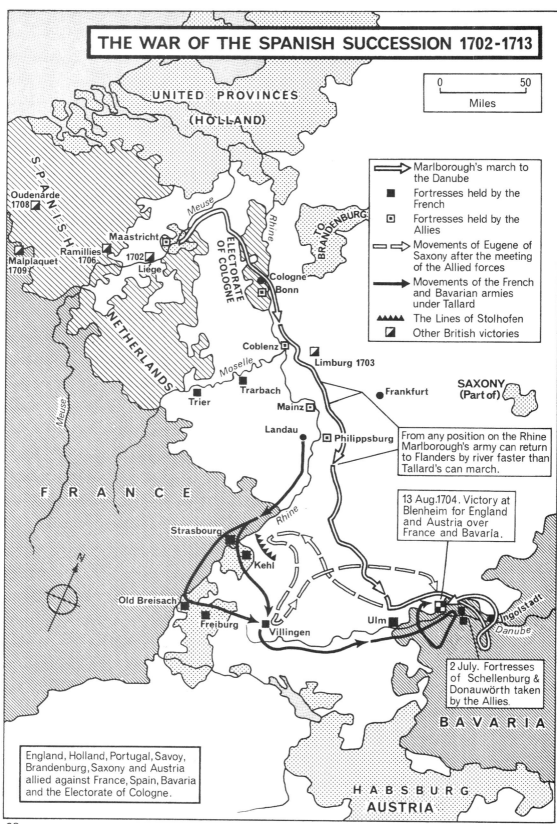

THE WAR OF THE SPANISH SUCCESSION 1702-1713

0   50
Miles

UNITED PROVINCES
(HOLLAND)

SPANISH

NETHERLANDS

Oudenarde 1708

Ramillies 1706

Malplaquet 1709

Maastricht

Liège

1702

ELECTORATE OF COLOGNE

Meuse

Rhine

TO BRANDENBURG

Cologne
Bonn

Coblenz

Limburg 1703

Moselle

Trarbach

Trier

Mainz

Frankfurt

SAXONY
(Part of)

Landau

Philippsburg

Meuse

F R A N C E

Rhine

Strasbourg

Kehl

Old Breisach

Freiburg

Villingen

Ulm

Ingolstadt

Danube

B A V A R I A

→ Marlborough's march to the Danube

■ Fortresses held by the French

▣ Fortresses held by the Allies

⇢ Movements of Eugene of Saxony after the meeting of the Allied forces

→ Movements of the French and Bavarian armies under Tallard

▲▲▲ The Lines of Stolhofen

◪ Other British victories

From any position on the Rhine Marlborough's army can return to Flanders by river faster than Tallard's can march.

13 Aug.1704. Victory at Blenheim for England and Austria over France and Bavaria.

2 July. Fortresses of Schellenburg & Donauwörth taken by the Allies.

England, Holland, Portugal, Savoy, Brandenburg, Saxony and Austria allied against France, Spain, Bavaria and the Electorate of Cologne.

H A B S B U R G
AUSTRIA

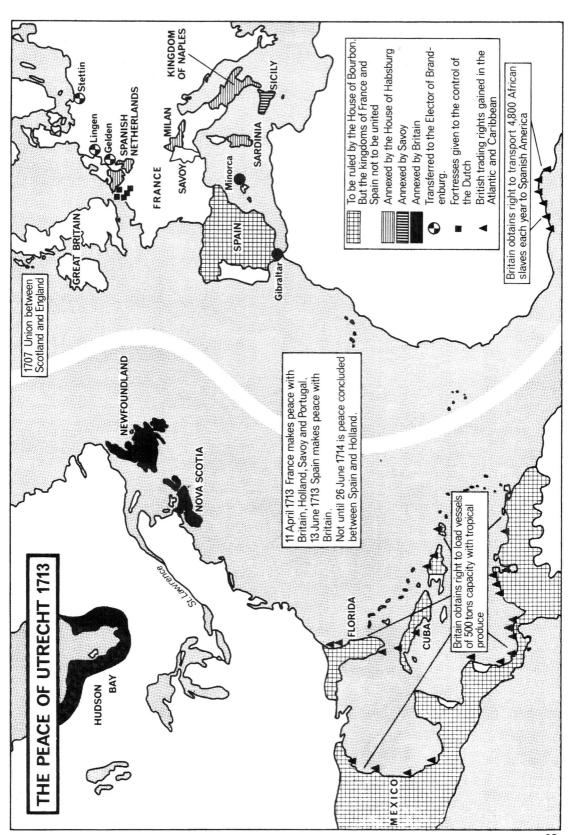

THE PEACE OF UTRECHT 1713

HUDSON BAY

St. Lawrence

NEWFOUNDLAND

NOVA SCOTIA

FLORIDA

CUBA

MEXICO

Britain obtains right to load vessels of 500 tons capacity with tropical produce

11 April 1713 France makes peace with Britain, Holland, Savoy and Portugal. 13 June 1713 Spain makes peace with Britain. Not until 26 June 1714 is peace concluded between Spain and Holland.

1707 Union between Scotland and England

GREAT BRITAIN

Stettin

Lingen
Gelden
SPANISH NETHERLANDS

FRANCE

SAVOY

MILAN

KINGDOM OF NAPLES

SICILY

SARDINIA

Minorca

SPAIN

Gibraltar

Britain obtains right to transport 4,800 African slaves each year to Spanish America

To be ruled by the House of Bourbon. But the kingdoms of France and Spain not to be united

Annexed by the House of Habsburg

Annexed by Savoy

Annexed by Britain

Transferred to the Elector of Brandenburg.

Fortresses given to the control of the Dutch

British trading rights gained in the Atlantic and Caribbean

69

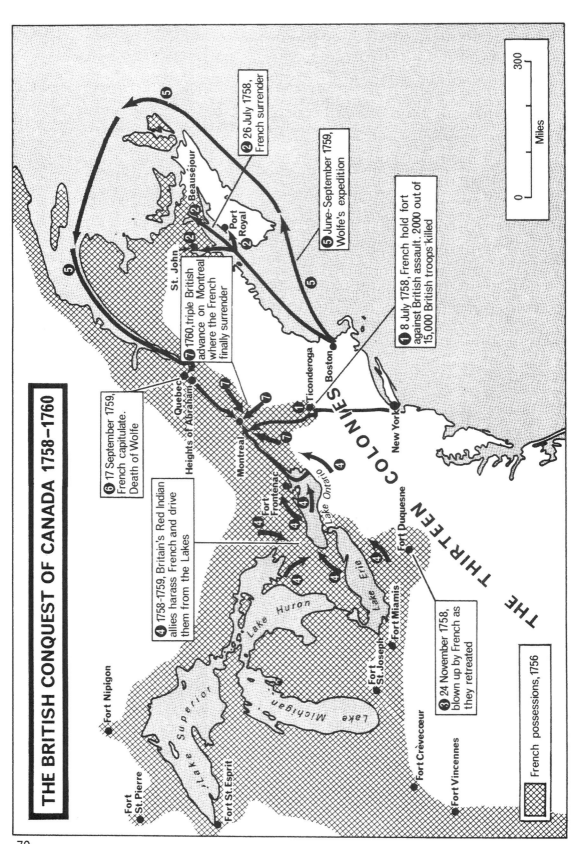

THE BRITISH CONQUEST OF CANADA 1758–1760

2 26 July 1758, French surrender

5 June–September 1759, Wolfe's expedition

1 8 July 1758, French hold fort against British assault. 2000 out of 15,000 British troops killed

7 1760, triple British advance on Montreal where the French finally surrender

6 17 September 1759, French capitulate. Death of Wolfe

4 1758-1759, Britain's Red Indian allies harass French and drive them from the Lakes

3 24 November 1758, blown up by French as they retreated

Fort Nipigon

Fort St. Pierre

Fort St. Esprit

Lake Superior

Lake Michigan

Lake Huron

Lake Erie

Lake Ontario

Fort St. Joseph

Fort Miamis

Fort Duquesne

Fort Crèvecoeur

Fort Vincennes

Fort Frontenac

Montreal

Quebec

Heights of Abraham

Ticonderoga

Boston

New York

THE THIRTEEN COLONIES

St. John

Beauséjour

Port Royal

French possessions, 1756

0   300
Miles

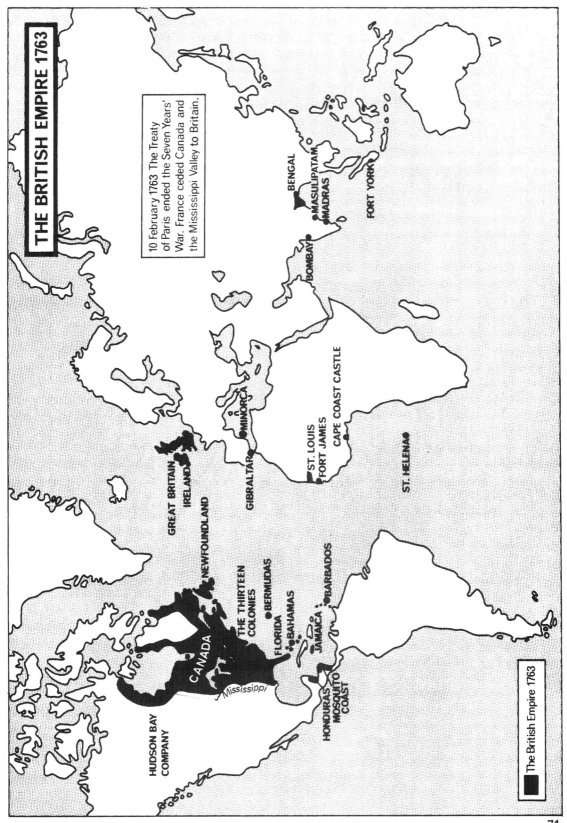

THE BRITISH EMPIRE 1763

10 February 1763 The Treaty of Paris ended the Seven Years' War. France ceded Canada and the Mississippi Valley to Britain.

BENGAL

MASULIPATAM
MADRAS

FORT YORK

BOMBAY

GREAT BRITAIN
IRELAND
NEWFOUNDLAND
MINORCA
GIBRALTAR
ST. LOUIS
FORT JAMES
CAPE COAST CASTLE

ST. HELENA

THE THIRTEEN COLONIES
BERMUDAS
FLORIDA
BAHAMAS
JAMAICA
BARBADOS

HUDSON BAY COMPANY

CANADA

Mississippi

HONDURAS
MOSQUITO COAST

■ The British Empire 1763

71

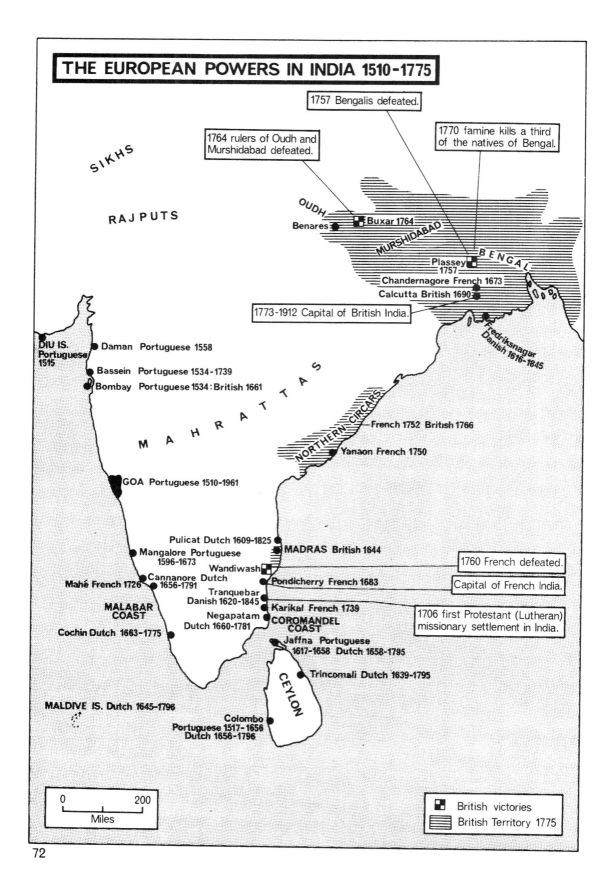

THE EUROPEAN POWERS IN INDIA 1510-1775

SIKHS

RAJPUTS

1757 Bengalis defeated.

1764 rulers of Oudh and Murshidabad defeated.

1770 famine kills a third of the natives of Bengal.

OUDH

Benares

Buxar 1764

MURSHIDABAD

BENGAL

Plassey 1757

Chandernagore French 1673

Calcutta British 1690

1773-1912 Capital of British India.

Fedriksnagar Danish 1616-1845

DIU IS. Portuguese 1515

Daman Portuguese 1558

Bassein Portuguese 1534-1739

Bombay Portuguese 1534: British 1661

M A H R A T T A S

NORTHERN CIRCARS

French 1752 British 1766

Yanaon French 1750

GOA Portuguese 1510-1961

Pulicat Dutch 1609-1825

MADRAS British 1844

Mangalore Portuguese 1596-1673

Wandiwash

1760 French defeated.

Capital of French India.

Mahé French 1726

Cannanore Dutch 1656-1791

Pondicherry French 1683

MALABAR COAST

Tranquebar Danish 1620-1845

Karikal French 1739

1706 first Protestant (Lutheran) missionary settlement in India.

Negapatam Dutch 1660-1781

COROMANDEL COAST

Cochin Dutch 1663-1775

Jaffna Portuguese 1617-1658 Dutch 1658-1795

Trincomali Dutch 1639-1795

MALDIVE IS. Dutch 1645-1796

CEYLON

Colombo Portuguese 1517-1656 Dutch 1656-1796

0   200
Miles

◨ British victories

▦ British Territory 1775

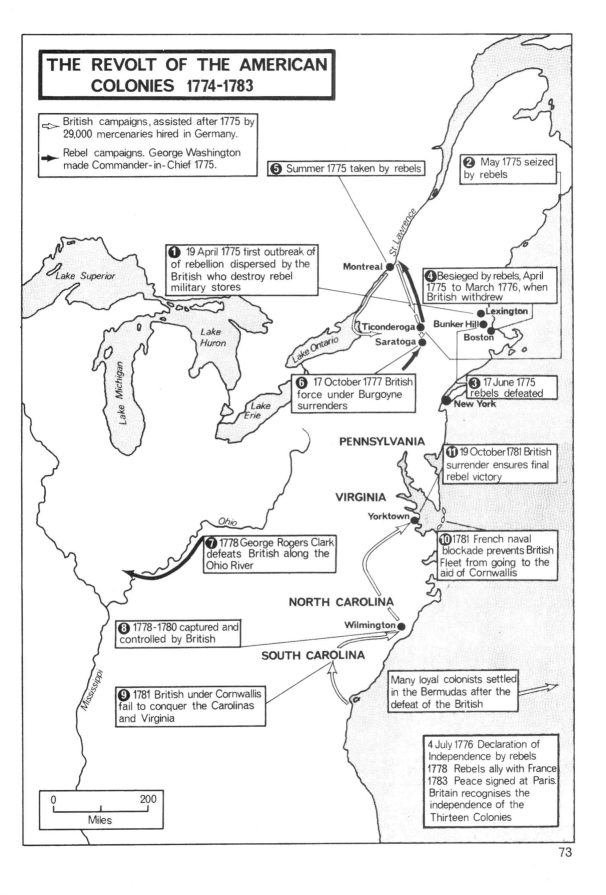

THE REVOLT OF THE AMERICAN COLONIES 1774-1783

➪ British campaigns, assisted after 1775 by 29,000 mercenaries hired in Germany.

➨ Rebel campaigns. George Washington made Commander-in-Chief 1775.

⑤ Summer 1775 taken by rebels

② May 1775 seized by rebels

① 19 April 1775 first outbreak of of rebellion dispersed by the British who destroy rebel military stores

④ Besieged by rebels, April 1775 to March 1776, when British withdrew

⑥ 17 October 1777 British force under Burgoyne surrenders

③ 17 June 1775 rebels defeated

⑪ 19 October 1781 British surrender ensures final rebel victory

⑦ 1778 George Rogers Clark defeats British along the Ohio River

⑩ 1781 French naval blockade prevents British Fleet from going to the aid of Cornwallis

⑧ 1778-1780 captured and controlled by British

Many loyal colonists settled in the Bermudas after the defeat of the British

⑨ 1781 British under Cornwallis fail to conquer the Carolinas and Virginia

4 July 1776 Declaration of Independence by rebels 1778 Rebels ally with France 1783 Peace signed at Paris. Britain recognises the independence of the Thirteen Colonies

Lake Superior
Lake Huron
Lake Michigan
Lake Erie
Lake Ontario
St. Lawrence
Montreal
Ticonderoga
Saratoga
Bunker Hill
Lexington
Boston
New York
PENNSYLVANIA
VIRGINIA
Yorktown
Ohio
NORTH CAROLINA
Wilmington
SOUTH CAROLINA
Mississippi

0   200
Miles

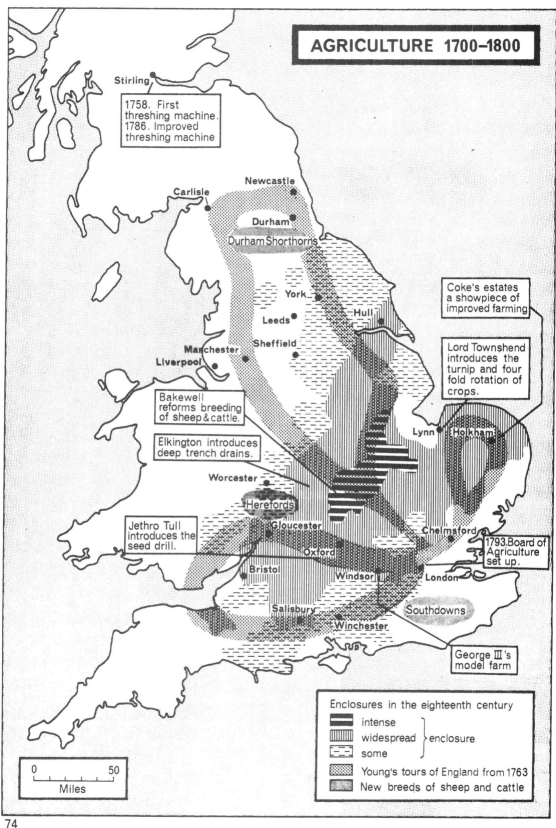

AGRICULTURE 1700–1800

Stirling

1758. First threshing machine. 1786. Improved threshing machine

Newcastle

Carlisle

Durham

Durham Shorthorns

York

Hull

Leeds

Sheffield

Manchester

Liverpool

Coke's estates a showpiece of improved farming

Lord Townshend introduces the turnip and four fold rotation of crops.

Lynn

Holkham

Bakewell reforms breeding of sheep & cattle.

Elkington introduces deep trench drains.

Worcester

Herefords

Jethro Tull introduces the seed drill.

Gloucester

Chelmsford

Oxford

1793. Board of Agriculture set up.

Bristol

Windsor

London

Salisbury

Southdowns

Winchester

George III's model farm

Enclosures in the eighteenth century

- ▬ intense
- ▥ widespread } enclosure
- ⎯ some
- ▦ Young's tours of England from 1763
- ▨ New breeds of sheep and cattle

0   50
Miles

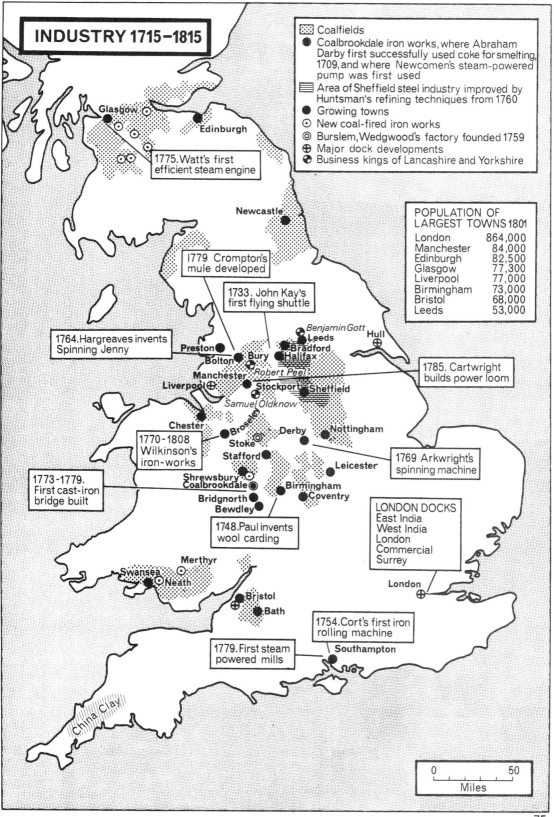

INDUSTRY 1715–1815

Coalfields
⬤ Coalbrookdale iron works, where Abraham Darby first successfully used coke for smelting, 1709, and where Newcomen's steam-powered pump was first used
▤ Area of Sheffield steel industry improved by Huntsman's refining techniques from 1760
⬤ Growing towns
⊙ New coal-fired iron works
◎ Burslem, Wedgwood's factory founded 1759
⊕ Major dock developments
✪ Business kings of Lancashire and Yorkshire

POPULATION OF LARGEST TOWNS 1801
London	864,000
Manchester	84,000
Edinburgh	82,500
Glasgow	77,300
Liverpool	77,000
Birmingham	73,000
Bristol	68,000
Leeds	53,000

1775. Watt's first efficient steam engine

1779 Crompton's mule developed

1733. John Kay's first flying shuttle

1764. Hargreaves invents Spinning Jenny

1785. Cartwright builds power loom

1770-1808 Wilkinson's iron-works

1769 Arkwright's spinning machine

1773-1779. First cast-iron bridge built

1748. Paul invents wool carding

LONDON DOCKS
East India
West India
London
Commercial
Surrey

1754. Cort's first iron rolling machine

1779. First steam powered mills

Glasgow
Edinburgh
Newcastle
Benjamin Gott
Hull
Preston
Leeds
Bradford
Bolton
Bury
Halifax
Manchester
Robert Peel
Liverpool
Stockport
Sheffield
Samuel Oldknow
Chester
Broseley
Derby
Nottingham
Stoke
Stafford
Leicester
Shrewsbury
Coalbrookdale
Birmingham
Bridgnorth
Coventry
Bewdley
Merthyr
Swansea
Neath
Bristol
Bath
London
Southampton

China Clay

0 — 50
Miles

75

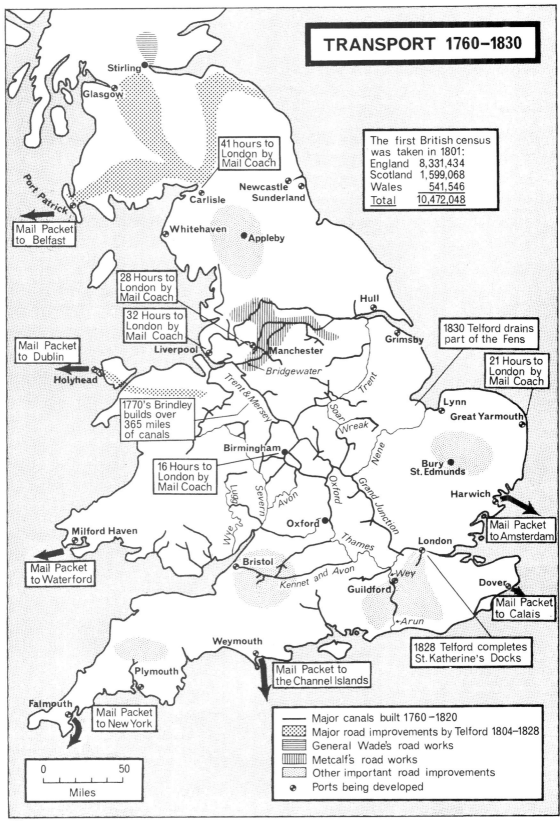

TRANSPORT 1760–1830

The first British census was taken in 1801:
England 8,331,434
Scotland 1,599,068
Wales 541,546
Total 10,472,048

Stirling

Glasgow

Port Patrick

Mail Packet to Belfast

41 hours to London by Mail Coach

Carlisle

Newcastle
Sunderland

Whitehaven

● Appleby

28 Hours to London by Mail Coach

32 Hours to London by Mail Coach

Mail Packet to Dublin

Holyhead

Liverpool

Manchester

Bridgewater

Hull

Grimsby

1830 Telford drains part of the Fens

21 Hours to London by Mail Coach

Lynn
Great Yarmouth

1770's Brindley builds over 365 miles of canals

Trent & Mersey

Soar

Wreak

Trent

Nene

Birmingham

16 Hours to London by Mail Coach

Lugg

Severn

Avon

Oxford

Grand Junction

Bury ●
St. Edmunds

Harwich

Wye

Oxford

Thames

London

Mail Packet to Amsterdam

Milford Haven

Mail Packet to Waterford

Bristol

Kennet and Avon

Wey

Guildford

Arun

Dover

Mail Packet to Calais

Weymouth

Mail Packet to the Channel Islands

1828 Telford completes St. Katherine's Docks

Plymouth

Falmouth

Mail Packet to New York

0   50
Miles

——— Major canals built 1760–1820

░░░ Major road improvements by Telford 1804–1828

General Wade's road works

‖‖‖ Metcalf's road works

Other important road improvements

● Ports being developed

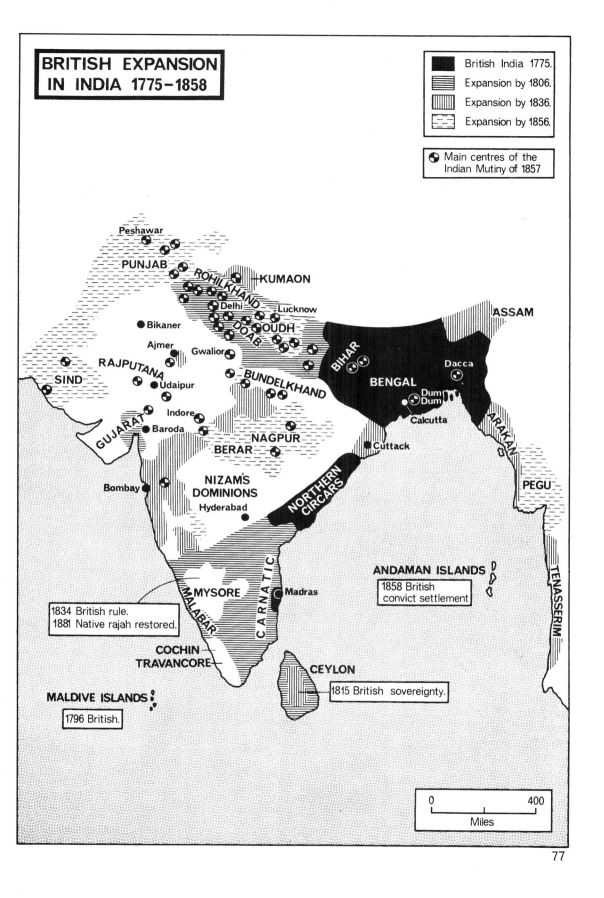

BRITISH EXPANSION IN INDIA 1775–1858

Legend:
- ■ British India 1775.
- Expansion by 1806.
- Expansion by 1836.
- Expansion by 1856.
- Main centres of the Indian Mutiny of 1857

Peshawar

PUNJAB

ROHILKHAND — KUMAON

Delhi   Lucknow

Bikaner

DOAB   OUDH

Ajmer   Gwalior

RAJPUTANA

SIND   Udaipur   BUNDELKHAND

BIHAR

ASSAM

BENGAL   Dacca

Indore

GUJARAT   Baroda

BERAR   NAGPUR

Dum
Dum

Cuttack   Calcutta

ARAKAN

Bombay

NIZAM'S
DOMINIONS

PEGU

Hyderabad

NORTHERN
CIRCARS

ANDAMAN ISLANDS

1858 British
convict settlement

MYSORE

MALABAR

CARNATIC

Madras

TENASSERIM

1834 British rule.
1881 Native rajah restored.

COCHIN
TRAVANCORE

CEYLON

1815 British sovereignty.

MALDIVE ISLANDS

1796 British.

0   400
Miles

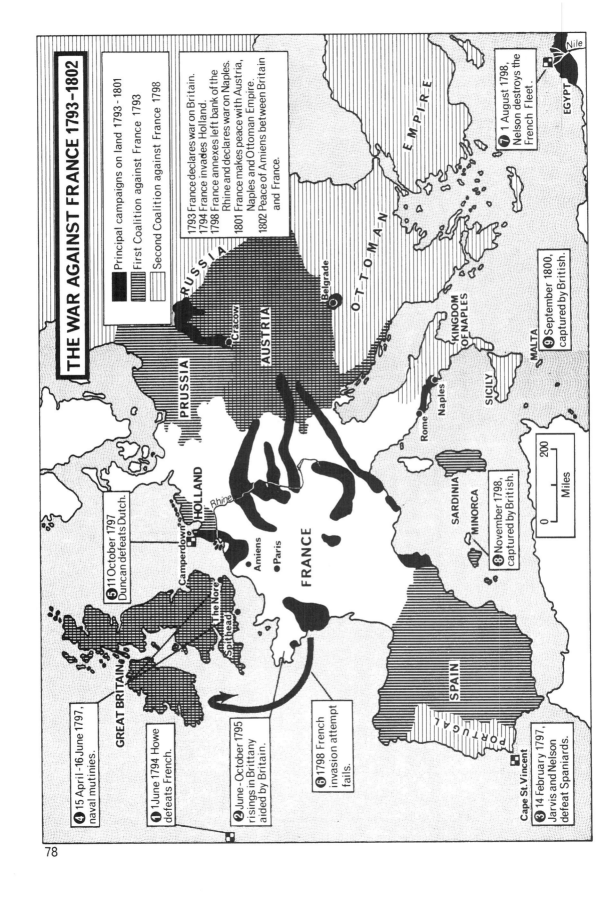

THE WAR AGAINST FRANCE 1793–1802

Principal campaigns on land 1793–1801

First Coalition against France 1793

Second Coalition against France 1798

1793 France declares war on Britain.
1794 France invades Holland.
1798 France annexes left bank of the Rhine and declares war on Naples.
1801 France makes peace with Austria, Naples and Ottoman Empire.
1802 Peace of Amiens between Britain and France.

7 1 August 1798, Nelson destroys the French Fleet.

9 September 1800, captured by British.

8 November 1798, captured by British.

5 11 October 1797 Duncan defeats Dutch.

4 15 April–16 June 1797, naval mutinies.

1 1 June 1794 Howe defeats French.

2 June–October 1795 risings in Brittany aided by Britain.

6 1798 French invasion attempt fails.

3 14 February 1797, Jarvis and Nelson defeat Spaniards.

Nile

EGYPT

OTTOMAN EMPIRE

Belgrade

Cracow

AUSTRIA

RUSSIA

PRUSSIA

HOLLAND

Rhine

Amiens

Paris

FRANCE

GREAT BRITAIN

Camperdown

The Nore

Spithead

Rome

Naples

KINGDOM OF NAPLES

SICILY

MALTA

SARDINIA

MINORCA

SPAIN

PORTUGAL

Cape St. Vincent

0   200
Miles

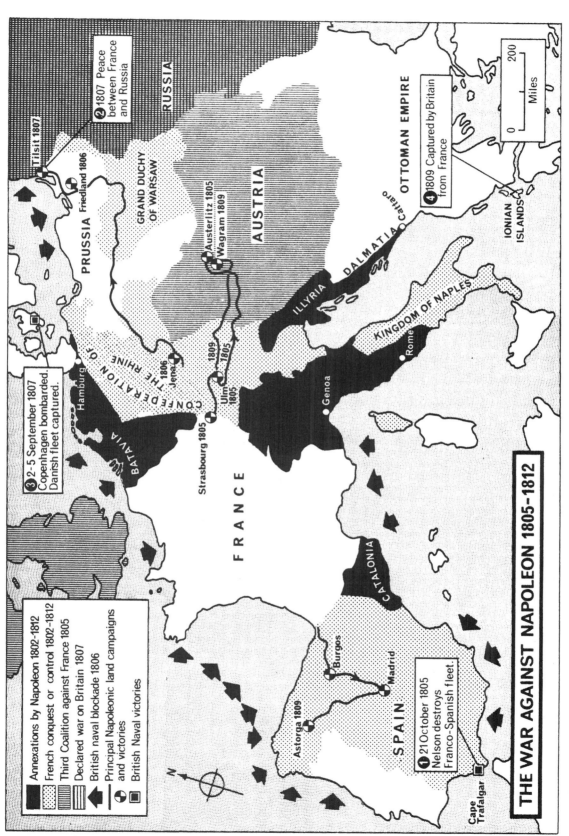

THE WAR AGAINST NAPOLEON 1805–1812

Annexations by Napoleon 1802–1812
French conquest or control 1802–1812
Third Coalition against France 1805
Declared war on Britain 1807
British naval blockade 1806
Principal Napoleonic land campaigns and victories
British Naval victories

❶ 21 October 1805 Nelson destroys Franco-Spanish fleet.

❷ 1807 Peace between France and Russia

❸ 2–5 September 1807 Copenhagen bombarded. Danish fleet captured.

❹ 1809 Captured by Britain from France

0 200 Miles

RUSSIA
PRUSSIA
GRAND DUCHY OF WARSAW
AUSTRIA
CONFEDERATION OF THE RHINE
FRANCE
SPAIN
BATAVIA
CATALONIA
ILLYRIA
DALMATIA
KINGDOM OF NAPLES
OTTOMAN EMPIRE
IONIAN ISLANDS

Tilsit 1807
Friedland 1806
Hamburg
Jena 1806
Strasbourg 1805
Ulm 1805
Austerlitz 1805
Wagram 1809
1809
1805
Genoa
Rome
Cattaro
Burgos
Madrid
Astorga 1809
Cape Trafalgar

N

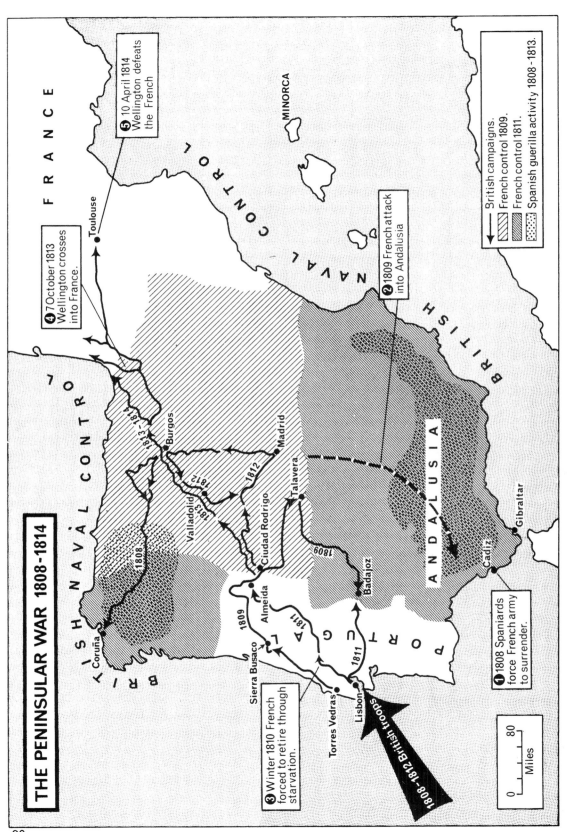

THE PENINSULAR WAR 1808-1814

FRANCE

FRENCH NAVAL CONTROL

BRITISH NAVAL CONTROL

BRITISH NAVAL CONTROL

PORTUGAL

ANDALUSIA

MINORCA

❹ 7 October 1813 Wellington crosses into France.

❺ 10 April 1814 Wellington defeats the French

❷ 1809 French attack into Andalusia

❸ Winter 1810 French forced to retire through starvation.

❶ 1808 Spaniards force French army to surrender.

1808-1812 British troops

Toulouse

Burgos

Madrid

Talavera

Valladolid

Ciudad Rodrigo

Badajoz

Cadiz

Gibraltar

Almeida

Sierra Busaco

Torres Vedras

Lisbon

Coruña

1808

1809

1811

1812

1813-1814

1813

1809

British campaigns.
French control 1809.
French control 1811.
Spanish guerilla activity 1808 - 1813.

0   80
Miles

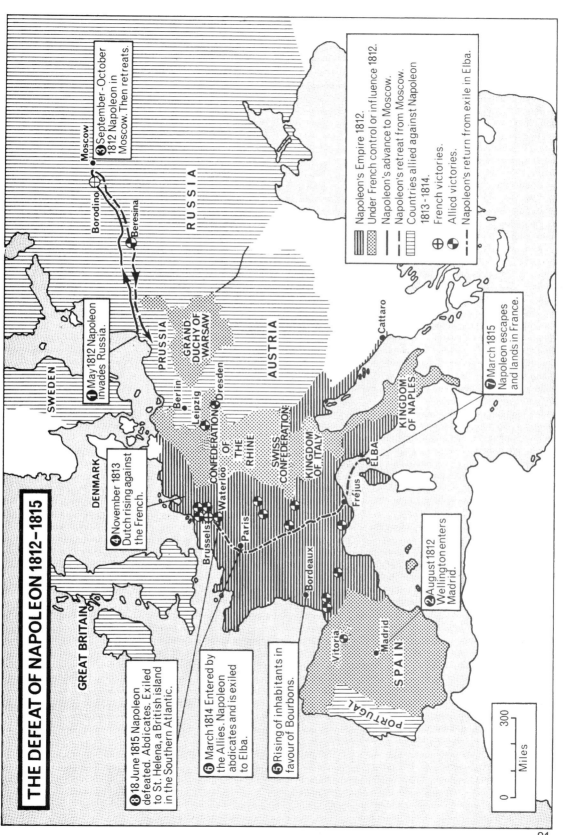

THE DEFEAT OF NAPOLEON 1812–1815

8 September – October 1812 Napoleon in Moscow. Then retreats.

1 May 1812 Napoleon invades Russia.

Napoleon's Empire 1812.
Under French control or influence 1812.
Napoleon's advance to Moscow.
Napoleon's retreat from Moscow.
Countries allied against Napoleon 1813 - 1814.
French victories.
Allied victories.
Napoleon's return from exile in Elba.

7 March 1815 Napoleon escapes and lands in France.

4 November 1813 Dutch rising against the French.

2 August 1812 Wellington enters Madrid.

8 18 June 1815 Napoleon defeated. Abdicates. Exiled to St. Helena, a British island in the Southern Atlantic.

6 March 1814 Entered by the Allies. Napoleon abdicates and is exiled to Elba.

5 Rising of inhabitants in favour of Bourbons.

RUSSIA

Moscow
Borodino
Beresina

SWEDEN

PRUSSIA
GRAND DUCHY OF WARSAW

AUSTRIA

Cattaro

Berlin
Leipzig
Dresden
CONFEDERATION OF THE RHINE
SWISS CONFEDERATION
KINGDOM OF ITALY
KINGDOM OF NAPLES

Waterloo
Brussels
Paris
Bordeaux

Fréjus
ELBA

DENMARK

GREAT BRITAIN

PORTUGAL
SPAIN
Vitoria
Madrid

0   300
Miles

81

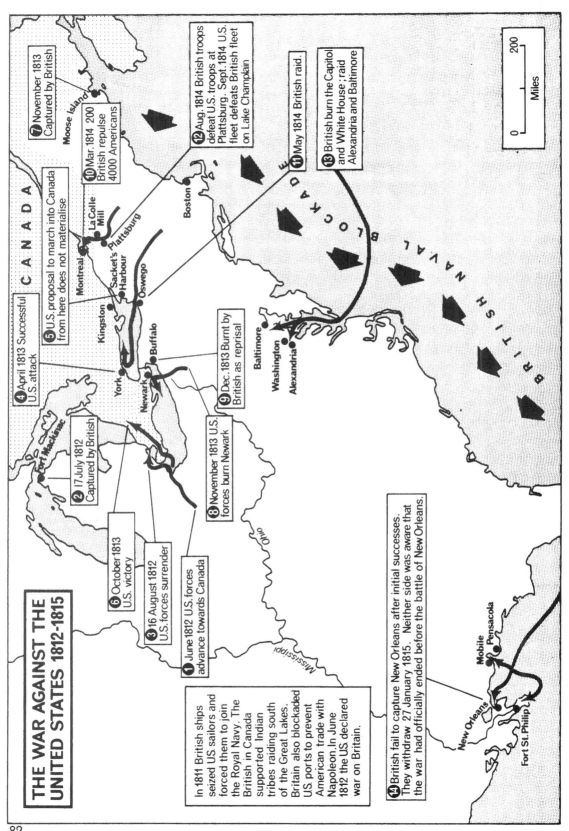

THE WAR AGAINST THE UNITED STATES 1812-1815

In 1811 British ships seized US sailors and forced them to join the Royal Navy. The British in Canada supported Indian tribes raiding south of the Great Lakes. Britain also blockaded US ports to prevent American trade with Napoleon. In June 1812 the US declared war on Britain.

1 June 1812 U.S. forces advance towards Canada

2 17 July 1812 Captured by British

3 16 August 1812 U.S. forces surrender

4 April 1813 Successful U.S. attack

5 U.S. proposal to march into Canada from here does not materialise

6 October 1813 U.S. victory

7 November 1813 Captured by British

8 November 1813 U.S. forces burn Newark

9 Dec. 1813 Burnt by British as reprisal

10 Mar. 1814 200 British repulse 4000 Americans

11 May 1814 British raid.

12 Aug.1814 British troops defeat U.S. troops at Plattsburg. Sept.1814 U.S. fleet defeats British fleet on Lake Champlain

13 British burn the Capitol and White House ; raid Alexandria and Baltimore

14 British fail to capture New Orleans after initial successes. They withdraw 27 January 1815. Neither side was aware that the war had officially ended before the battle of New Orleans.

BRITISH NAVAL BLOCKADE

CANADA

Moose Island

Montreal

La Colle Mill

Plattsburg

Sacket's Harbour

Kingston

Oswego

Boston

York

Newark

Buffalo

Baltimore

Washington

Alexandria

Fort Mackinac

Ohio

Mississippi

Mobile

Pensacola

New Orleans

Fort St. Philip

0   200

Miles

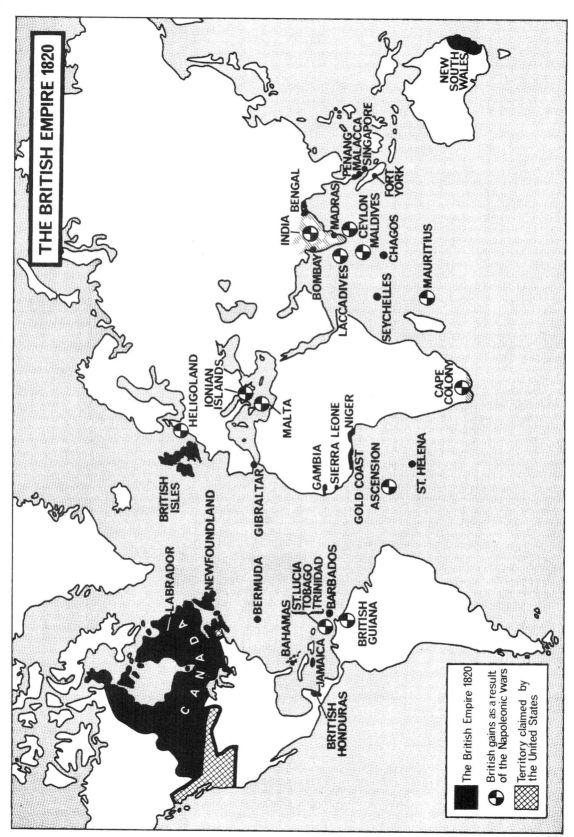

THE BRITISH EMPIRE 1820

NEW SOUTH WALES

PENANG
MALACCA
SINGAPORE
FORT YORK

INDIA
BENGAL
MADRAS
CEYLON
MALDIVES
CHAGOS
MAURITIUS
BOMBAY
LACCADIVES
SEYCHELLES

HELIGOLAND
IONIAN ISLANDS
MALTA
NIGER
CAPE COLONY

BRITISH ISLES
GIBRALTAR
GAMBIA
SIERRA LEONE
GOLD COAST
ASCENSION
ST. HELENA

LABRADOR
NEWFOUNDLAND
BERMUDA
BAHAMAS
JAMAICA
ST. LUCIA
TOBAGO
TRINIDAD
BARBADOS
BRITISH GUIANA
BRITISH HONDURAS
CANADA

The British Empire 1820

British gains as a result
of the Napoleonic wars

Territory claimed by
the United States

83

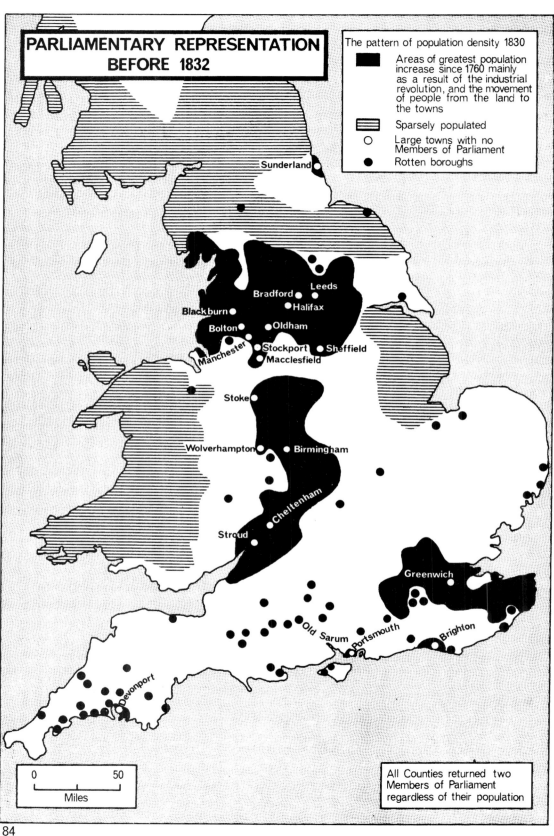

PARLIAMENTARY REPRESENTATION BEFORE 1832

The pattern of population density 1830

Areas of greatest population increase since 1760 mainly as a result of the industrial revolution, and the movement of people from the land to the towns

Sparsely populated

○ Large towns with no Members of Parliament

● Rotten boroughs

Sunderland

Bradford ● Leeds
Blackburn ● ● Halifax
Bolton ● ● Oldham
Manchester ● Stockport ● Sheffield
Macclesfield

Stoke

Wolverhampton ● Birmingham

Cheltenham

Stroud

Greenwich

Old Sarum Portsmouth Brighton

Devonport

All Counties returned two Members of Parliament regardless of their population

0   50
Miles

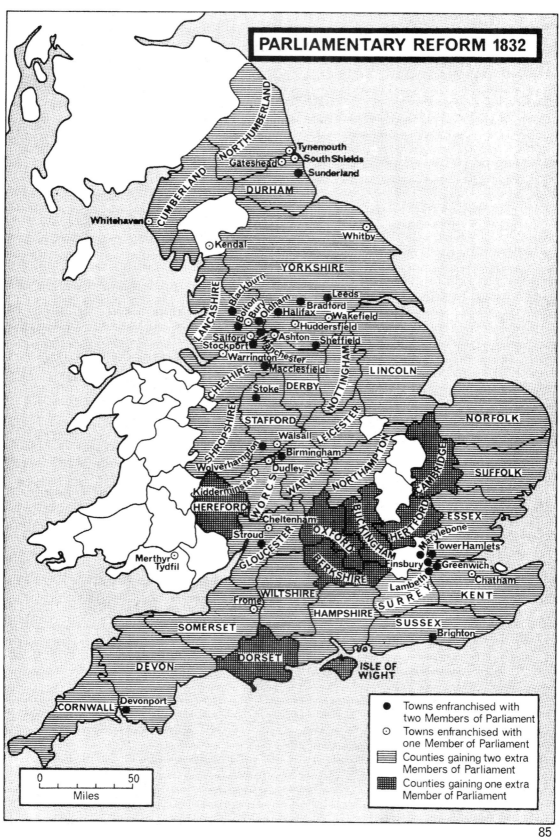

PARLIAMENTARY REFORM 1832

NORTHUMBERLAND

CUMBERLAND

Tynemouth
Gateshead · South Shields
· Sunderland

DURHAM

Whitehaven

Kendal

Whitby

YORKSHIRE

LANCASHIRE
Blackburn
Bolton · Bury · Oldham
Leeds
Bradford
Halifax · Wakefield
Huddersfield
Salford · Ashton
Stockport · Manchester · Sheffield
Warrington
Macclesfield

CHESHIRE

LINCOLN

Stoke

DERBY

SHROPSHIRE

STAFFORD

NOTTINGHAM

NORFOLK

Walsall
Wolverhampton
Birmingham
LEICESTER
Kidderminster · Dudley
WARWICK
NORTHAMPTON
CAMBRIDGE
SUFFOLK

HEREFORD

WORCS

Cheltenham
Stroud

OXFORD
BUCKINGHAM
HERTFORD

ESSEX

Marylebone
Tower Hamlets

GLOUCESTER
BERKSHIRE
Finsbury
Greenwich
Lambeth
Chatham

Merthyr
Tydfil

WILTSHIRE
SURREY
KENT

Frome
HAMPSHIRE
SUSSEX

SOMERSET

Brighton

DORSET

ISLE OF
WIGHT

DEVON

CORNWALL
Devonport

Legend

● Towns enfranchised with two Members of Parliament

⊙ Towns enfranchised with one Member of Parliament

▦ Counties gaining two extra Members of Parliament

▨ Counties gaining one extra Member of Parliament

0   50
Miles

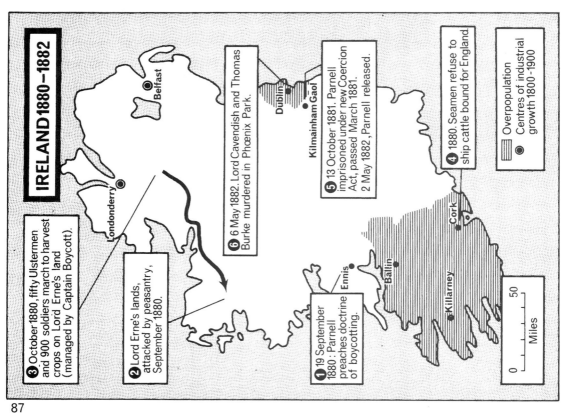

IRELAND 1880–1882

3 October 1880, fifty Ulstermen and 900 soldiers march to harvest crops on Lord Erne's land (managed by Captain Boycott).

2 Lord Erne's lands, attacked by peasantry, September 1880.

6 6 May 1882. Lord Cavendish and Thomas Burke murdered in Phœnix Park.

5 13 October 1881. Parnell imprisoned under new Coercion Act, passed March 1881. 2 May 1882 ,Parnell released.

4 1880. Seamen refuse to ship cattle bound for England.

1 19 September 1880 : Parnell preaches doctrine of boycotting.

Belfast

Londonderry

Dublin

Kilmainham Gaol

Cork

Ennis

Ballin

Killarney

☐ Overpopulation
◉ Centres of industrial growth 1800-1900

0   50
Miles

87

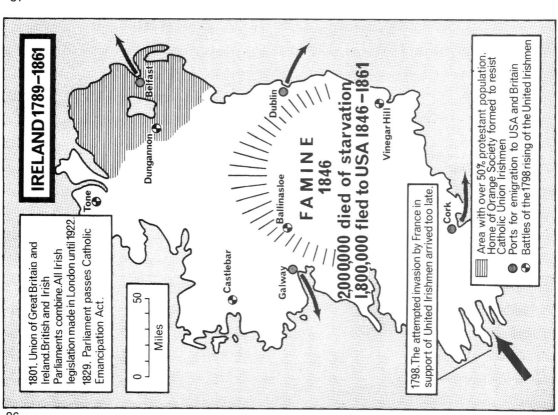

IRELAND 1789–1861

1801. Union of Great Britain and Ireland.British and Irish Parliaments combine.All Irish legislation made in London until 1922.

1829. Parliament passes Catholic Emancipation Act.

FAMINE 1846
2000000 died of starvation
1,800,000 fled to USA 1846–1861

Belfast

Dublin

Dungannon

Vinegar Hill

Tone

Ballinasloe

Cork

Castlebar

Galway

1798.The attempted invasion by France in support of United Irishmen arrived too late.

▥ Area with over 50% protestant population. Home of Orange Society formed to resist Catholic Union Irishmen
◐ Ports for emigration to USA and Britain
✦ Battles of the1798 rising of the United Irishmen

0   50
Miles

86

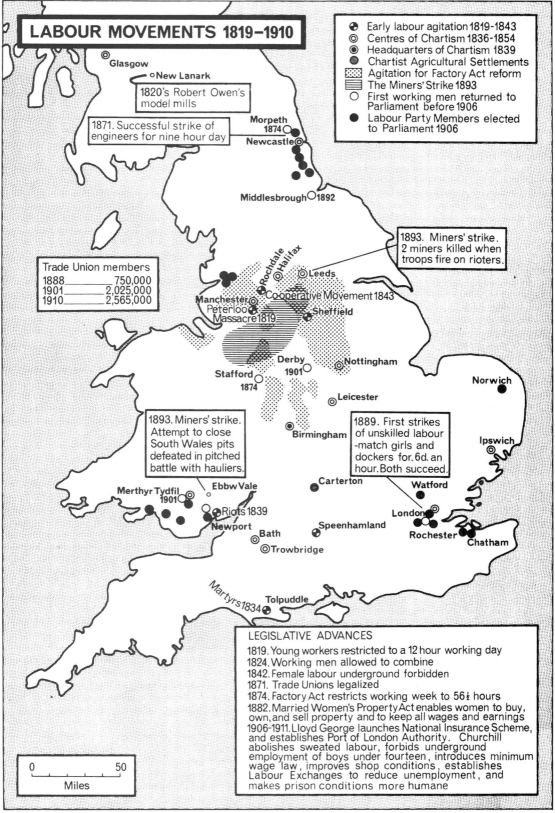

LABOUR MOVEMENTS 1819–1910

Legend:
- ⊕ Early labour agitation 1819-1843
- ◎ Centres of Chartism 1836-1854
- ◉ Headquarters of Chartism 1839
- ⊖ Chartist Agricultural Settlements
- ▦ Agitation for Factory Act reform
- ▤ The Miners' Strike 1893
- ○ First working men returned to Parliament before 1906
- ● Labour Party Members elected to Parliament 1906

Glasgow

New Lanark

1820's Robert Owen's model mills

1871. Successful strike of engineers for nine hour day

Morpeth 1874
Newcastle

Middlesbrough 1892

1893. Miners' strike. 2 miners killed when troops fire on rioters.

Trade Union members
1888————750,000
1901————2,025,000
1910————2,565,000

Rochdale Halifax
Leeds
Manchester Co-operative Movement 1843
Peterloo Sheffield
Massacre 1819

Derby 1901

Stafford 1874

Nottingham

Norwich

Leicester

1893. Miners' strike. Attempt to close South Wales pits defeated in pitched battle with hauliers.

Birmingham

1889. First strikes of unskilled labour -match girls and dockers for 6d. an hour. Both succeed.

Ipswich

Carterton

Watford

Merthyr Tydfil 1901

Ebbw Vale
Riots 1839
Newport

Bath
Trowbridge

Speenhamland

London
Rochester
Chatham

Martyrs 1834
Tolpuddle

LEGISLATIVE ADVANCES
1819. Young workers restricted to a 12 hour working day
1824. Working men allowed to combine
1842. Female labour underground forbidden
1871. Trade Unions legalized
1874. Factory Act restricts working week to 56½ hours
1882. Married Women's Property Act enables women to buy, own, and sell property and to keep all wages and earnings
1906-1911. Lloyd George launches National Insurance Scheme, and establishes Port of London Authority. Churchill abolishes sweated labour, forbids underground employment of boys under fourteen, introduces minimum wage law, improves shop conditions, establishes Labour Exchanges to reduce unemployment, and makes prison conditions more humane

0   50
Miles

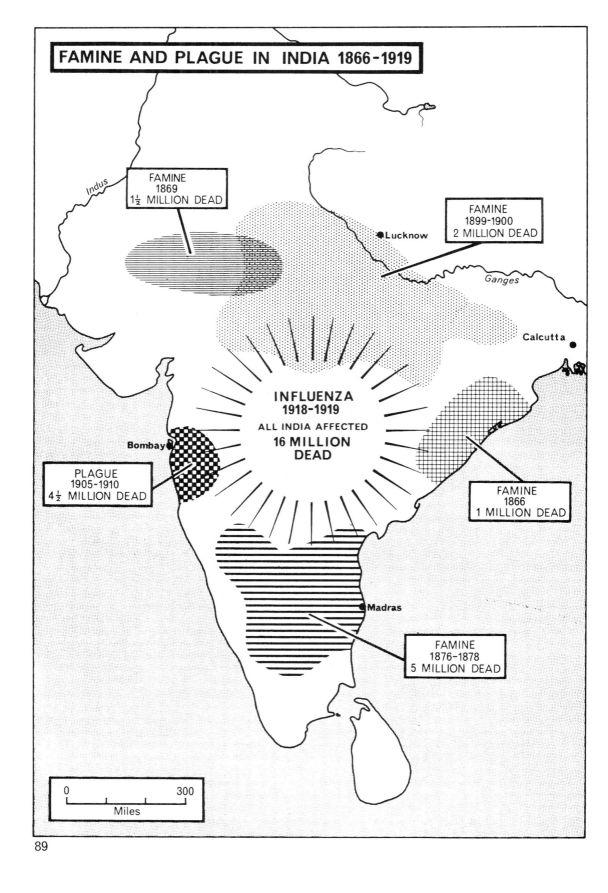

FAMINE AND PLAGUE IN INDIA 1866-1919

FAMINE
1869
1½ MILLION DEAD

FAMINE
1899-1900
2 MILLION DEAD

●Lucknow

Indus

Ganges

●Calcutta

INFLUENZA
1918-1919
ALL INDIA AFFECTED
16 MILLION
DEAD

Bombay●

PLAGUE
1905-1910
4½ MILLION DEAD

FAMINE
1866
1 MILLION DEAD

●Madras

FAMINE
1876-1878
5 MILLION DEAD

0   300
Miles

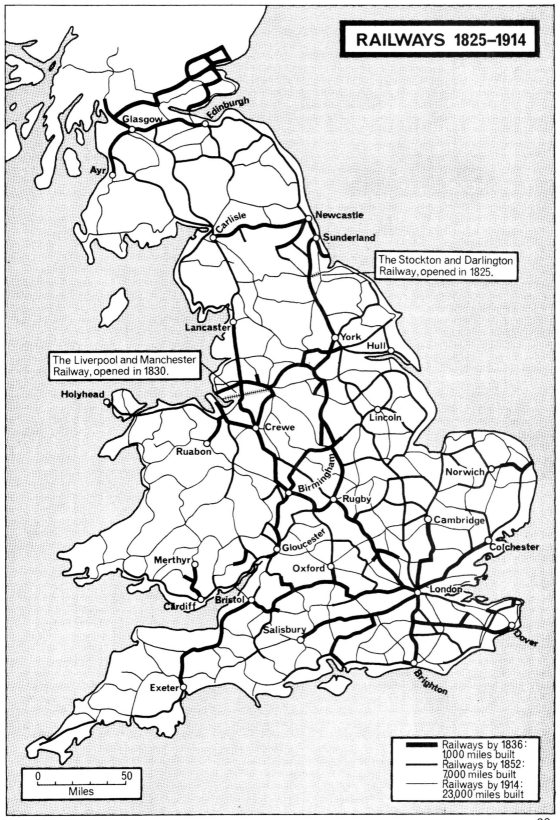

RAILWAYS 1825–1914

The Stockton and Darlington Railway, opened in 1825.

The Liverpool and Manchester Railway, opened in 1830.

Glasgow
Edinburgh
Ayr
Carlisle
Newcastle
Sunderland
Lancaster
York
Hull
Holyhead
Crewe
Lincoln
Ruabon
Birmingham
Norwich
Rugby
Cambridge
Gloucester
Colchester
Merthyr
Oxford
Cardiff
Bristol
London
Salisbury
Dover
Exeter
Brighton

0 50
Miles

Railways by 1836: 1,000 miles built
Railways by 1852: 7,000 miles built
Railways by 1914: 23,000 miles built

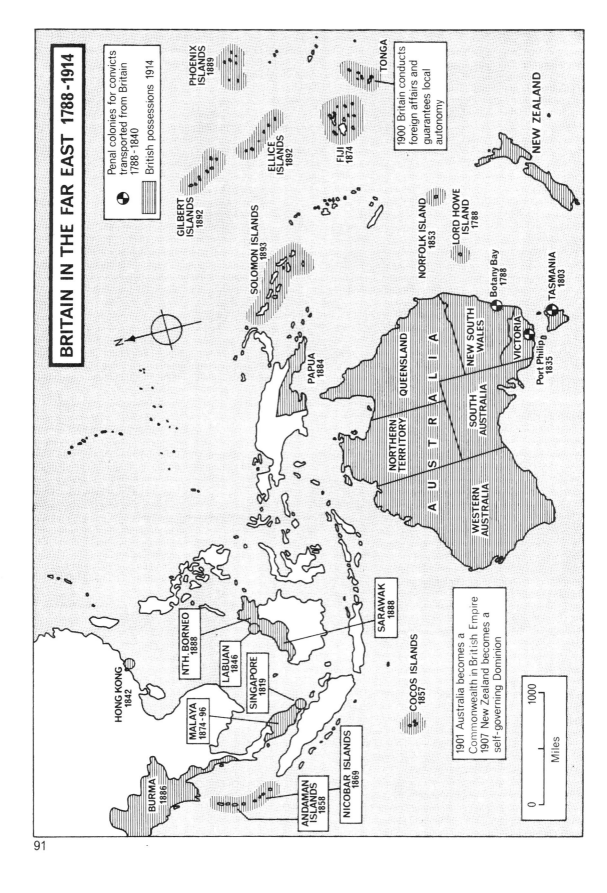

BRITAIN IN THE FAR EAST 1788-1914

Penal colonies for convicts transported from Britain 1788-1840

British possessions 1914

PHOENIX ISLANDS 1889

TONGA

1900 Britain conducts foreign affairs and guarantees local autonomy

GILBERT ISLANDS 1892

ELLICE ISLANDS 1892

FIJI 1874

NEW ZEALAND

SOLOMON ISLANDS 1893

NORFOLK ISLAND 1853

LORD HOWE ISLAND 1788

PAPUA 1884

QUEENSLAND

NORTHERN TERRITORY

WESTERN AUSTRALIA

SOUTH AUSTRALIA

NEW SOUTH WALES

A U S T R A L I A

VICTORIA

Botany Bay 1788

Port Philip 1835

TASMANIA 1803

HONG KONG 1842

NTH. BORNEO 1888

LABUAN 1846

SINGAPORE 1819

SARAWAK 1888

COCOS ISLANDS 1857

MALAYA 1874-96

BURMA 1886

ANDAMAN ISLANDS 1858

NICOBAR ISLANDS 1869

1901 Australia becomes a Commonwealth in British Empire
1907 New Zealand becomes a self-governing Dominion

0   1000
Miles

N

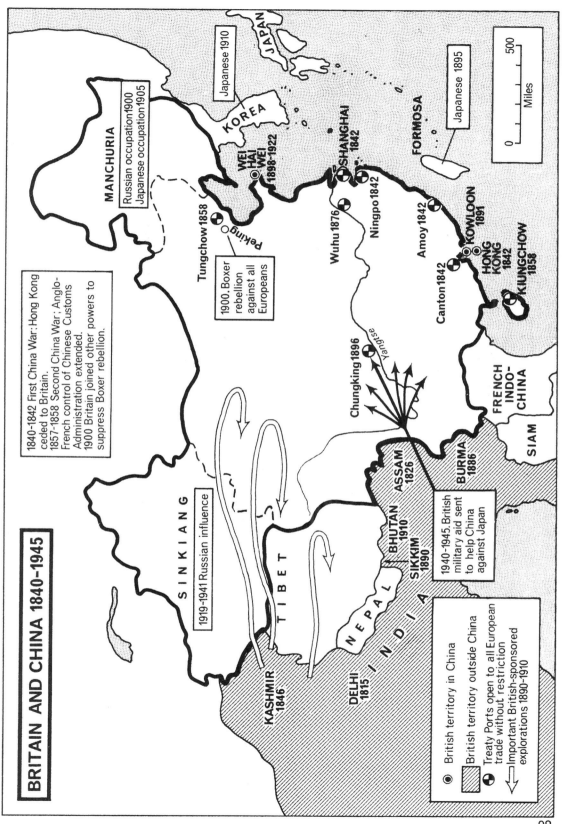

BRITAIN AND CHINA 1840–1945

MANCHURIA

Russian occupation 1900
Japanese occupation 1905

Japanese 1910

KOREA

JAPAN

Japanese 1895

FORMOSA

500
Miles
0

SHANGHAI 1842

WEI HAI WEI 1898-1922

Ningpo 1842

Amoy 1842

KOWLOON 1891

HONG KONG 1842

KIUNGCHOW 1858

Wuhu 1876

Tungchow 1858

Peking

1900, Boxer rebellion against all Europeans

Canton 1842

1840-1842 First China War; Hong Kong ceded to Britain.
1857-1858 Second China War; Anglo-French control of Chinese Customs Administration extended.
1900 Britain joined other powers to suppress Boxer rebellion.

Chungking 1896

Yangtse

FRENCH INDO-CHINA

SIAM

BURMA 1886

ASSAM 1826

1940-1945. British military aid sent to help China against Japan

SINKIANG

1919-1941 Russian influence

T I B E T

BHUTAN 1910

SIKKIM 1890

N E P A L

I N D I A

KASHMIR 1846

DELHI 1815

● British territory in China

British territory outside China

Treaty Ports open to all European trade without restriction

Important British-sponsored explorations 1890-1910

92

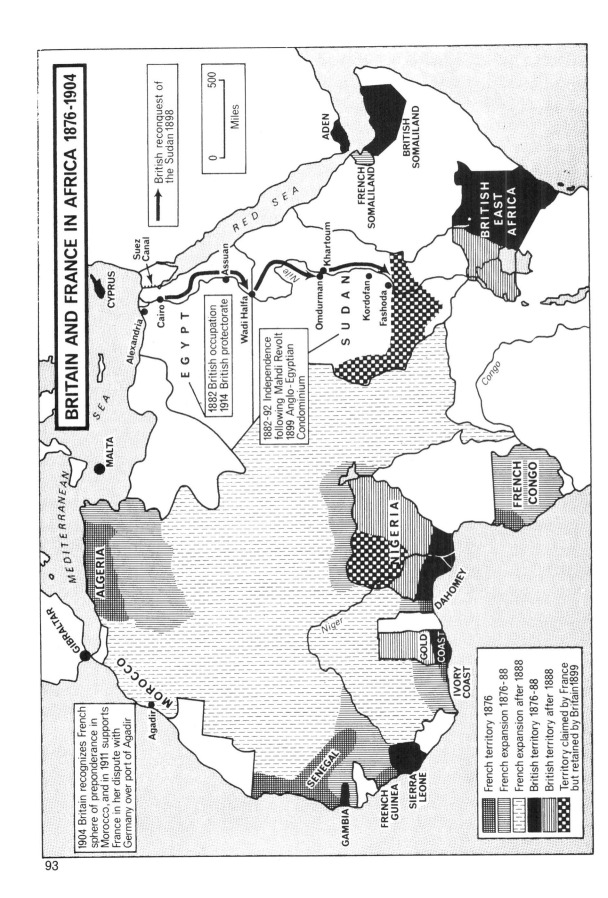

BRITAIN AND FRANCE IN AFRICA 1876-1904

British reconquest of the Sudan 1898

500

0

Miles

ADEN

RED SEA

BRITISH SOMALILAND

FRENCH SOMALILAND

BRITISH EAST AFRICA

Suez Canal

Assuan

Khartoum

Alexandria

Cairo

EGYPT

Wadi Halfa

Nile

Omdurman

Kordofan

Fashoda

SUDAN

Congo

CYPRUS

1882 British occupation
1914 British protectorate

1882-92 Independence
following Mahdi Revolt
1899 Anglo-Egyptian
Condominium

MALTA

MEDITERRANEAN SEA

FRENCH CONGO

ALGERIA

NIGERIA

GIBRALTAR

DAHOMEY

Niger

GOLD COAST

IVORY COAST

MOROCCO

Agadir

SENEGAL

FRENCH GUINEA

SIERRA LEONE

GAMBIA

1904 Britain recognizes French
sphere of preponderance in
Morocco, and in 1911 supports
France in her dispute with
Germany over port of Agadir

French territory 1876

French expansion 1876-88

French expansion after 1888

British territory 1876-88

British territory after 1888

Territory claimed by France
but retained by Britain 1899

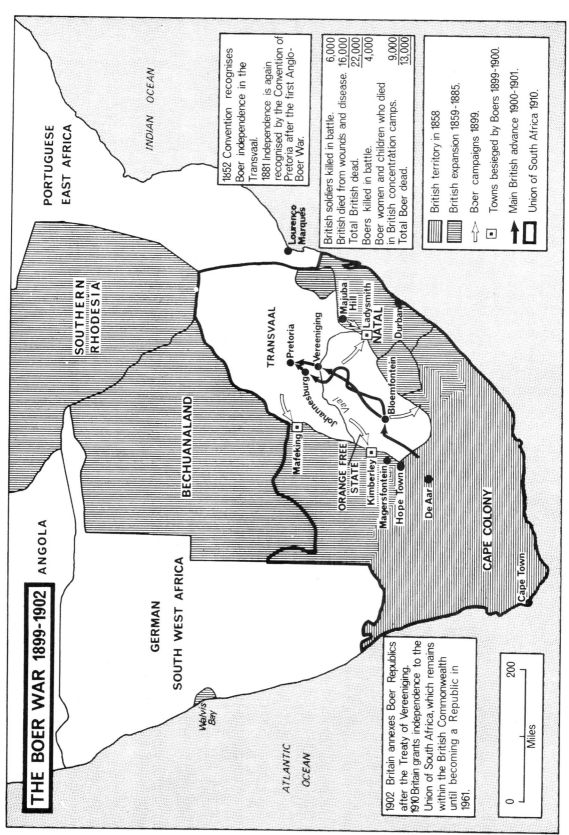

THE BOER WAR 1899-1902

INDIAN OCEAN

PORTUGUESE EAST AFRICA

1852 Convention recognises Boer independence in the Transvaal.
1881 Independence is again recognised by the Convention of Pretoria after the first Anglo-Boer War.

British soldiers killed in battle.	6,000
British died from wounds and disease.	16,000
Total British dead.	22,000
Boers killed in battle.	4,000
Boer women and children who died in British concentration camps.	9,000
Total Boer dead.	13,000

▨	British territory in 1858
▨	British expansion 1859-1885.
↗	Boer campaigns 1899.
▫	Towns besieged by Boers 1899-1900.
⬆	Main British advance 1900-1901.
▯	Union of South Africa 1910.

Lourenço Marquês

SOUTHERN RHODESIA

Majuba Hill
Ladysmith
NATAL
Durban

TRANSVAAL

Pretoria
Vereeniging

Johannesburg
Vaal

BECHUANALAND

Bloemfontein

Mafeking

ORANGE FREE STATE

Kimberley
Magersfontein
Hope Town

De Aar

GERMAN SOUTH WEST AFRICA

ANGOLA

CAPE COLONY

Walvis Bay

Cape Town

ATLANTIC OCEAN

1902 Britain annexes Boer Republics after the Treaty of Vereeniging.
1910 Britain grants independence to the Union of South Africa, which remains within the British Commonwealth until becoming a Republic in 1961.

0		200

Miles

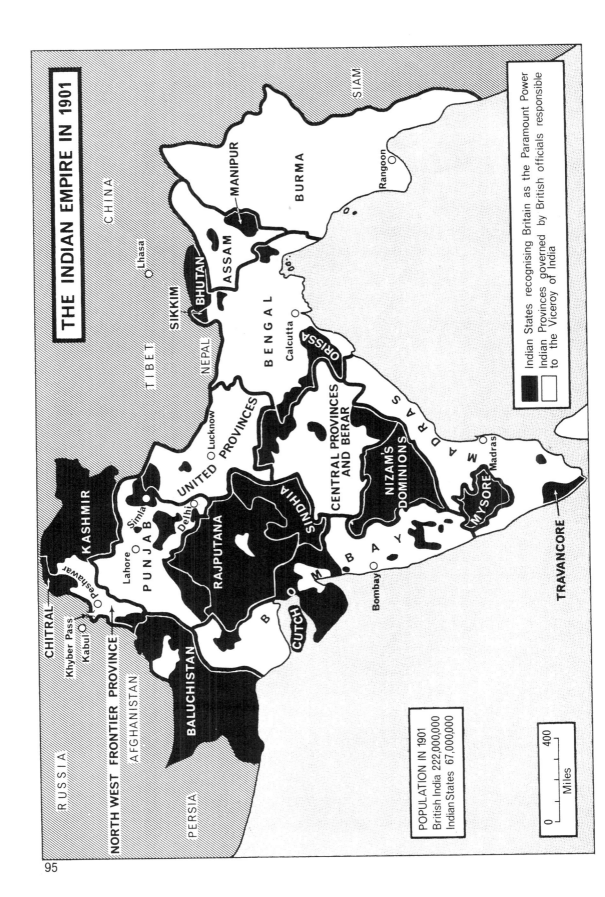

THE INDIAN EMPIRE IN 1901

RUSSIA

PERSIA

AFGHANISTAN

NORTH WEST FRONTIER PROVINCE

CHITRAL

Khyber Pass

Kabul

Peshawar

BALUCHISTAN

KASHMIR

CHINA

TIBET

Lhasa

NEPAL

SIKKIM

BHUTAN

ASSAM

MANIPUR

BURMA

SIAM

Rangoon

PUNJAB

Lahore

Simla

Delhi

UNITED PROVINCES

Lucknow

RAJPUTANA

SINDHIA

BENGAL

Calcutta

ORISSA

CENTRAL PROVINCES AND BERAR

NIZAM'S DOMINIONS

M A D R A S

CUTCH

B

B A Y

Bombay

MYSORE

Madras

TRAVANCORE

POPULATION IN 1901
British India 222,000,000
Indian States 67,000,000

Indian States recognising Britain as the Paramount Power

Indian Provinces governed by British officials responsible to the Viceroy of India

0   400
Miles

95

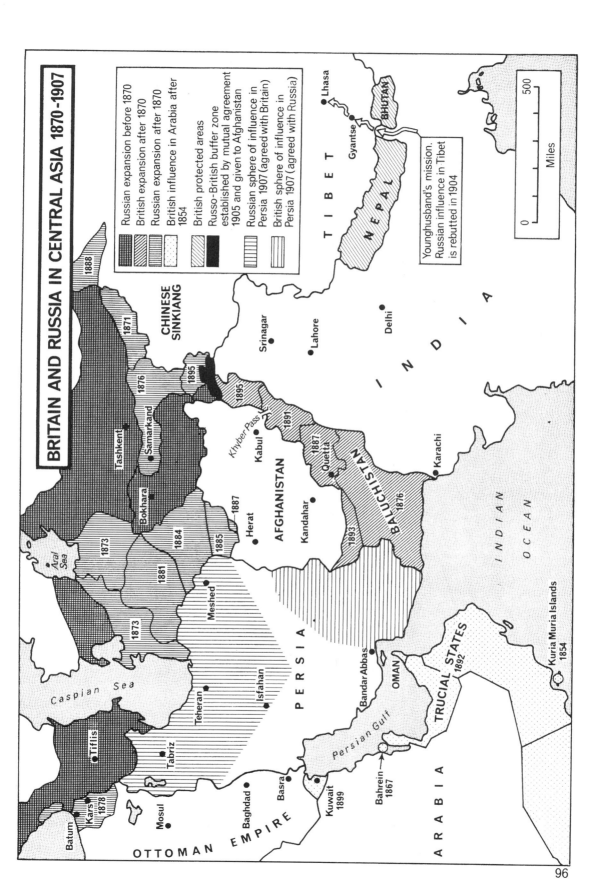

BRITAIN AND RUSSIA IN CENTRAL ASIA 1870-1907

Russian expansion before 1870

British expansion after 1870

Russian expansion after 1870

British influence in Arabia after 1854

British protected areas

Russo-British buffer zone established by mutual agreement 1905 and given to Afghanistan

Russian sphere of influence in Persia 1907 (agreed with Britain)

British sphere of influence in Persia 1907 (agreed with Russia)

Younghusband's mission. Russian influence in Tibet is rebutted in 1904

Miles

0   500

TIBET

Lhasa

Gyantse

BHUTAN

NEPAL

CHINESE SINKIANG

1888

1871

1876

1895

1893

Srinagar

Lahore

Delhi

INDIA

Tashkent

Samarkand

Khyber Pass

Kabul

1891

1887

Quetta

1876

BALUCHISTAN

Karachi

Bokhara

1887

1873

1884

1885

Herat

AFGHANISTAN

Kandahar

1893

Aral Sea

1881

Meshed

INDIAN OCEAN

1873

PERSIA

Teheran

Isfahan

Bandar Abbas

OMAN

TRUCIAL STATES

1892

Kuria Muria Islands

1854

Caspian Sea

Tiflis

Tabriz

Persian Gulf

Bahrein

1867

ARABIA

Kars

1878

Batum

Mosul

Baghdad

Basra

Kuwait

1899

OTTOMAN EMPIRE

96

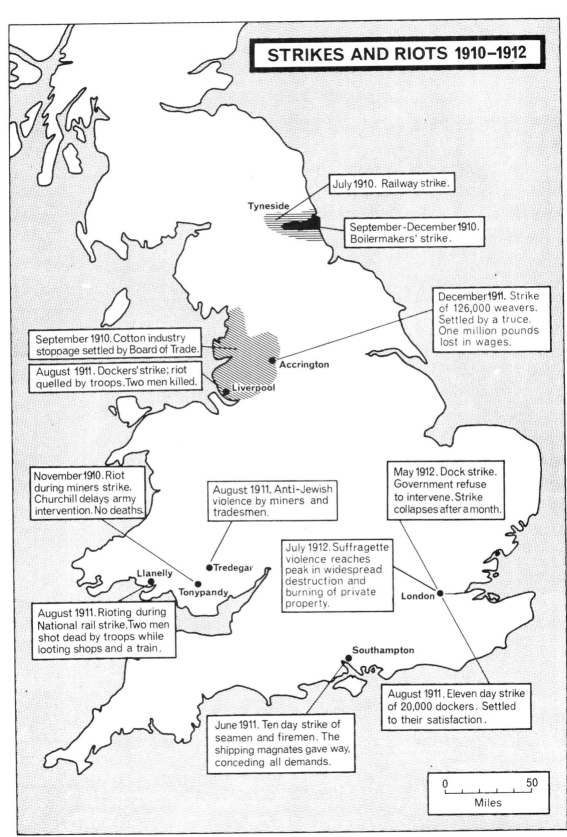

STRIKES AND RIOTS 1910–1912

July 1910. Railway strike.

Tyneside

September–December 1910. Boilermakers' strike.

December 1911. Strike of 126,000 weavers. Settled by a truce. One million pounds lost in wages.

September 1910. Cotton industry stoppage settled by Board of Trade.

August 1911. Dockers' strike; riot quelled by troops. Two men killed.

Accrington

Liverpool

November 1910. Riot during miners strike. Churchill delays army intervention. No deaths.

August 1911. Anti-Jewish violence by miners and tradesmen.

May 1912. Dock strike. Government refuse to intervene. Strike collapses after a month.

July 1912. Suffragette violence reaches peak in widespread destruction and burning of private property.

Tredegar

Llanelly

Tonypandy

London

August 1911. Rioting during National rail strike. Two men shot dead by troops while looting shops and a train.

Southampton

August 1911. Eleven day strike of 20,000 dockers. Settled to their satisfaction.

June 1911. Ten day strike of seamen and firemen. The shipping magnates gave way, conceding all demands.

0   50
Miles

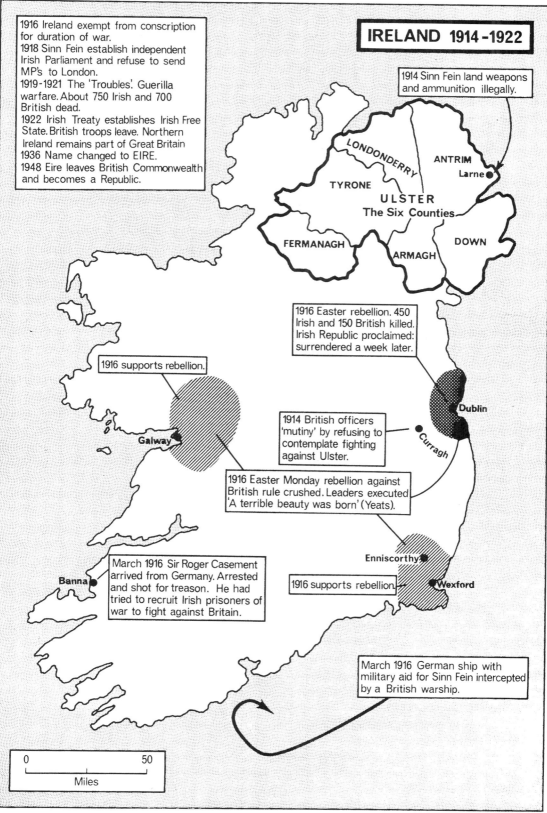

IRELAND 1914-1922

1916 Ireland exempt from conscription for duration of war.
1918 Sinn Fein establish independent Irish Parliament and refuse to send MP's to London.
1919-1921 The 'Troubles'. Guerilla warfare. About 750 Irish and 700 British dead.
1922 Irish Treaty establishes Irish Free State. British troops leave. Northern Ireland remains part of Great Britain
1936 Name changed to EIRE.
1948 Eire leaves British Commonwealth and becomes a Republic.

1914 Sinn Fein land weapons and ammunition illegally.

LONDONDERRY

ANTRIM

Larne

TYRONE

ULSTER
The Six Counties

FERMANAGH

ARMAGH

DOWN

1916 Easter rebellion. 450 Irish and 150 British killed. Irish Republic proclaimed: surrendered a week later.

1916 supports rebellion.

1914 British officers 'mutiny' by refusing to contemplate fighting against Ulster.

Dublin

Galway

Curragh

1916 Easter Monday rebellion against British rule crushed. Leaders executed 'A terrible beauty was born' (Yeats).

Enniscorthy

March 1916 Sir Roger Casement arrived from Germany. Arrested and shot for treason. He had tried to recruit Irish prisoners of war to fight against Britain.

1916 supports rebellion.

Wexford

Banna

March 1916 German ship with military aid for Sinn Fein intercepted by a British warship.

0   50
    Miles

98

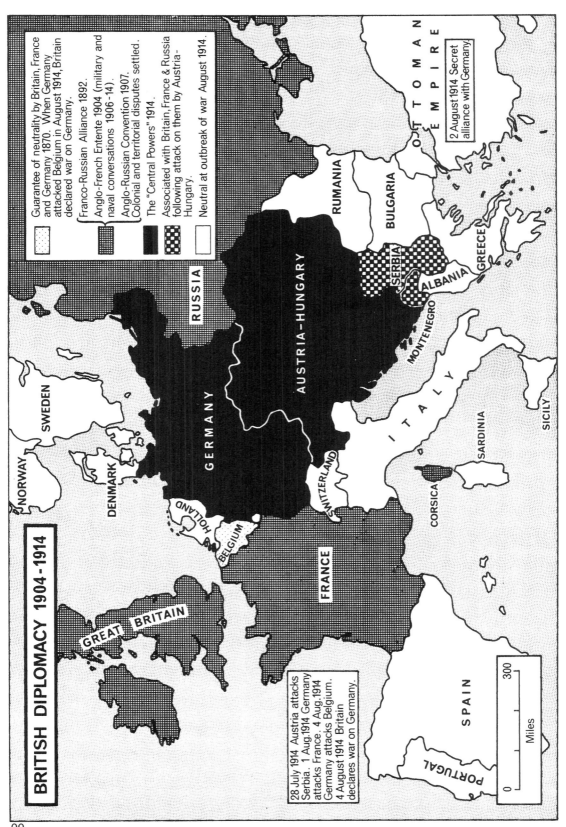

BRITISH DIPLOMACY 1904-1914

Guarantee of neutrality by Britain, France and Germany 1870. When Germany attacked Belgium in August 1914, Britain declared war on Germany.

Franco-Russian Alliance 1892.

Anglo-French Entente 1904 (military and naval conversations 1906-14).

Anglo-Russian Convention 1907. Colonial and territorial disputes settled.

The "Central Powers" 1914.

Associated with Britain, France & Russia following attack on them by Austria-Hungary.

Neutral at outbreak of war August 1914.

2 August 1914 Secret alliance with Germany.

28 July 1914 Austria attacks Serbia. 1 Aug.1914 Germany attacks France. 4 Aug.1914 Germany attacks Belgium. 4 August 1914 Britain declares war on Germany.

NORWAY

SWEDEN

DENMARK

GREAT BRITAIN

HOLLAND

BELGIUM

FRANCE

GERMANY

SWITZERLAND

RUSSIA

AUSTRIA-HUNGARY

ITALY

RUMANIA

BULGARIA

SERBIA

ALBANIA

MONTENEGRO

GREECE

OTTOMAN EMPIRE

SPAIN

PORTUGAL

CORSICA

SARDINIA

SICILY

Miles

0   300

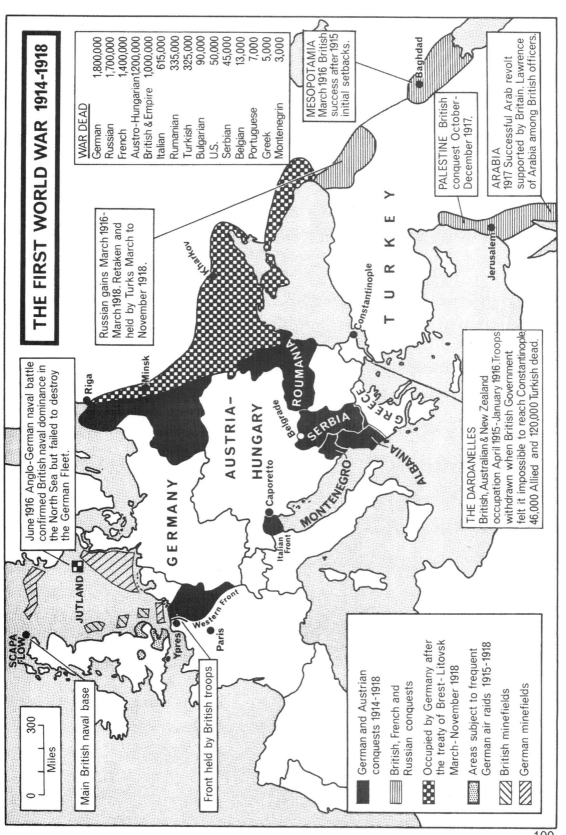

THE FIRST WORLD WAR 1914-1918

WAR DEAD

German	1,800,000
Russian	1,700,000
French	1,400,000
Austro-Hungarian	1,200,000
British & Empire	1,000,000
Italian	615,000
Rumanian	335,000
Turkish	325,000
Bulgarian	90,000
U.S.	50,000
Serbian	45,000
Belgian	13,000
Portuguese	7,000
Greek	5,000
Montenegrin	3,000

MESOPOTAMIA March 1916 British success after 1915 initial setbacks.

PALESTINE British conquest October–December 1917.

ARABIA 1917 Successful Arab revolt supported by Britain. Lawrence of Arabia among British officers.

Russian gains March 1916-March 1918. Retaken and held by Turks March to November 1918.

June 1916 Anglo-German naval battle confirmed British naval dominance in the North Sea but failed to destroy the German Fleet.

THE DARDANELLES British, Australian & New Zealand occupation April 1915-January 1916.Troops withdrawn when British Government felt it impossible to reach Constantinople. 46,000 Allied and 120,000 Turkish dead.

Baghdad

Jerusalem

Constantinople

T U R K E Y

G R E E C E

ALBANIA

MONTENEGRO

SERBIA

Belgrade

ROUMANIA

AUSTRIA–HUNGARY

GERMANY

Kharkov

Minsk

Riga

Caporetto

Italian Front

Western Front

Paris

Ypres

JUTLAND

SCAPA FLOW

Main British naval base

Front held by British troops

■ German and Austrian conquests 1914-1918

▥ British, French and Russian conquests

▦ Occupied by Germany after the treaty of Brest-Litovsk March-November 1918

⬚ Areas subject to frequent German air raids 1915-1918

▨ British minefields

▧ German minefields

0 300

Miles

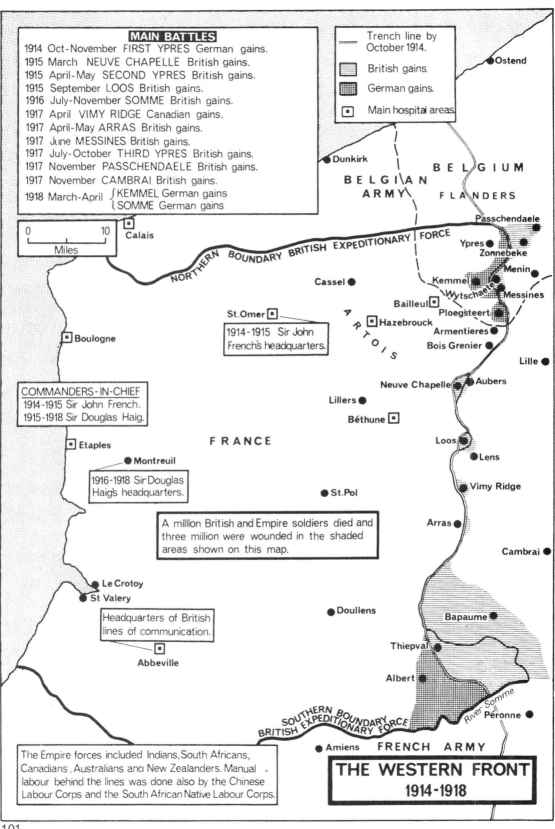

MAIN BATTLES

1914 Oct-November FIRST YPRES German gains.
1915 March NEUVE CHAPELLE British gains.
1915 April-May SECOND YPRES British gains.
1915 September LOOS British gains.
1916 July-November SOMME British gains.
1917 April VIMY RIDGE Canadian gains.
1917 April-May ARRAS British gains.
1917 June MESSINES British gains.
1917 July-October THIRD YPRES British gains.
1917 November PASSCHENDAELE British gains.
1917 November CAMBRAI British gains.
1918 March-April { KEMMEL German gains
                  { SOMME German gains

Trench line by
October 1914.

British gains

German gains

Main hospital areas.

0   10
Miles

NORTHERN BOUNDARY BRITISH EXPEDITIONARY FORCE

Ostend

BELGIUM

BELGIAN
ARMY

FLANDERS

Dunkirk

Passchendaele
Ypres
Zonnebeke
Menin
Kemmel
Wytschaete
Messines
Ploegsteert
Armentieres
Bois Grenier
Lille

Calais

Cassel

St.Omer

1914-1915 Sir John
French's headquarters.

Bailleul
Hazebrouck

ARTOIS

Boulogne

Neuve Chapelle
Aubers

COMMANDERS-IN-CHIEF
1914-1915 Sir John French.
1915-1918 Sir Douglas Haig.

Lillers

Béthune

Etaples

Montreuil

FRANCE

1916-1918 Sir Douglas
Haig's headquarters.

St.Pol

Loos
Lens
Vimy Ridge
Arras
Cambrai

A million British and Empire soldiers died and
three million were wounded in the shaded
areas shown on this map.

Le Crotoy
St Valery

Doullens

Bapaume

Headquarters of British
lines of communication.

Thiepval

Abbeville

Albert

River Somme
Péronne

SOUTHERN BOUNDARY
BRITISH EXPEDITIONARY FORCE

The Empire forces included Indians, South Africans,
Canadians, Australians and New Zealanders. Manual
labour behind the lines was done also by the Chinese
Labour Corps and the South African Native Labour Corps.

Amiens   FRENCH ARMY

THE WESTERN FRONT
1914-1918

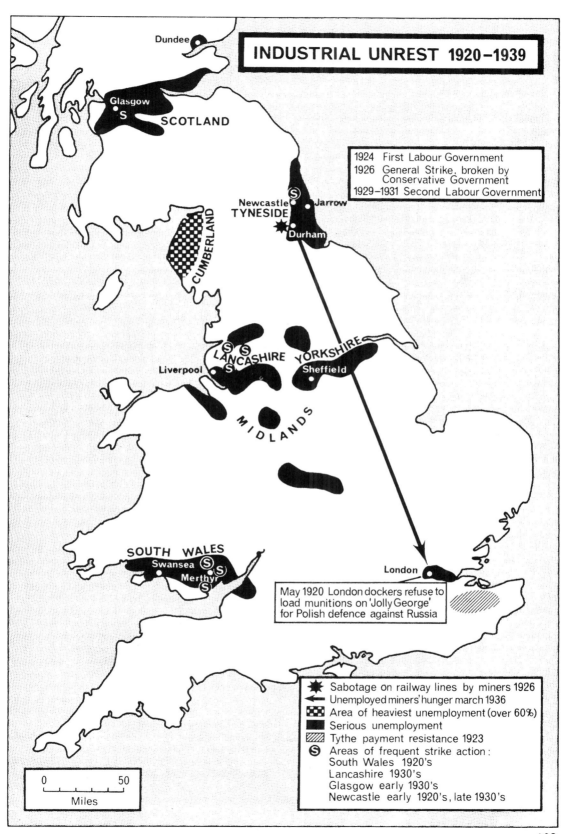

INDUSTRIAL UNREST 1920-1939

Dundee

Glasgow
S

SCOTLAND

1924 First Labour Government
1926 General Strike, broken by
        Conservative Government
1929–1931 Second Labour Government

CUMBERLAND

Newcastle Ⓢ Jarrow
TYNESIDE
✦ Durham

LANCASHIRE ⓈⓈ YORKSHIRE
Liverpool Ⓢ Sheffield

M I D L A N D S

SOUTH WALES
Swansea Ⓢ Ⓢ
Merthyr
Ⓢ

London

May 1920 London dockers refuse to
load munitions on 'Jolly George'
for Polish defence against Russia

✦ Sabotage on railway lines by miners 1926
← Unemployed miners' hunger march 1936
▨ Area of heaviest unemployment (over 60%)
■ Serious unemployment
▨ Tythe payment resistance 1923
Ⓢ Areas of frequent strike action:
   South Wales 1920's
   Lancashire 1930's
   Glasgow early 1930's
   Newcastle early 1920's, late 1930's

0   50
Miles

102

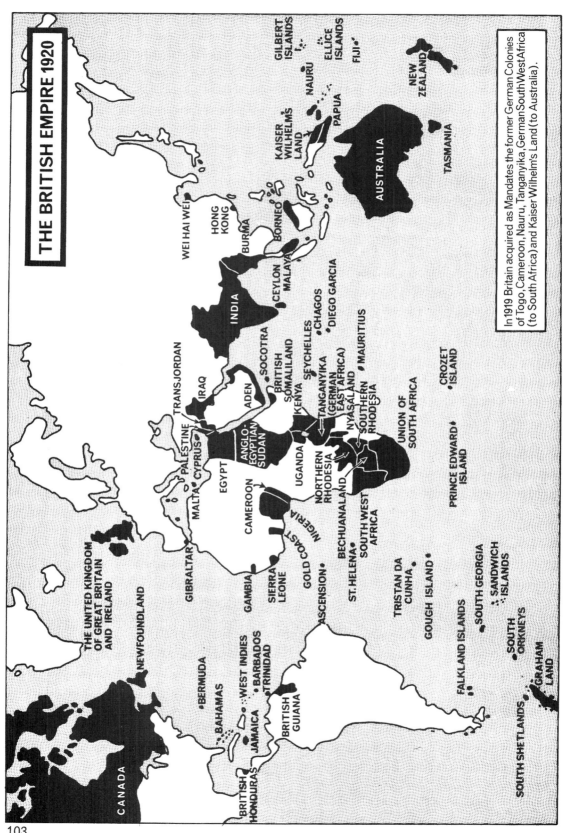

THE BRITISH EMPIRE 1920

In 1919 Britain acquired as Mandates the former German Colonies of Togo, Cameroon, Nauru, Tanganyika, German South West Africa (to South Africa) and Kaiser Wilhelm's Land (to Australia).

CANADA

THE UNITED KINGDOM OF GREAT BRITAIN AND IRELAND

NEWFOUNDLAND

BERMUDA

BAHAMAS

WEST INDIES

JAMAICA

BARBADOS

TRINIDAD

BRITISH HONDURAS

BRITISH GUIANA

FALKLAND ISLANDS

SOUTH GEORGIA

SANDWICH ISLANDS

SOUTH ORKNEYS

SOUTH SHETLANDS

GRAHAM LAND

GIBRALTAR

GAMBIA

SIERRA LEONE

GOLD COAST

NIGERIA

CAMEROON

ASCENSION

ST. HELENA

TRISTAN DA CUNHA

GOUGH ISLAND

PALESTINE

MALTA

CYPRUS

TRANSJORDAN

IRAQ

ADEN

EGYPT

ANGLO-EGYPTIAN SUDAN

UGANDA

BRITISH SOMALILAND

KENYA

TANGANYIKA (GERMAN EAST AFRICA)

NYASALAND

NORTHERN RHODESIA

SOUTHERN RHODESIA

BECHUANALAND

SOUTH WEST AFRICA

UNION OF SOUTH AFRICA

PRINCE EDWARD ISLAND

CROZET ISLAND

SOCOTRA

SEYCHELLES

CHAGOS

DIEGO GARCIA

MAURITIUS

INDIA

CEYLON

MALAYA

BORNEO

BURMA

WEI HAI WEI

HONG KONG

AUSTRALIA

TASMANIA

KAISER WILHELM'S LAND

PAPUA

NAURU

GILBERT ISLANDS

ELLICE ISLANDS

FIJI

NEW ZEALAND

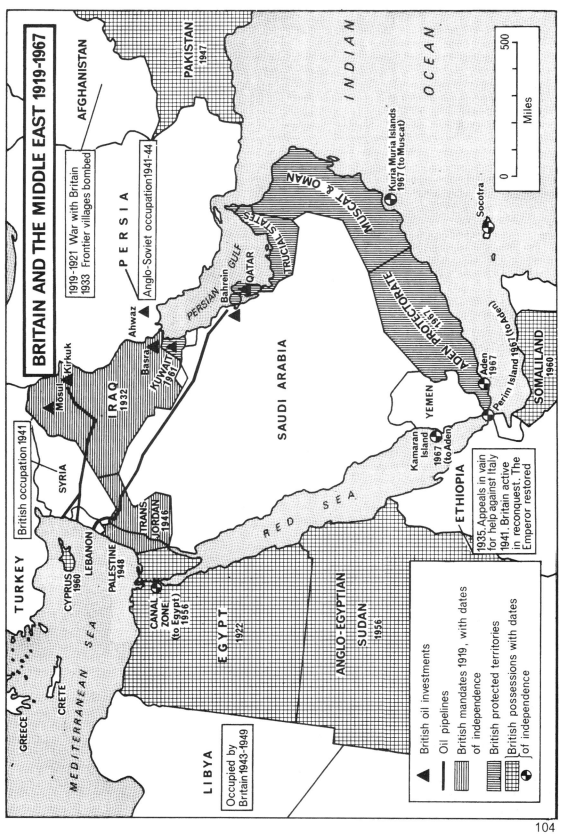

BRITAIN AND THE MIDDLE EAST 1919-1967

AFGHANISTAN

PAKISTAN
1947

PERSIA

1919-1921 War with Britain
1933 Frontier villages bombed

Anglo-Soviet occupation 1941-44

Kuria Muria Islands
1967 (to Muscat)

INDIAN OCEAN

Socotra

OMAN

MUSCAT & OMAN

TRUCIAL STATES

Ahwaz

Kirkuk
Mosul

IRAQ
1932

Basra

KUWAIT
1961

Bahrein
QATAR

PERSIAN GULF

ADEN PROTECTORATE
1967

Aden
1967

Perim Island 1967 (to Aden)

SOMALILAND
1960

SYRIA

British occupation 1941

TURKEY

LEBANON

CYPRUS
1960

PALESTINE
1948

TRANS-
JORDAN
1946

SAUDI ARABIA

YEMEN

Kamaran
Island
1967
(to Aden)

ETHIOPIA

1935. Appeals in vain
for help against Italy
1941. Britain active
in reconquest. The
Emperor restored

RED SEA

CRETE

GREECE

MEDITERRANEAN SEA

CANAL
ZONE
(to Egypt)
1956

EGYPT
1922

ANGLO-EGYPTIAN
SUDAN
1956

LIBYA

Occupied by
Britain 1943-1949

Miles
0   500

British oil investments

Oil pipelines

British mandates 1919, with dates
of independence

British protected territories

British possessions with dates
of independence

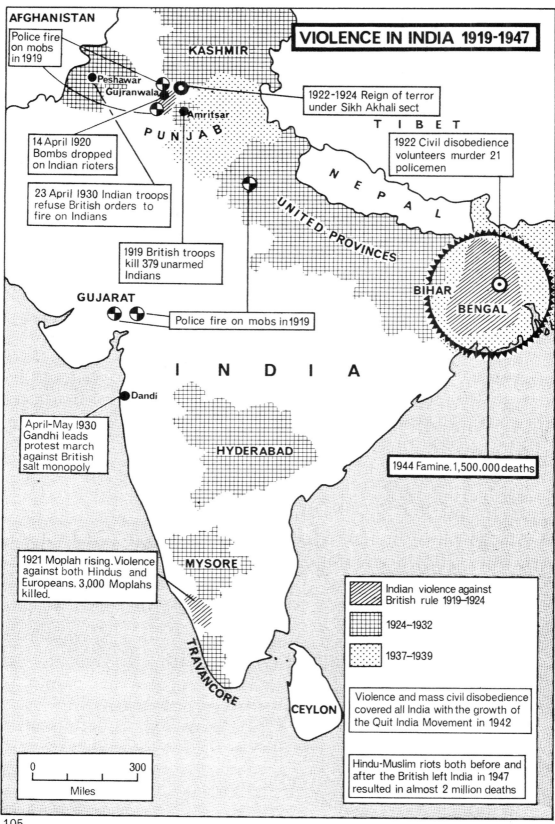

VIOLENCE IN INDIA 1919-1947

AFGHANISTAN

Police fire on mobs in 1919

KASHMIR

Peshawar
Gujranwala

1922-1924 Reign of terror under Sikh Akhali sect

Amritsar

PUNJAB

TIBET

14 April 1920 Bombs dropped on Indian rioters

1922 Civil disobedience volunteers murder 21 policemen

23 April 1930 Indian troops refuse British orders to fire on Indians

NEPAL

UNITED PROVINCES

1919 British troops kill 379 unarmed Indians

BIHAR

GUJARAT

BENGAL

Police fire on mobs in 1919

I N D I A

Dandi

April-May 1930 Gandhi leads protest march against British salt monopoly

HYDERABAD

1944 Famine. 1,500,000 deaths

1921 Moplah rising. Violence against both Hindus and Europeans. 3,000 Moplahs killed.

MYSORE

TRAVANCORE

CEYLON

Indian violence against British rule 1919–1924

1924–1932

1937–1939

Violence and mass civil disobedience covered all India with the growth of the Quit India Movement in 1942

Hindu-Muslim riots both before and after the British left India in 1947 resulted in almost 2 million deaths

0   300

Miles

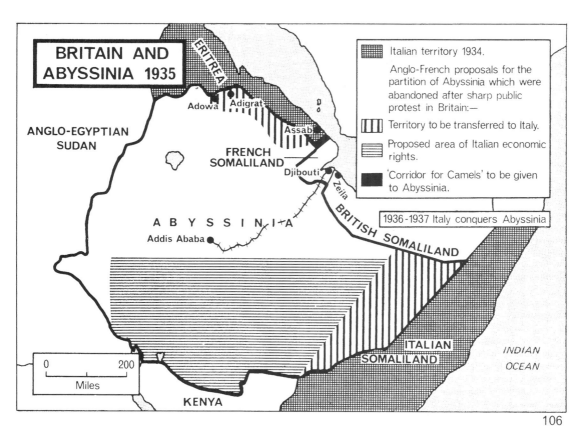

BRITAIN AND ABYSSINIA 1935

Italian territory 1934.

Anglo-French proposals for the partition of Abyssinia which were abandoned after sharp public protest in Britain:—

Territory to be transferred to Italy.

Proposed area of Italian economic rights.

'Corridor for Camels' to be given to Abyssinia.

1936-1937 Italy conquers Abyssinia

ERITREA

ANGLO-EGYPTIAN SUDAN

Adowa   Adigrat

Assab

FRENCH SOMALILAND

Djibouti

Zeila

BRITISH SOMALILAND

A B Y S S I N I A

Addis Ababa

ITALIAN SOMALILAND

INDIAN OCEAN

0   200
Miles

KENYA

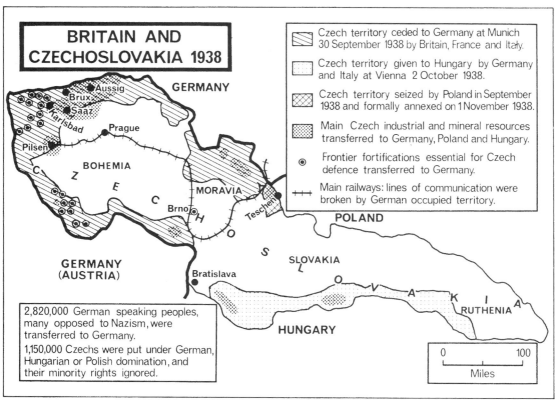

BRITAIN AND CZECHOSLOVAKIA 1938

Czech territory ceded to Germany at Munich 30 September 1938 by Britain, France and Italy.

Czech territory given to Hungary by Germany and Italy at Vienna 2 October 1938.

Czech territory seized by Poland in September 1938 and formally annexed on 1 November 1938.

Main Czech industrial and mineral resources transferred to Germany, Poland and Hungary.

Frontier fortifications essential for Czech defence transferred to Germany.

Main railways: lines of communication were broken by German occupied territory.

GERMANY

Aussig
Brux
Saaz
Karlsbad
Prague
Pilsen

BOHEMIA

C Z E C H

MORAVIA

Brno

Teschen

POLAND

GERMANY (AUSTRIA)

Bratislava

O S L O V A K I A

SLOVAKIA

RUTHENIA

HUNGARY

2,820,000 German speaking peoples, many opposed to Nazism, were transferred to Germany.

1,150,000 Czechs were put under German, Hungarian or Polish domination, and their minority rights ignored.

0   100
Miles

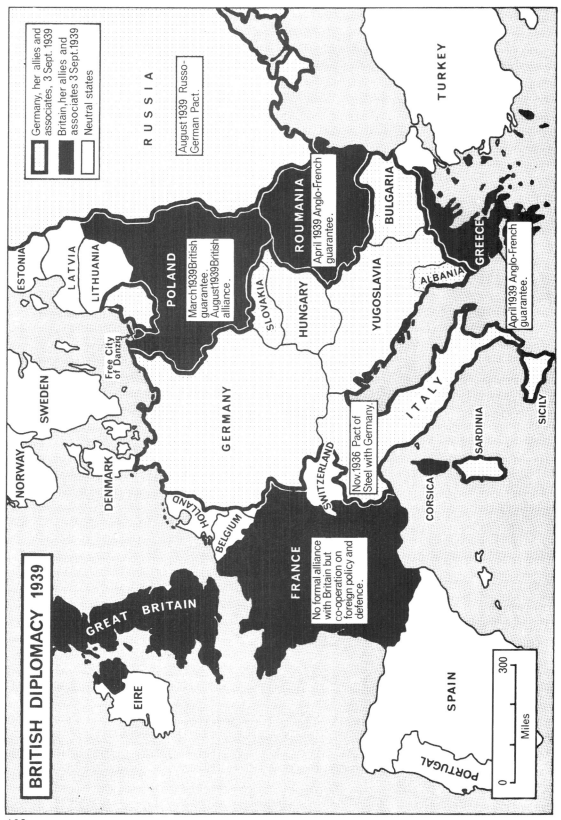

BRITISH DIPLOMACY 1939

Germany, her allies and associates, 3 Sept. 1939

Britain, her allies and associates 3 Sept.1939

Neutral states

August 1939 Russo-German Pact.

RUSSIA

TURKEY

NORWAY

SWEDEN

ESTONIA

LATVIA

LITHUANIA

Free City of Danzig

POLAND
March1939British guarantee. August1939British alliance.

ROUMANIA
April 1939 Anglo-French guarantee.

BULGARIA

GREECE
April1939 Anglo-French guarantee.

SLOVAKIA

HUNGARY

YUGOSLAVIA

ALBANIA

DENMARK

GERMANY

HOLLAND

BELGIUM

SWITZERLAND

Nov.1936 Pact of Steel with Germany.

ITALY

CORSICA

SARDINIA

SICILY

GREAT BRITAIN

EIRE

FRANCE
No formal alliance with Britain but co-operation on foreign policy and defence.

SPAIN

PORTUGAL

300

Miles

0

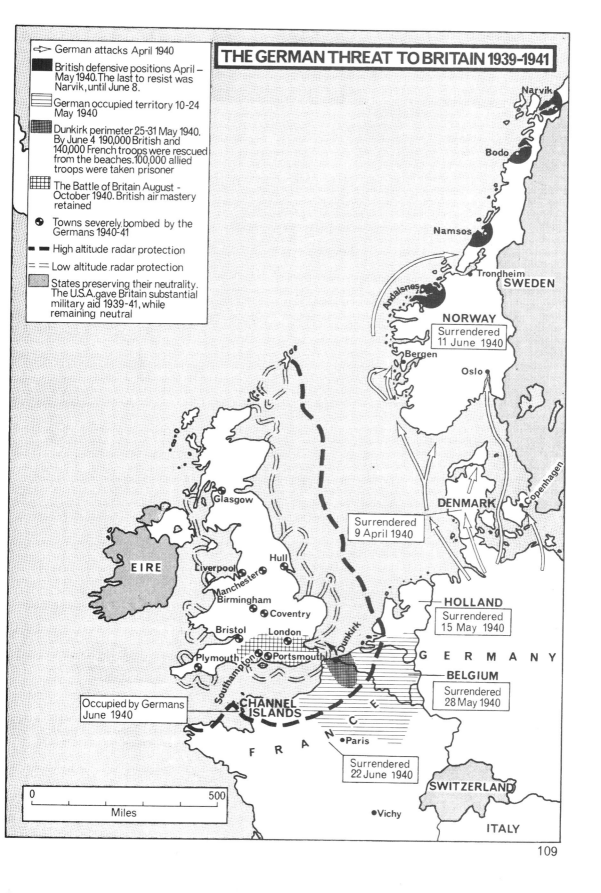

THE GERMAN THREAT TO BRITAIN 1939-1941

Legend:

- ⇨ German attacks April 1940
- British defensive positions April – May 1940. The last to resist was Narvik, until June 8.
- German occupied territory 10-24 May 1940
- Dunkirk perimeter 25-31 May 1940. By June 4 190,000 British and 140,000 French troops were rescued from the beaches.100,000 allied troops were taken prisoner
- The Battle of Britain August – October 1940. British air mastery retained
- Towns severely bombed by the Germans 1940-41
- High altitude radar protection
- Low altitude radar protection
- States preserving their neutrality. The U.S.A.gave Britain substantial military aid 1939-41, while remaining neutral

Narvik

Bodo

Namsos

Andalsnes

Trondheim

SWEDEN

NORWAY
Surrendered 11 June 1940

Bergen

Oslo

DENMARK
Surrendered 9 April 1940

Copenhagen

EIRE

Glasgow

Hull

Liverpool

Manchester

Birmingham

Coventry

Bristol

London

Plymouth

Southampton

Portsmouth

Dunkirk

HOLLAND
Surrendered 15 May 1940

G E R M A N Y

BELGIUM
Surrendered 28 May 1940

Occupied by Germans June 1940

CHANNEL ISLANDS

F R A N C E

Paris

Surrendered 22 June 1940

SWITZERLAND

Vichy

ITALY

0 ————————— 500
Miles

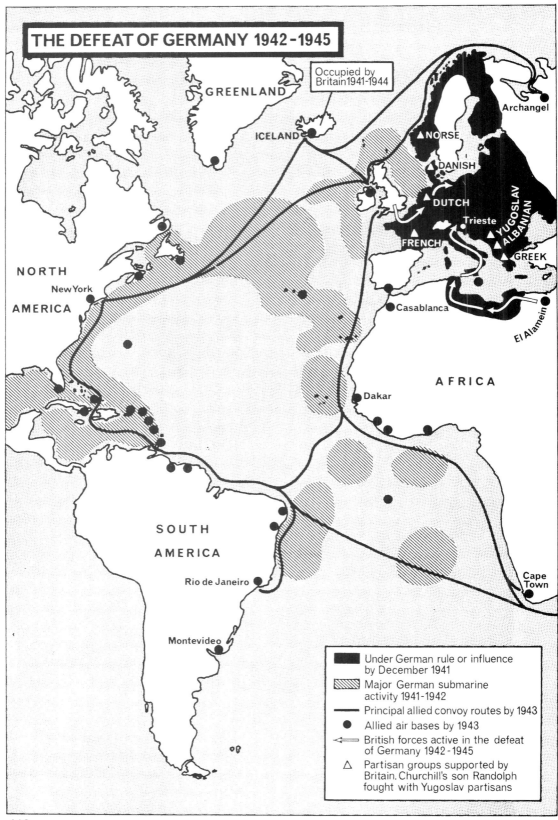

THE DEFEAT OF GERMANY 1942-1945

Occupied by
Britain 1941-1944

GREENLAND

ICELAND

Archangel

NORSE

DANISH

DUTCH

Trieste

YUGOSLAV

ALBANIAN

FRENCH

GREEK

NORTH
AMERICA

New York

Casablanca

El Alamein

AFRICA

Dakar

SOUTH
AMERICA

Rio de Janeiro

Cape
Town

Montevideo

■ Under German rule or influence
by December 1941

▨ Major German submarine
activity 1941-1942

— Principal allied convoy routes by 1943

● Allied air bases by 1943

⟸ British forces active in the defeat
of Germany 1942-1945

△ Partisan groups supported by
Britain. Churchill's son Randolph
fought with Yugoslav partisans

110

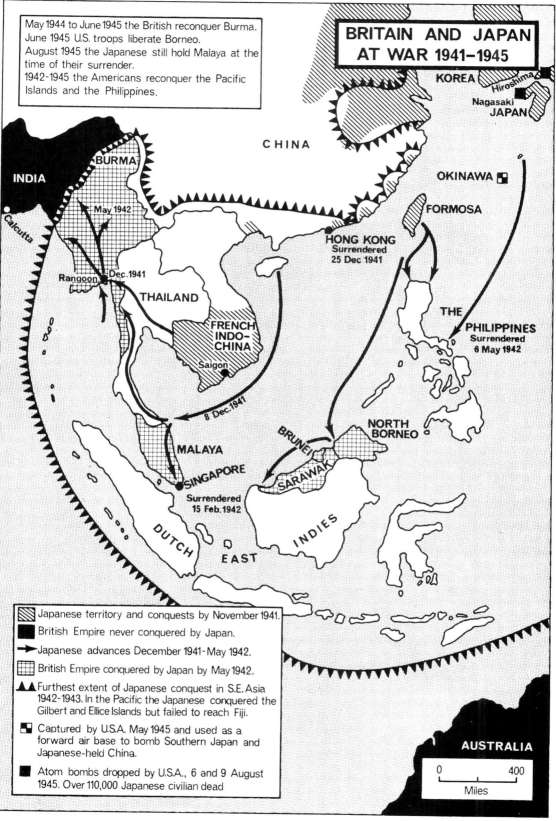

May 1944 to June 1945 the British reconquer Burma.
June 1945 U.S. troops liberate Borneo.
August 1945 the Japanese still hold Malaya at the time of their surrender.
1942-1945 the Americans reconquer the Pacific Islands and the Philippines.

BRITAIN AND JAPAN AT WAR 1941–1945

KOREA

Hiroshima
Nagasaki
JAPAN

CHINA

OKINAWA

INDIA

BURMA

Calcutta

FORMOSA

May 1942

HONG KONG
Surrendered
25 Dec 1941

Rangoon
Dec. 1941

THAILAND

THE PHILIPPINES
Surrendered
6 May 1942

FRENCH INDO-CHINA

Saigon

8 Dec. 1941

MALAYA

NORTH BORNEO

BRUNEI

SINGAPORE
Surrendered
15 Feb. 1942

SARAWAK

DUTCH

EAST

INDIES

Japanese territory and conquests by November 1941.

British Empire never conquered by Japan.

Japanese advances December 1941-May 1942.

British Empire conquered by Japan by May 1942.

Furthest extent of Japanese conquest in S.E. Asia 1942-1943. In the Pacific the Japanese conquered the Gilbert and Ellice Islands but failed to reach Fiji.

Captured by U.S.A. May 1945 and used as a forward air base to bomb Southern Japan and Japanese-held China.

Atom bombs dropped by U.S.A., 6 and 9 August 1945. Over 110,000 Japanese civilian dead

AUSTRALIA

0   400
Miles

111

British occupation zones in Germany and Austria 1945 – 48.

European Free Trade Association (EFTA) 1958.

Associate Members of EFTA.

The "Iron Curtain".

European Common Market established by the Treaty of Rome 1957. Britain's first application in 1962 rejected. Second application made in 1967.

Members of the North Atlantic Treaty Organisation (NATO) established 1949. The USA and Canada are also members. Turkey was admitted 1951.

0   400

Miles

FINLAND
February 1947 Anglo–Soviet Peace Treaty limits Army to 34,000 men and Air Force to 60 machines

SWEDEN

NORWAY

U. S. S. R.

DENMARK

EIRE

GREAT BRITAIN

NETHERLANDS

Berlin

P O L A N D

GERMAN DEMOCRATIC REPUBLIC

GERMAN

BELGIUM

LUXEMBOURG

FEDERAL

REPUBLIC

CZECHOSLOVAKIA

HUNGARY

RUMANIA

AUSTRIA

FRANCE

SWITZ.

YUGOSLAVIA

BULGARIA

I T A L Y

ALBANIA

P O R T U G A L

SPAIN

GREECE

GIBRALTAR
Anglo–Spanish dispute over sovereignty

BRITAIN AND EUROPE 1945–1965

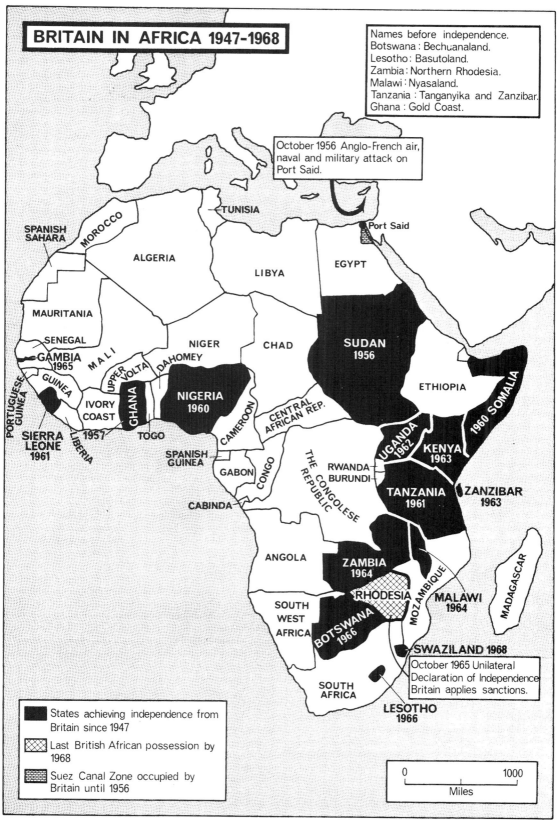

BRITAIN IN AFRICA 1947-1968

Names before independence.
Botswana : Bechuanaland.
Lesotho : Basutoland.
Zambia : Northern Rhodesia.
Malawi : Nyasaland.
Tanzania : Tanganyika and Zanzibar.
Ghana : Gold Coast.

October 1956 Anglo-French air, naval and military attack on Port Said.

SPANISH SAHARA

MOROCCO

TUNISIA

Port Said

ALGERIA

LIBYA

EGYPT

MAURITANIA

SENEGAL

NIGER

CHAD

SUDAN
1956

ETHIOPIA

GAMBIA
1965

MALI

1960 SOMALIA

GUINEA

UPPER VOLTA

DAHOMEY

GHANA

NIGERIA
1960

PORTUGUESE GUINEA

IVORY COAST

CAMEROON

CENTRAL AFRICAN REP.

UGANDA
1962

KENYA
1963

SIERRA LEONE
1961

LIBERIA

1957

TOGO

SPANISH GUINEA

GABON

CONGO

THE CONGOLESE REPUBLIC

RWANDA

BURUNDI

TANZANIA
1961

ZANZIBAR
1963

CABINDA

ANGOLA

ZAMBIA
1964

MALAWI
1964

MADAGASCAR

SOUTH WEST AFRICA

RHODESIA

MOZAMBIQUE

BOTSWANA
1966

SWAZILAND 1968

October 1965 Unilateral Declaration of Independence Britain applies sanctions.

SOUTH AFRICA

LESOTHO
1966

States achieving independence from Britain since 1947

Last British African possession by 1968

Suez Canal Zone occupied by Britain until 1956

0   1000

Miles

113

UNIVERSITY FOUNDATIONS 1264–1967

0 ___ 50
Miles

Aberdeen 1495

Dundee 1967

St. Andrews 1410

1967 Stirling

Glasgow 1451
Strathclyde 1964

Edinburgh 1583

Heriot-Watt 1966

Newcastle 1963

Durham 1832

Lancaster 1964

York 1963

Leeds 1904

Hull 1954

Bradford 1966

Liverpool 1903

Manchester 1851

Salford 1967

Sheffield 1905

Bangor

Keele 1962

Nottingham 1938

1966 Loughborough

Leicester 1957

East Anglia 1964

Aston 1966

Birmingham 1900

University of
Wales 1893

Warwick 1965

Cambridge 1284

Aberystwyth

Essex 1965

Swansea

Cardiff

Oxford 1264

Brunel 1966

Reading 1926

Surrey 1966

London 1836

Kent 1965

Bristol 1909

Bath 1966

The City University 1966

Southampton 1952

Sussex 1961

Exeter 1955

● Founded 1264–1583
⊖ Nineteenth century foundations
◕ Founded 1900–1938
◉ Founded 1952–1967

114

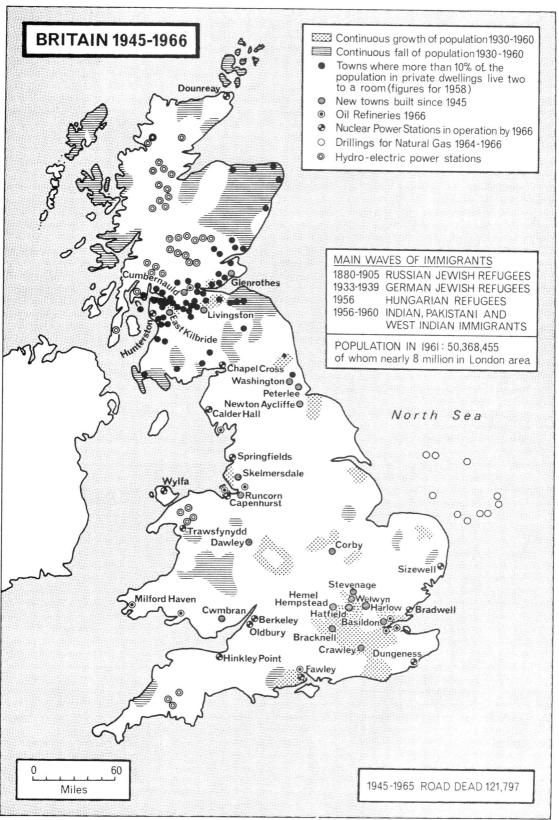

BRITAIN 1945-1966

Legend:
- ▒ Continuous growth of population 1930-1960
- ▤ Continuous fall of population 1930-1960
- ● Towns where more than 10% of the population in private dwellings live two to a room (figures for 1958)
- ⊖ New towns built since 1945
- ⊙ Oil Refineries 1966
- ◒ Nuclear Power Stations in operation by 1966
- ○ Drillings for Natural Gas 1964-1966
- ◎ Hydro-electric power stations

MAIN WAVES OF IMMIGRANTS
1880-1905	RUSSIAN JEWISH REFUGEES
1933-1939	GERMAN JEWISH REFUGEES
1956	HUNGARIAN REFUGEES
1956-1960	INDIAN, PAKISTANI AND WEST INDIAN IMMIGRANTS

POPULATION IN 1961: 50,368,455
of whom nearly 8 million in London area

North Sea

Dounreay
Cumbernauld
Glenrothes
Livingston
East Kilbride
Hunterston
Chapel Cross
Washington
Peterlee
Newton Aycliffe
Calder Hall
Springfields
Skelmersdale
Wylfa
Runcorn
Capenhurst
Trawsfynydd
Dawley
Corby
Sizewell
Stevenage
Hemel Hempstead
Welwyn
Harlow
Bradwell
Hatfield
Basildon
Milford Haven
Cwmbran
Berkeley
Oldbury
Bracknell
Crawley
Dungeness
Hinkley Point
Fawley

0 ⊢———⊣ 60
Miles

1945-1965 ROAD DEAD 121,797

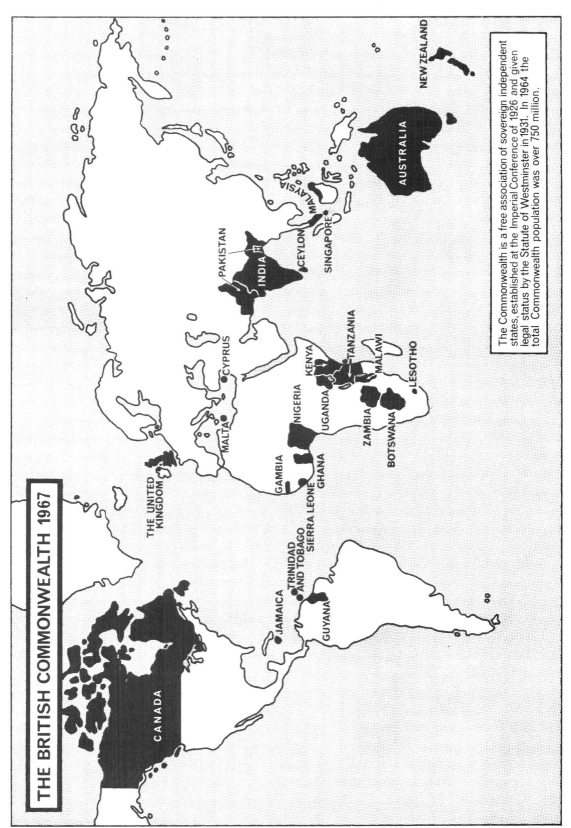

THE BRITISH COMMONWEALTH 1967

CANADA

THE UNITED KINGDOM

JAMAICA
TRINIDAD AND TOBAGO
GUYANA

MALTA
CYPRUS

GAMBIA
SIERRA LEONE
GHANA
NIGERIA
UGANDA
KENYA
TANZANIA
MALAWI
ZAMBIA
BOTSWANA
LESOTHO

PAKISTAN
INDIA
CEYLON
SINGAPORE
MALAYSIA

AUSTRALIA

NEW ZEALAND

The Commonwealth is a free association of sovereign independent states, established at the Imperial Conference of 1926 and given legal status by the Statute of Westminster in 1931. In 1964 the total Commonwealth population was over 750 million.

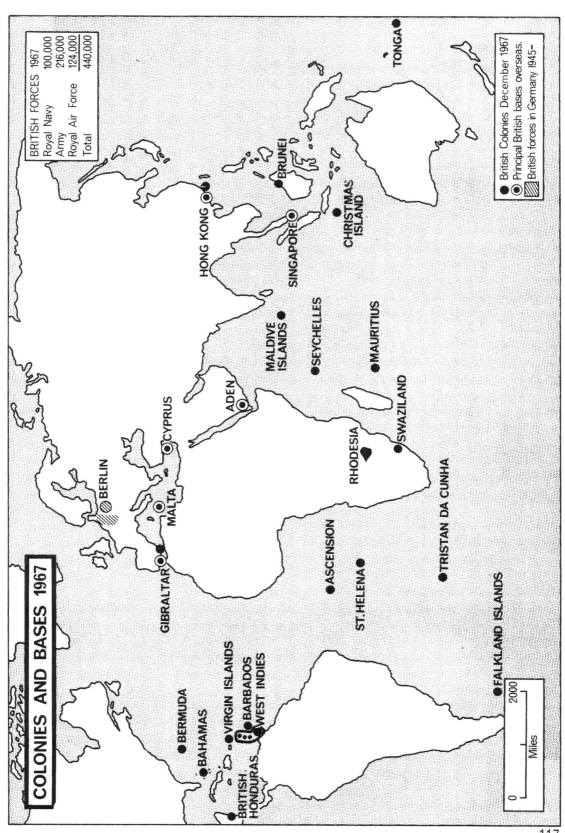

COLONIES AND BASES 1967

BRITISH FORCES 1967	
Royal Navy	100,000
Army	216,000
Royal Air Force	124,000
Total	440,000

Legend:
● British Colonies December 1967
◉ Principal British bases overseas.
▨ British forces in Germany 1945–

TONGA

BRUNEI

HONG KONG

SINGAPORE

CHRISTMAS ISLAND

MALDIVE ISLANDS

SEYCHELLES

MAURITIUS

ADEN

CYPRUS

BERLIN

MALTA

SWAZILAND

RHODESIA

GIBRALTAR

ASCENSION

ST.HELENA

TRISTAN DA CUNHA

FALKLAND ISLANDS

BERMUDA

BAHAMAS

VIRGIN ISLANDS

BARBADOS

WEST INDIES

BRITISH HONDURAS

0   2000

Miles

THE WESTERN PACIFIC SINCE 1945

ALASKA
49th U.S. STATE

ALEUTIAN ISLANDS

U.S.S.R.

50th U.S. STATE

HAWAIIAN ISLANDS

MIDWAY

JOHNSTON

JAPAN

CHINA

Hong Kong

U.S. MILITARY ADMINISTRATION

BONIN
OKINAWA ● **DAITO**
● **VOLCANO** **MARCUS**

WAKE

FORMOSA

VIET-NAM

PHILLIPINES

MARIANAS ISLANDS
● **GUAM**

ISLANDS
BIKINI

ENIWETOK

U.S. TRUST TERRITORY

Brunei

● **YAP**
● **PALAU**

CAROLINE

TRUK
MARSHALL ISLANDS

BORNEO

HOWLAND
BAKER

GILBERT ISLANDS
1892

CANTON ISLAND
● 1939

INDONESIA

NEW GUINEA

TO AUSTRALIA

OCEAN ISLAND
1900

ELLICE ISLANDS

PHOENIX ISLANDS
1937

SOLOMON ISLANDS 1893

SANTA CRUZ ISLANDS 1898

NEW HEBRIDES
1887
FRENCH

FRENCH

AUSTRALIA

FIJI 1874

SAMOA
TUTUILA

NEW CALEDONIA

TONGA 1900

TO NEW ZEALAND

KERMADEC
TO NEW ZEALAND

COOK

NEW ZEALAND

TO NEW ZEALAND
CHATHAM

British possessions with date of acquisition.

Anglo-French Condominium.

Anglo-American joint sovereignty.

United States possessions.

Commonwealth possessions.

0   500

Miles approx.

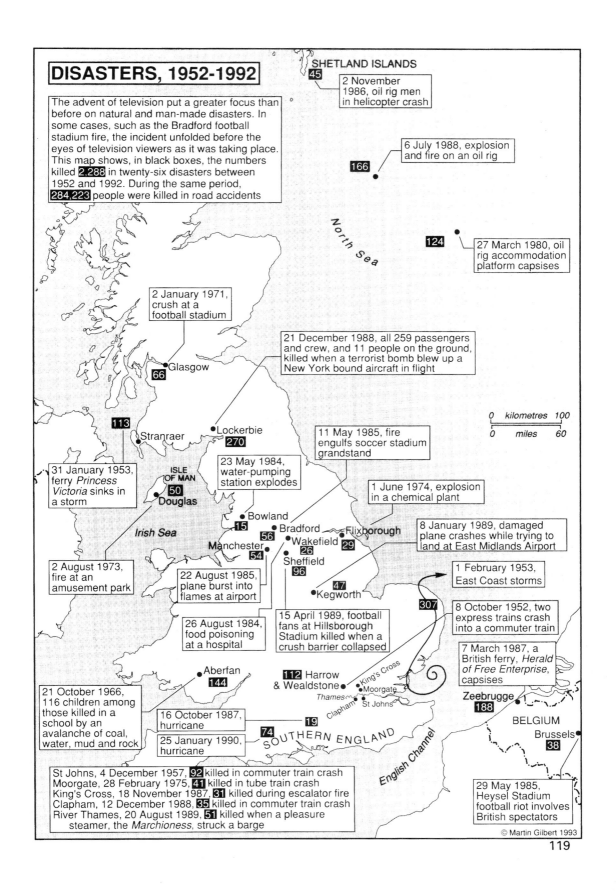

DISASTERS, 1952-1992

The advent of television put a greater focus than before on natural and man-made disasters. In some cases, such as the Bradford football stadium fire, the incident unfolded before the eyes of television viewers as it was taking place. This map shows, in black boxes, the numbers killed **2,288** in twenty-six disasters between 1952 and 1992. During the same period, **284,223** people were killed in road accidents

SHETLAND ISLANDS
45

2 November 1986, oil rig men in helicopter crash

6 July 1988, explosion and fire on an oil rig
166

North Sea

27 March 1980, oil rig accommodation platform capsizes
124

2 January 1971, crush at a football stadium

21 December 1988, all 259 passengers and crew, and 11 people on the ground, killed when a terrorist bomb blew up a New York bound aircraft in flight

●Glasgow
66

0   kilometres   100
0   miles   60

113
Stranraer

●Lockerbie
270

11 May 1985, fire engulfs soccer stadium grandstand

23 May 1984, water-pumping station explodes

1 June 1974, explosion in a chemical plant

31 January 1953, ferry *Princess Victoria* sinks in a storm

ISLE OF MAN
50
Douglas

Irish Sea

8 January 1989, damaged plane crashes while trying to land at East Midlands Airport

●Bowland
15
●Bradford
Manchester● **56**
54 ●Wakefield **26**
Sheffield
96

Flixborough
29

2 August 1973, fire at an amusement park

22 August 1985, plane burst into flames at airport

47
●Kegworth

1 February 1953, East Coast storms

307

8 October 1952, two express trains crash into a commuter train

26 August 1984, food poisoning at a hospital

15 April 1989, football fans at Hillsborough Stadium killed when a crush barrier collapsed

7 March 1987, a British ferry, *Herald of Free Enterprise*, capsises

●Aberfan
144

112 Harrow
& Wealdstone● ●King's Cross
●Moorgate
Thames● ●
Clapham● St Johns

Zeebrugge
188

BELGIUM

21 October 1966, 116 children among those killed in a school by an avalanche of coal, water, mud and rock

16 October 1987, hurricane

25 January 1990, hurricane

74
19

SOUTHERN ENGLAND

Brussels●
38

English Channel

St Johns, 4 December 1957, **92** killed in commuter train crash
Moorgate, 28 February 1975, **41** killed in tube train crash
King's Cross, 18 November 1987, **31** killed during escalator fire
Clapham, 12 December 1988, **35** killed in commuter train crash
River Thames, 20 August 1989, **51** killed when a pleasure steamer, the *Marchioness*, struck a barge

29 May 1985, Heysel Stadium football riot involves British spectators

© Martin Gilbert 1993

119

THE QUEEN AND THE COMMONWEALTH

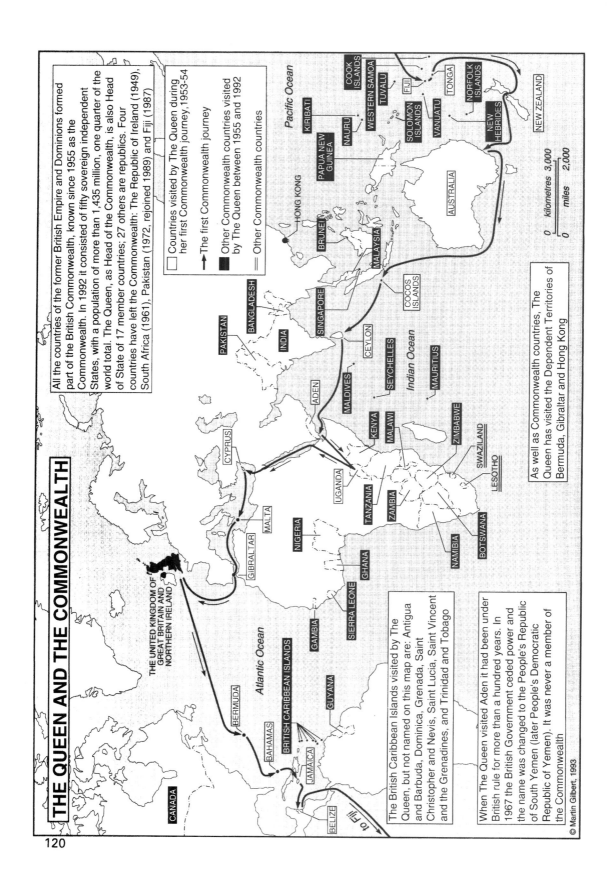

All the countries of the former British Empire and Dominions formed part of the British Commonwealth, known since 1955 as the Commonwealth. In 1992 it consisted of fifty sovereign independent States, with a population of more than 1,435 million, one quarter of the world total. The Queen, as Head of the Commonwealth, is also Head of State of 17 member countries; 27 others are republics. Four countries have left the Commonwealth: The Republic of Ireland (1949), South Africa (1961), Pakistan (1972, rejoined 1989) and Fiji (1987)

☐ Countries visited by The Queen during her first Commonwealth journey, 1953-54

→ The first Commonwealth journey

■ Other Commonwealth countries visited by The Queen between 1955 and 1992

═ Other Commonwealth countries

The British Caribbean Islands visited by The Queen, but not named on this map are: Antigua and Barbuda, Dominica, Grenada, Saint Christopher and Nevis, Saint Lucia, Saint Vincent and the Grenadines, and Trinidad and Tobago

When The Queen visited Aden it had been under British rule for more than a hundred years. In 1967 the British Government ceded power and the name was changed to the People's Republic of South Yemen (later People's Democratic Republic of Yemen). It was never a member of the Commonwealth

As well as Commonwealth countries, The Queen has visited the Dependent Territories of Bermuda, Gibraltar and Hong Kong

© Martin Gilbert, 1993

Pacific Ocean

Indian Ocean

Atlantic Ocean

THE UNITED KINGDOM OF GREAT BRITAIN AND NORTHERN IRELAND

CANADA · BERMUDA · BAHAMAS · JAMAICA · BELIZE · BRITISH CARIBBEAN ISLANDS · GUYANA · to Fiji

GIBRALTAR · MALTA · CYPRUS · GAMBIA · SIERRA LEONE · GHANA · NIGERIA · NAMIBIA · BOTSWANA · LESOTHO · SWAZILAND · ZIMBABWE

ADEN · UGANDA · KENYA · TANZANIA · ZAMBIA · MALAWI · MALDIVES · SEYCHELLES · MAURITIUS

PAKISTAN · BANGLADESH · INDIA · CEYLON · SINGAPORE · COCOS ISLANDS · BRUNEI · MALAYSIA · HONG KONG

HONG KONG · BRUNEI · PAPUA NEW GUINEA · KIRIBATI · NAURU · SOLOMON ISLANDS · VANUATU · COOK ISLANDS · WESTERN SAMOA · TUVALU · FIJI · TONGA · NORFOLK ISLANDS · NEW HEBRIDES · NEW ZEALAND · AUSTRALIA

0 kilometres 3,000
0 miles 2,000

OLD ENEMIES, NEW NATIONS: STATE VISITS 1955-1992

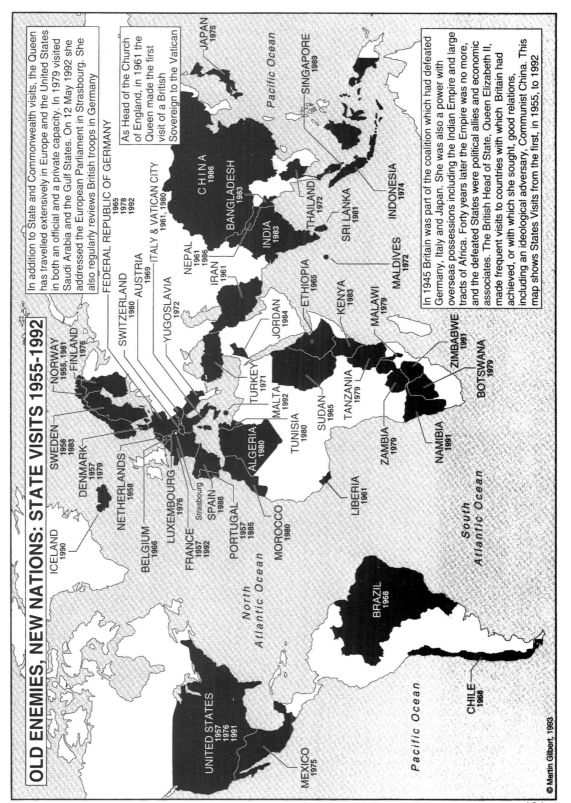

In addition to State and Commonwealth visits, the Queen has travelled extensively in Europe and the United States in both an official and a private capacity. In 1979 visited Saudi Arabia and the Gulf States. On 12 May 1992 she addressed the European Parliament in Strasbourg. She also regularly reviews British troops in Germany.

As Head of the Church of England, in 1961 the Queen made the first visit of a British Sovereign to the Vatican.

In 1945 Britain was part of the coalition which had defeated Germany, Italy and Japan. She was also a power with overseas possessions including the Indian Empire and large tracts of Africa. Forty years later the Empire was no more, and the defeated States were political allies and economic associates. The British Head of State, Queen Elizabeth II, made frequent visits to countries with which Britain had achieved, or with which she sought, good relations, including an ideological adversary, Communist China. This map shows States Visits from the first, in 1955, to 1992.

JAPAN 1975

SINGAPORE 1989

CHINA 1986

BANGLADESH 1983

THAILAND 1972

SRI LANKA 1981

INDONESIA 1974

MALDIVES 1972

INDIA 1983

NEPAL 1961 1986

IRAN 1961

FEDERAL REPUBLIC OF GERMANY 1965 1978 1992

ITALY & VATICAN CITY 1961, 1980

AUSTRIA 1969

SWITZERLAND 1980

YUGOSLAVIA 1972

ETHIOPIA 1965

KENYA 1983

MALAWI 1979

ZIMBABWE 1991

BOTSWANA 1979

JORDAN 1984

TURKEY 1971

MALTA 1992

SUDAN 1965

TANZANIA 1979

ZAMBIA 1979

NAMIBIA 1991

NORWAY 1955, 1981

FINLAND 1976

SWEDEN 1956 1983

DENMARK 1957 1979

NETHERLANDS 1958

BELGIUM 1966

LUXEMBOURG 1976

Strasbourg

FRANCE 1957 1992

SPAIN 1988

PORTUGAL 1957 1985

MOROCCO 1980

ALGERIA 1980

TUNISIA 1980

LIBERIA 1961

ICELAND 1990

UNITED STATES 1957 1976 1991

MEXICO 1975

BRAZIL 1968

CHILE 1968

Pacific Ocean

North Atlantic Ocean

South Atlantic Ocean

Pacific Ocean

© Martin Gilbert, 1993

121

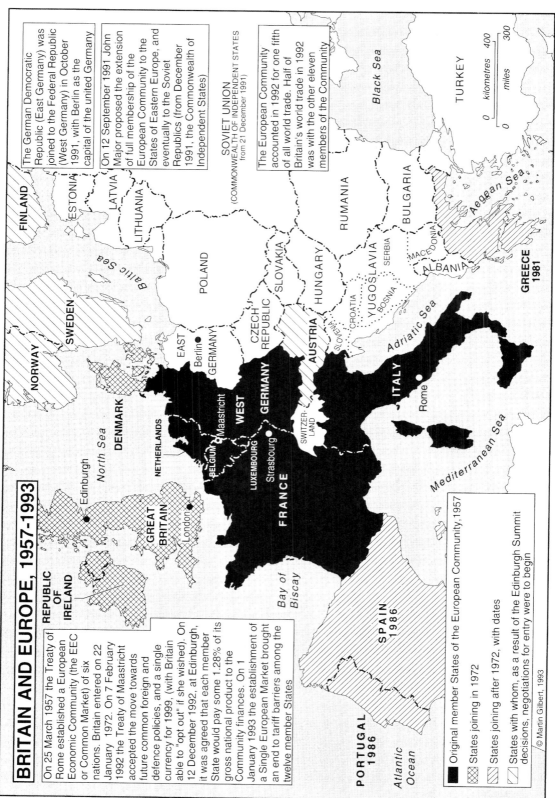

BRITAIN AND EUROPE, 1957-1993

On 25 March 1957 the Treaty of Rome established a European Economic Community (the EEC or Common Market) of six nations. Britain entered on 22 January 1972. On 7 February 1992 the Treaty of Maastricht accepted the move towards future common foreign and defence policies, and a single currency for 1999, (with Britain able to "opt out" if she wished). On 12 December 1992, at Edinburgh, it was agreed that each member State would pay some 1.28% of its gross national product to the Community finances. On 1 January 1993 the establishment of a Single European Market brought an end to tariff barriers among the twelve member States

The German Democratic Republic (East Germany) was joined to the Federal Republic (West Germany) in October 1991, with Berlin as the capital of the united Germany

On 12 September 1991 John Major proposed the extension of full membership of the European Community to the States of Eastern Europe, and eventually to the Soviet Republics (from December 1991, the Commonwealth of Independent States)

The European Community accounted in 1992 for one fifth of all world trade. Half of Britain's world trade in 1992 was with the other eleven members of the Community

SOVIET UNION
(COMMONWEALTH OF INDEPENDENT STATES from 21 December 1991)

Legend:
- Original member States of the European Community, 1957
- States joining in 1972
- States joining after 1972, with dates
- States with whom, as a result of the Edinburgh Summit decisions, negotiations for entry were to begin

© Martin Gilbert, 1993

GREECE 1981

SPAIN 1986

PORTUGAL 1986

GREAT BRITAIN

REPUBLIC OF IRELAND

NORWAY

SWEDEN

FINLAND

DENMARK

NETHERLANDS

BELGIUM

LUXEMBOURG

FRANCE

WEST GERMANY

EAST GERMANY

SWITZER-LAND

ITALY

AUSTRIA

CZECH REPUBLIC

SLOVAKIA

HUNGARY

POLAND

ESTONIA

LATVIA

LITHUANIA

RUMANIA

BULGARIA

YUGOSLAVIA

SLOVENIA

CROATIA

BOSNIA

SERBIA

MACEDONIA

ALBANIA

TURKEY

Edinburgh

London

Berlin

Maastricht

Strasbourg

Rome

North Sea

Baltic Sea

Bay of Biscay

Atlantic Ocean

Mediterranean Sea

Adriatic Sea

Aegean Sea

Black Sea

0   kilometres   400
0   miles   300

NORTHERN IRELAND, 1969-1993

Since 1922, the six counties of Ulster (Northern Ireland) have been an integral part of the United Kingdom. Of the total population of 1,532,000, just under two-thirds is Protestant and just over one-third Roman Catholic. The Irish Republican Army (IRA) undertook acts of violence to bring an end to British rule. A wave of violence began in 1969, when IRA killings were countered by various Protestant para-military groups. In 1992 there were 19,400 British troops in the Province. Some of the main outbreaks of violence are shown on this map

On 30 January 1972, "Bloody Sunday", British troops killed 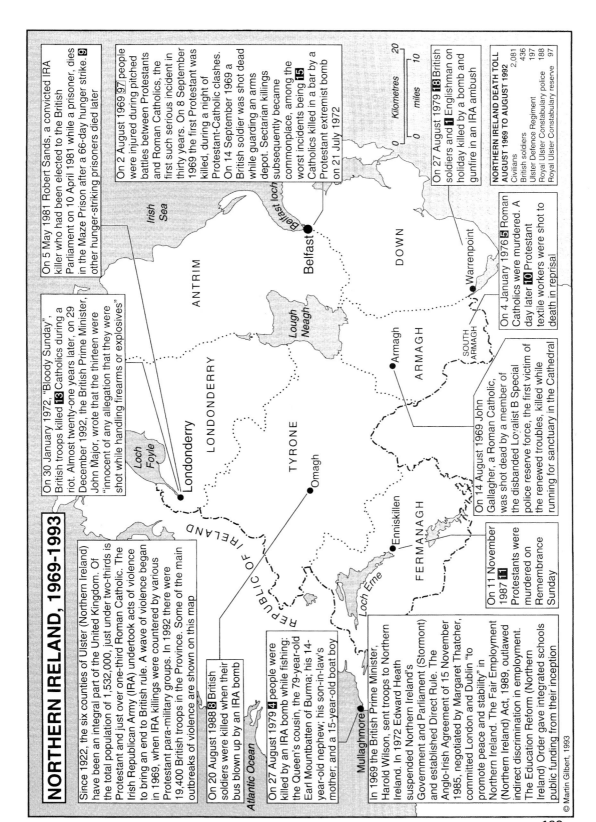**13** Catholics during a riot. Almost twenty-one years later, on 29 December 1992, the British Prime Minister, John Major, wrote that the thirteen were "innocent of any allegation that they were shot while handling firearms or explosives"

On 5 May 1981 Robert Sands, a convicted IRA killer who had been elected to the British Parliament on 10 April 1981 while a prisoner, dies in the Maze Prison after a 66-day hunger strike. **9** other hunger-striking prisoners died later

On 2 August 1969 **97** people were injured during pitched battles between Protestants and Roman Catholics, the first such serious incident in thirty years. On 8 September 1969 the first Protestant was killed, during a night of Protestant-Catholic clashes. On 14 September 1969 a British soldier was shot dead while guarding an arms depot. Sectarian killings subsequently became commonplace, among the worst incidents being **15** Catholics killed in a bar by a Protestant extremist bomb on 21 July 1972

On 27 August 1979 **18** British soldiers and **1** Englishman on holiday killed by a bomb and gunfire in an IRA ambush

NORTHERN IRELAND DEATH TOLL AUGUST 1969 TO AUGUST 1992
Civilians	2,081
British soldiers	436
Ulster Defence Regiment	197
Royal Ulster Constabulary police	188
Royal Ulster Constabulary reserve	97

On 4 January 1976 **5** Roman Catholics were murdered. A day later **10** Protestant textile workers were shot to death in reprisal

On 20 August 1988 **8** British soldiers were killed when their bus blown up by an IRA bomb

On 27 August 1979 **4** people were killed by an IRA bomb while fishing: the Queen's cousin, the 79-year-old Earl Mountbatten of Burma; his 14-year-old nephew; his son-in-law's mother; and a 15-year-old boat boy

On 14 August 1969 John Gallagher, a Roman Catholic, was shot dead by a member of the disbanded Loyalist B Special police reserve force, the first victim of the renewed troubles, killed while running for sanctuary in the Cathedral

On 11 November 1987 **11** Protestants were murdered on Remembrance Sunday

In 1969 the British Prime Minister, Harold Wilson, sent troops to Northern Ireland. In 1972 Edward Heath suspended Northern Ireland's Government and Parliament (Stormont) and established Direct Rule. The Anglo-Irish Agreement of 15 November 1985, negotiated by Margaret Thatcher, committed London and Dublin "to promote peace and stability" in Northern Ireland. The Fair Employment (Northern Ireland) Act, 1989, outlawed indirect discrimination in employment. The Education Reform (Northern Ireland) Order gave integrated schools public funding from their inception

Irish Sea

Belfast lough

ANTRIM

DOWN

● Belfast

● Warrenpoint

Lough Neagh

LONDONDERRY

● Armagh

ARMAGH

SOUTH ARMAGH

● Londonderry

Loch Foyle

TYRONE

● Omagh

REPUBLIC OF IRELAND

FERMANAGH

● Enniskillen

Loch Erne

Atlantic Ocean

● Mullaghmore

0 10
Kilometres

0 10 20
miles

© Martin Gilbert, 1993

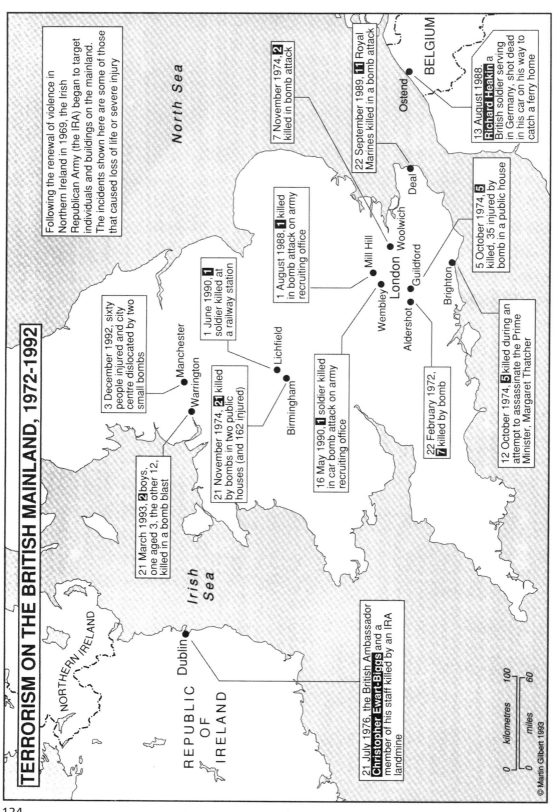

TERRORISM ON THE BRITISH MAINLAND, 1972-1992

Following the renewal of violence in Northern Ireland in 1969, the Irish Republican Army (the IRA) began to target individuals and buildings on the mainland. The incidents shown here are some of those that caused loss of life or severe injury

North Sea

7 November 1974, **2** killed in bomb attack

22 September 1989, **11** Royal Marines killed in a bomb attack

13 August 1988. **Richard Heakin** a British soldier serving in Germany, shot dead in his car on his way to catch a ferry home

BELGIUM

Ostend

Deal

5 October 1974, **5** killed, 35 injured by bomb in a public house

3 December 1992, sixty people injured and city centre dislocated by two small bombs

1 August 1988. **1** killed in bomb attack on army recruiting office

1 June 1990, **1** soldier killed at a railway station

Manchester

Warrington

Mill Hill
Woolwich
Wembley
London
Aldershot
Guildford

Brighton

12 October 1974, **5** killed during an attempt to assassinate the Prime Minister, Margaret Thatcher

21 March 1993, **2** boys, one aged 3, the other 12, killed in a bomb blast

21 November 1974, **21** killed by bombs in two public houses (and 162 injured)

Lichfield

Birmingham

16 May 1990, **1** soldier killed in car bomb attack on army recruiting office

22 February 1972, **7** killed by bomb

Irish Sea

NORTHERN IRELAND

Dublin

REPUBLIC
OF
IRELAND

21 July 1976, the British Ambassador **Christopher Ewart-Biggs** and a member of his staff killed by an IRA landmine

kilometres 100

miles 60

0

© Martin Gilbert 1993

124

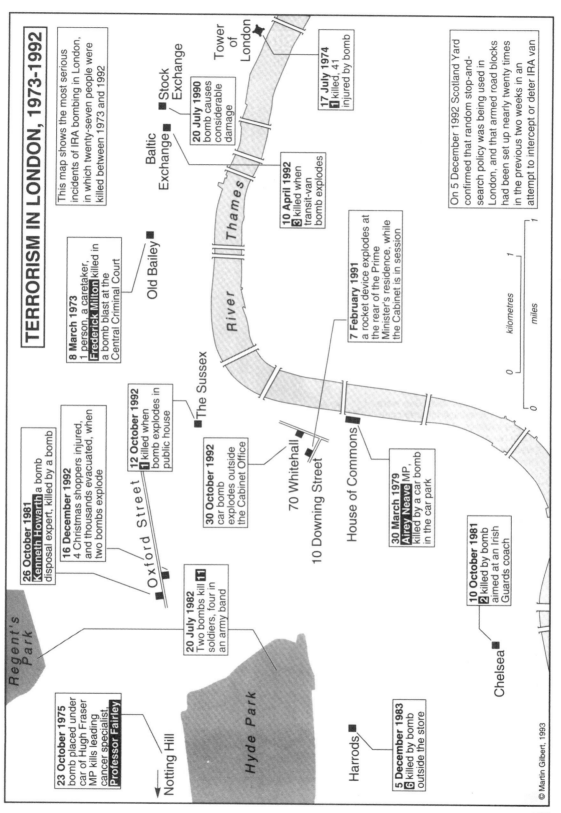

TERRORISM IN LONDON, 1973-1992

This map shows the most serious incidents of IRA bombing in London, in which twenty-seven people were killed between 1973 and 1992

8 March 1973 1 person, a caretaker, **Frederick Milton** killed in a bomb blast at the Central Criminal Court

17 July 1974 1 killed, 41 injured by bomb

20 July 1990 bomb causes considerable damage

10 April 1992 3 killed when transit-van bomb explodes

7 February 1991 a rocket device explodes at the rear of the Prime Minister's residence, while the Cabinet is in session

On 5 December 1992 Scotland Yard confirmed that random stop-and-search policy was being used in London, and that armed road blocks had been set up nearly twenty times in the previous two weeks in an attempt to intercept or deter IRA van

Tower of London

Stock Exchange

Baltic Exchange

Old Bailey

The Sussex

River Thames

26 October 1981 **Kenneth Howarth** a bomb disposal expert, killed by a bomb

16 December 1992 4 Christmas shoppers injured, and thousands evacuated, when two bombs explode

12 October 1992 1 killed when bomb explodes in public house

30 October 1992 car bomb explodes outside the Cabinet Office

70 Whitehall

10 Downing Street

House of Commons

30 March 1979 **Airey Neave** MP, killed by a car bomb in the car park

20 July 1982 Two bombs kill soldiers, four in an army band

10 October 1981 2 killed by bomb aimed at an Irish Guards coach

Chelsea

Oxford Street

Regent's Park

Hyde Park

Notting Hill

23 October 1975 bomb placed under car of Hugh Fraser MP kills leading cancer specialist, **Professor Fairley**

Harrods

5 December 1983 6 killed by bomb outside the store

0   kilometres   1

0   miles   1

© Martin Gilbert, 1993

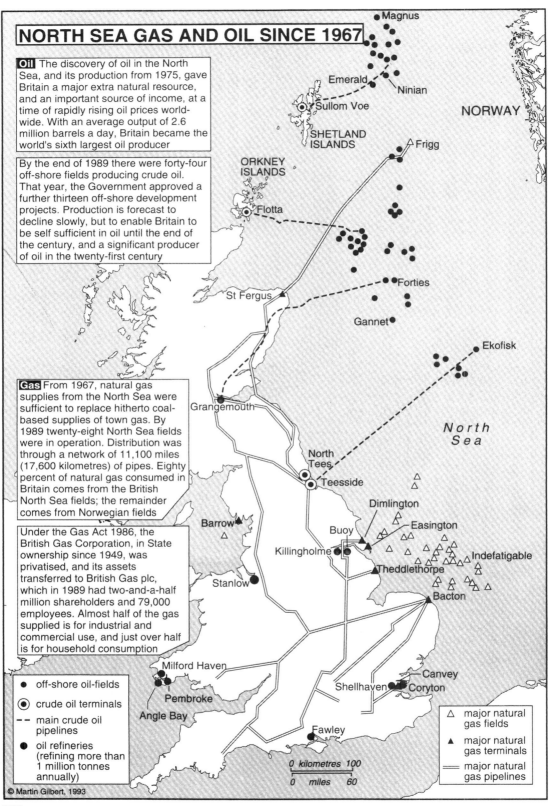

NORTH SEA GAS AND OIL SINCE 1967

Oil The discovery of oil in the North Sea, and its production from 1975, gave Britain a major extra natural resource, and an important source of income, at a time of rapidly rising oil prices world-wide. With an average output of 2.6 million barrels a day, Britain became the world's sixth largest oil producer

By the end of 1989 there were forty-four off-shore fields producing crude oil. That year, the Government approved a further thirteen off-shore development projects. Production is forecast to decline slowly, but to enable Britain to be self sufficient in oil until the end of the century, and a significant producer of oil in the twenty-first century

Gas From 1967, natural gas supplies from the North Sea were sufficient to replace hitherto coal-based supplies of town gas. By 1989 twenty-eight North Sea fields were in operation. Distribution was through a network of 11,100 miles (17,600 kilometres) of pipes. Eighty percent of natural gas consumed in Britain comes from the British North Sea fields; the remainder comes from Norwegian fields

Under the Gas Act 1986, the British Gas Corporation, in State ownership since 1949, was privatised, and its assets transferred to British Gas plc, which in 1989 had two-and-a-half million shareholders and 79,000 employees. Almost half of the gas supplied is for industrial and commercial use, and just over half is for household consumption

Magnus

Emerald
Ninian
Sullom Voe
SHETLAND ISLANDS
NORWAY

ORKNEY ISLANDS
Frigg

Flotta

St Fergus
Forties

Gannet

Ekofisk

North Sea

Grangemouth

North Tees
Teesside

Dimlington
Easington
Buoy
Indefatigable
Killingholme
Theddlethorpe
Bacton

Barrow

Stanlow

Milford Haven
Canvey
Pembroke
Shellhaven
Coryton
Angle Bay

Fawley

- ● off-shore oil-fields
- ◉ crude oil terminals
- ‑ ‑ main crude oil pipelines
- ● oil refineries (refining more than 1 million tonnes annually)

△ major natural gas fields
▲ major natural gas terminals
═ major natural gas pipelines

0 kilometres 100
0 miles 60

© Martin Gilbert, 1993

126

BRITAIN AND THE PACIFIC OCEAN, 1968-1980

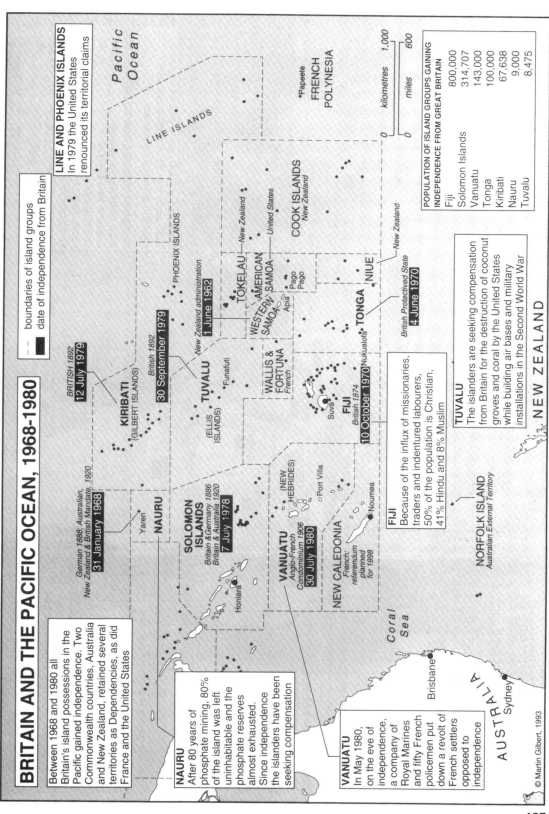

Between 1968 and 1980 all Britain's island possessions in the Pacific gained independence. Two Commonwealth countries, Australia and New Zealand, retained several territories as Dependencies, as did France and the United States

LINE AND PHOENIX ISLANDS
In 1979 the United States renounced its territorial claims

Pacific Ocean

LINE ISLANDS

POPULATION OF ISLAND GROUPS GAINING INDEPENDENCE FROM GREAT BRITAIN

Fiji	800,000
Solomon Islands	314,707
Vanuatu	143,000
Tonga	100,000
Kiribati	67,638
Nauru	9,000
Tuvalu	8,475

•Papeete
FRENCH POLYNESIA

PHOENIX ISLANDS

British 1892
30 September 1979

KIRIBATI
(GILBERT ISLANDS)

BRITISH 1892
12 July 1979

TOKELAU — *New Zealand*

WESTERN — AMERICAN
SAMOA• SAMOA — *United States*
Apia• •Pago Pago

COOK ISLANDS
New Zealand

NIUE
British Protected State
4 June 1970

New Zealand

New Zealand administration
1 June 1962

TUVALU
(ELLIS ISLANDS)
•Funafuti

WALLIS & FORTUNA
French

TONGA
Nukualofa•

•Suva
FIJI
British 1874
10 October 1970

TUVALU
The islanders are seeking compensation from Britain for the destruction of coconut groves and coral by the United States while building air bases and military installations in the Second World War

FIJI
Because of the influx of missionaries, traders and indentured labourers, 50% of the population is Christian, 41% Hindu and 8% Muslim

German 1888: Australian, New Zealand & British Mandate, 1920
31 January 1968

•Yaren
NAURU

SOLOMON ISLANDS
Britain & Germany 1886
Britain & Australia 1920
7 July 1978

(NEW HEBRIDES)
•Port Villa

VANUATU
Anglo-French Condominium 1906
30 July 1980

•Honiara

•Noumea
NEW CALEDONIA
French: referendum planned for 1998

NORFOLK ISLAND
Australian External Territory

NAURU
After 80 years of phosphate mining, 80% of the island was left uninhabitable and the phosphate reserves almost exhausted. Since independence the islanders have been seeking compensation

VANUATU
In May 1980, on the eve of independence, a company of Royal Marines and fifty French policemen put down a revolt of French settlers opposed to independence

Coral Sea

NEW ZEALAND

AUSTRALIA
•Brisbane
•Sydney

— — boundaries of island groups
▬ date of independence from Britain

kilometres 1,000 600
0 miles
0

© Martin Gilbert, 1993

127

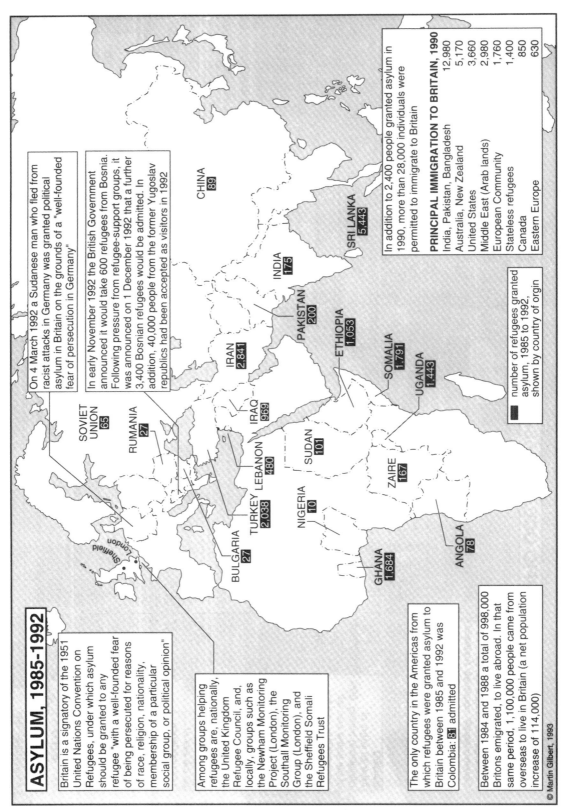

ASYLUM, 1985-1992

Britain is a signatory of the 1951 United Nations Convention on Refugees, under which asylum should be granted to any refugee "with a well-founded fear of being persecuted for reasons of race, religion, nationality, membership of a particular social group, or political opinion"

On 4 March 1992 a Sudanese man who fled from racist attacks in Germany was granted political asylum in Britain on the grounds of a "well-founded fear of persecution in Germany"

In early November 1992 the British Government announced it would take 600 refugees from Bosnia. Following pressure from refugee-support groups, it was announced on 1 December 1992 that a further 3,400 Bosnian refugees would be admitted. In addition, 40,000 people from the former Yugoslav republics had been accepted as visitors in 1992

In addition to 2,400 people granted asylum in 1990, more than 28,000 individuals were permitted to immigrate to Britain

PRINCIPAL IMMIGRATION TO BRITAIN, 1990

India, Pakistan, Bangladesh	12,980
Australia, New Zealand	5,170
United States	3,660
Middle East (Arab lands)	2,980
European Community	1,760
Stateless refugees	1,400
Canada	850
Eastern Europe	630

Among groups helping refugees are, nationally, the United Kingdom Refugee Council, and, locally, groups such as the Newham Monitoring Project (London), the Southall Monitoring Group (London), and the Sheffield Somali Refugees Trust

The only country in the Americas from which refugees were granted asylum to Britain between 1985 and 1992 was Colombia: **81** admitted

Between 1984 and 1988 a total of 998,000 Britons emigrated, to live abroad. In that same period, 1,100,000 people came from overseas to live in Britain (a net population increase of 114,000)

■ number of refugees granted asylum, 1985 to 1992, shown by country of orgin

CHINA **89**

SRI LANKA **5,443**

INDIA **175**

PAKISTAN **200**

IRAN **2,841**

ETHIOPIA **1,053**

SOMALIA **1,791**

UGANDA **1,443**

IRAQ **969**

SUDAN **101**

ZAIRE **167**

LEBANON **480**

TURKEY **2,038**

NIGERIA **10**

ANGOLA **78**

GHANA **1,684**

BULGARIA **27**

RUMANIA **27**

SOVIET UNION **65**

London

Sheffield

© Martin Gilbert, 1993

128

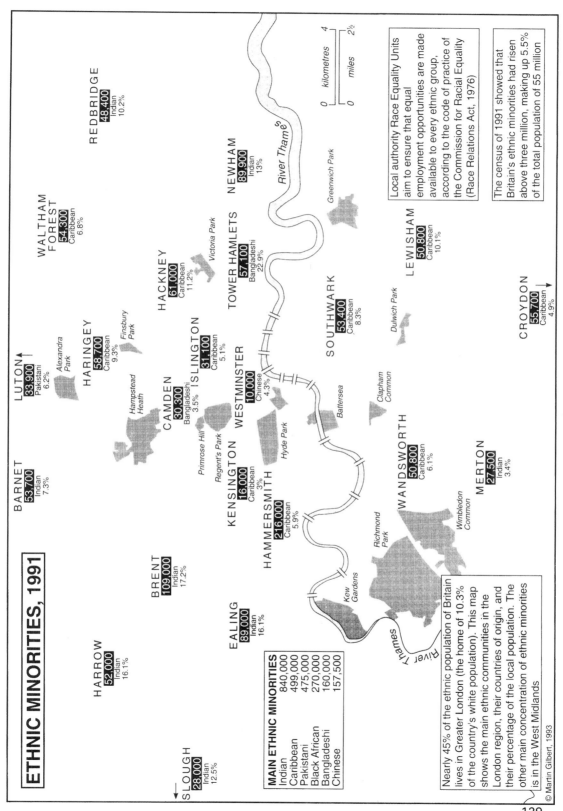

ETHNIC MINORITIES, 1991

SLOUGH
28,000
Indian
12.5%

HARROW
52,000
Indian
16.1%

BRENT
109,000
Indian
17.2%

EALING
89,000
Indian
16.1%

BARNET
53,700
Indian
7.3%

LUTON
33,900
Pakistani
6.2%

HARINGEY
58,700
Caribbean
9.3%

Alexandra Park

Finsbury Park

CAMDEN
30,300
Bangladeshi
3.5%

ISLINGTON
31,100
Caribbean
5.1%

Hampstead Heath

Primrose Hill

Regent's Park

KENSINGTON
16,000
Caribbean
3%

HAMMERSMITH
216,000
Caribbean
5.9%

WESTMINSTER
10,000
Chinese
4.3%

Hyde Park

REDBRIDGE
48,400
Indian
10.2%

WALTHAM FOREST
54,300
Caribbean
6.8%

HACKNEY
61,000
Caribbean
11.2%

Victoria Park

TOWER HAMLETS
57,100
Bangladeshi
22.9%

NEWHAM
89,900
Indian
13%

River Thames

Greenwich Park

LEWISHAM
50,800
Caribbean
10.1%

SOUTHWARK
53,400
Caribbean
8.3%

Dulwich Park

Battersea

Clapham Common

WANDSWORTH
50,800
Caribbean
6.1%

Richmond Park

Wimbledon Common

MERTON
27,500
Indian
3.4%

CROYDON
55,700
Caribbean
4.9%

Kew Gardens

River Thames

MAIN ETHNIC MINORITIES

Indian	840,000
Caribbean	499,000
Pakistani	475,000
Black African	270,000
Bangladeshi	160,000
Chinese	157,500

Local authority Race Equality Units aim to ensure that equal employment opportunities are made available to every ethnic group, according to the code of practice of the Commission for Racial Equality (Race Relations Act, 1976)

The census of 1991 showed that Britain's ethnic minorities had risen above three million, making up 5.5% of the total population of 55 million

Nearly 45% of the ethnic population of Britain lives in Greater London (the home of 10.3% of the country's white population). This map shows the main ethnic communities in the London region, their countries of origin, and their percentage of the local population. The other main concentration of ethnic minorities is in the West Midlands

0 kilometres 4
0 miles 2½

© Martin Gilbert, 1993

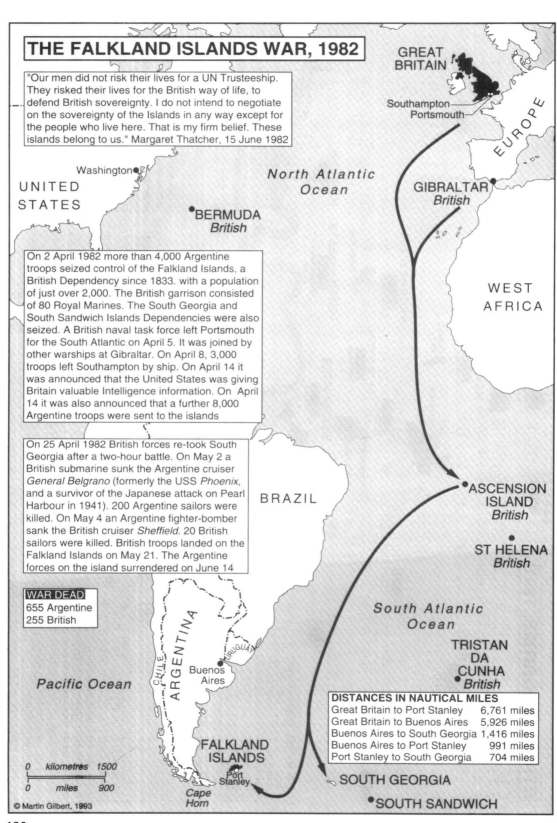

THE FALKLAND ISLANDS WAR, 1982

GREAT BRITAIN

"Our men did not risk their lives for a UN Trusteeship. They risked their lives for the British way of life, to defend British sovereignty. I do not intend to negotiate on the sovereignty of the Islands in any way except for the people who live here. That is my firm belief. These islands belong to us." Margaret Thatcher, 15 June 1982

Southampton
Portsmouth

EUROPE

Washington

North Atlantic Ocean

GIBRALTAR
British

UNITED
STATES

BERMUDA
British

WEST
AFRICA

On 2 April 1982 more than 4,000 Argentine troops seized control of the Falkland Islands, a British Dependency since 1833. with a population of just over 2,000. The British garrison consisted of 80 Royal Marines. The South Georgia and South Sandwich Islands Dependencies were also seized. A British naval task force left Portsmouth for the South Atlantic on April 5. It was joined by other warships at Gibraltar. On April 8, 3,000 troops left Southampton by ship. On April 14 it was announced that the United States was giving Britain valuable Intelligence information. On April 14 it was also announced that a further 8,000 Argentine troops were sent to the islands

On 25 April 1982 British forces re-took South Georgia after a two-hour battle. On May 2 a British submarine sunk the Argentine cruiser *General Belgrano* (formerly the USS *Phoenix*, and a survivor of the Japanese attack on Pearl Harbour in 1941). 200 Argentine sailors were killed. On May 4 an Argentine fighter-bomber sank the British cruiser *Sheffield*. 20 British sailors were killed. British troops landed on the Falkland Islands on May 21. The Argentine forces on the island surrendered on June 14

BRAZIL

ASCENSION
ISLAND
British

ST HELENA
British

WAR DEAD
655 Argentine
255 British

South Atlantic Ocean

TRISTAN
DA
CUNHA
British

Pacific Ocean

ARGENTINA

CHILE

URUGUAY

Buenos
Aires

DISTANCES IN NAUTICAL MILES	
Great Britain to Port Stanley	6,761 miles
Great Britain to Buenos Aires	5,926 miles
Buenos Aires to South Georgia	1,416 miles
Buenos Aires to Port Stanley	991 miles
Port Stanley to South Georgia	704 miles

0 kilometres 1500

0 miles 900

© Martin Gilbert, 1993

FALKLAND
ISLANDS

Port
Stanley

Cape
Horn

SOUTH GEORGIA

SOUTH SANDWICH

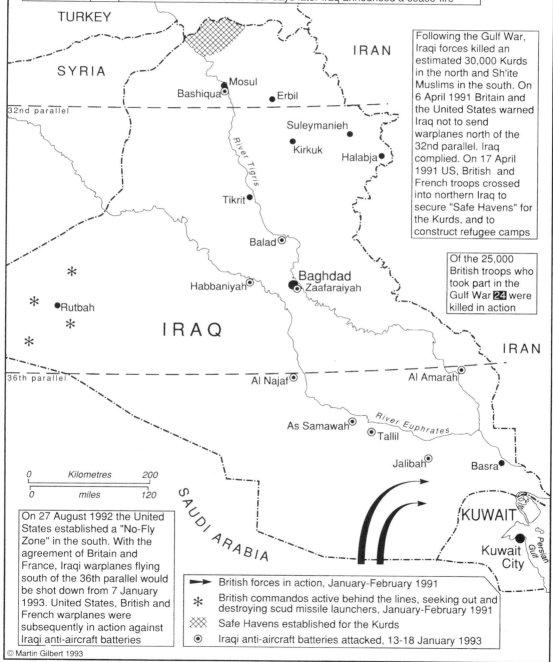

BRITAIN, THE GULF WAR AND ITS AFTERMATH, 1990-1993

On 2 August 1990 Iraqi forces occupied Kuwait. The United Nations Security Council demanded immediate withdrawal. On 29 November 1990 the Security Council authorised UN members to use force to expel Iraq from Kuwait. On 17 January 1991 Allied air forces, British among them, attacked strategic targets throughout Iraq and Iraqi-occupied Kuwait. On 24 February 1991 British forces participated in the land offensive. Four days later Iraq announced a cease-fire

TURKEY

SYRIA

IRAN

Mosul
Bashiqua
Erbil

32nd parallel

Suleymanieh
Kirkuk
Halabja

River Tigris

Tikrit

Balad

Habbaniyah
Baghdad
Zaafaraiyah

*

* ●Rutbah

*

IRAQ

*

IRAN

36th parallel
Al Najaf
Al Amarah

River Euphrates

As Samawah
Tallil

Jalibah
Basra

Following the Gulf War, Iraqi forces killed an estimated 30,000 Kurds in the north and Sh'ite Muslims in the south. On 6 April 1991 Britain and the United States warned Iraq not to send warplanes north of the 32nd parallel. Iraq complied. On 17 April 1991 US, British and French troops crossed into northern Iraq to secure "Safe Havens" for the Kurds, and to construct refugee camps

Of the 25,000 British troops who took part in the Gulf War **24** were killed in action

0	Kilometres	200
0	miles	120

SAUDI ARABIA

KUWAIT
Kuwait City

Persian Gulf

On 27 August 1992 the United States established a "No-Fly Zone" in the south. With the agreement of Britain and France, Iraqi warplanes flying south of the 36th parallel would be shot down from 7 January 1993. United States, British and French warplanes were subsequently in action against Iraqi anti-aircraft batteries

➤ British forces in action, January-February 1991

* British commandos active behind the lines, seeking out and destroying scud missile launchers, January-February 1991

✕✕✕ Safe Havens established for the Kurds

⊙ Iraqi anti-aircraft batteries attacked, 13-18 January 1993

© Martin Gilbert 1993

HOMELESSNESS, 1977-1993

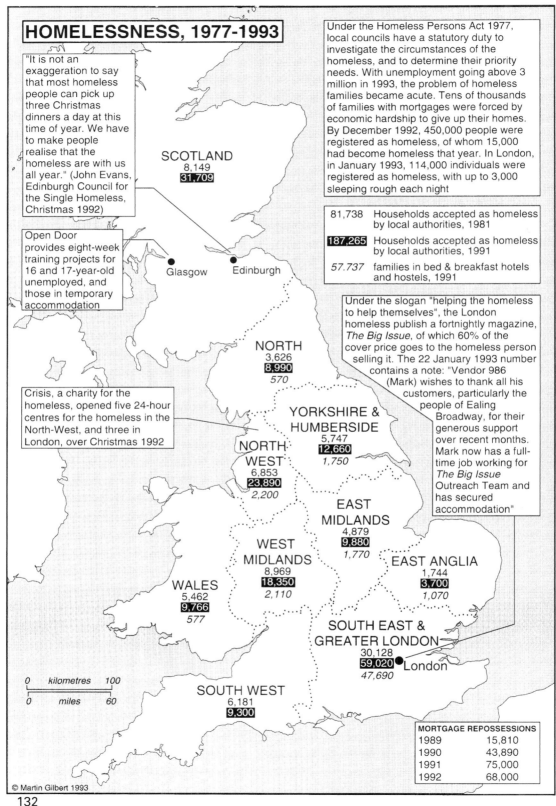

"It is not an exaggeration to say that most homeless people can pick up three Christmas dinners a day at this time of year. We have to make people realise that the homeless are with us all year." (John Evans, Edinburgh Council for the Single Homeless, Christmas 1992)

Open Door provides eight-week training projects for 16 and 17-year-old unemployed, and those in temporary accommodation

Crisis, a charity for the homeless, opened five 24-hour centres for the homeless in the North-West, and three in London, over Christmas 1992

Under the Homeless Persons Act 1977, local councils have a statutory duty to investigate the circumstances of the homeless, and to determine their priority needs. With unemployment going above 3 million in 1993, the problem of homeless families became acute. Tens of thousands of families with mortgages were forced by economic hardship to give up their homes. By December 1992, 450,000 people were registered as homeless, of whom 15,000 had become homeless that year. In London, in January 1993, 114,000 individuals were registered as homeless, with up to 3,000 sleeping rough each night

81,738	Households accepted as homeless by local authorities, 1981
187,265	Households accepted as homeless by local authorities, 1991
57.737	families in bed & breakfast hotels and hostels, 1991

Under the slogan "helping the homeless to help themselves", the London homeless publish a fortnightly magazine, *The Big Issue*, of which 60% of the cover price goes to the homeless person selling it. The 22 January 1993 number contains a note: "Vendor 986 (Mark) wishes to thank all his customers, particularly the people of Ealing Broadway, for their generous support over recent months. Mark now has a full-time job working for *The Big Issue* Outreach Team and has secured accommodation"

SCOTLAND
8,149
31,709

Glasgow   Edinburgh

NORTH
3,626
8,990
570

YORKSHIRE & HUMBERSIDE
5,747
12,660
1,750

NORTH WEST
6,853
23,890
2,200

EAST MIDLANDS
4,879
9,880
1,770

WEST MIDLANDS
8,969
18,350
2,110

EAST ANGLIA
1,744
3,700
1,070

WALES
5,462
9,766
577

SOUTH EAST & GREATER LONDON
30,128
59,020 London
47,690

SOUTH WEST
6,181
9,300

| 0 | kilometres | 100 |
| 0 | miles | 60 |

MORTGAGE REPOSSESSIONS	
1989	15,810
1990	43,890
1991	75,000
1992	68,000

© Martin Gilbert 1993

HOMES FOR THE HOMELESS, 1992-1993

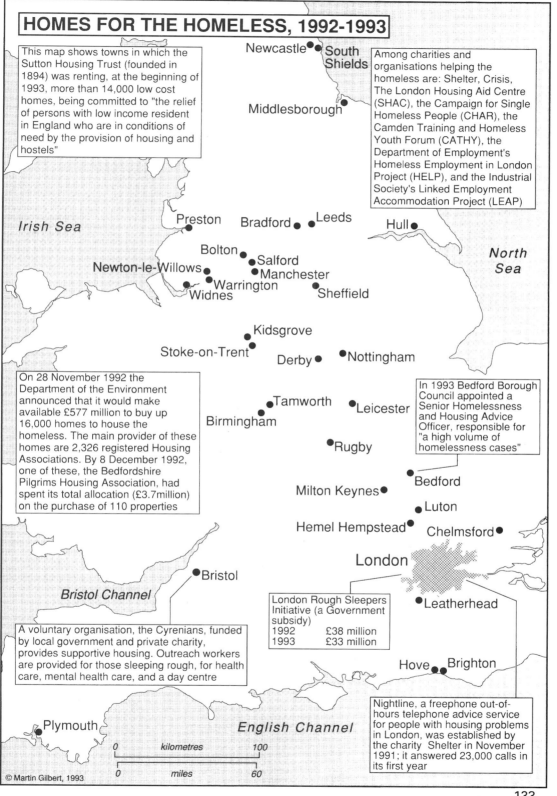

This map shows towns in which the Sutton Housing Trust (founded in 1894) was renting, at the beginning of 1993, more than 14,000 low cost homes, being committed to "the relief of persons with low income resident in England who are in conditions of need by the provision of housing and hostels"

Among charities and organisations helping the homeless are: Shelter, Crisis, The London Housing Aid Centre (SHAC), the Campaign for Single Homeless People (CHAR), the Camden Training and Homeless Youth Forum (CATHY), the Department of Employment's Homeless Employment in London Project (HELP), and the Industrial Society's Linked Employment Accommodation Project (LEAP)

Newcastle • • South Shields
Middlesborough •

Irish Sea

Preston • Bradford • • Leeds   Hull •

North Sea

Bolton •
Newton-le-Willows • • Salford
• • Manchester
Warrington •
Widnes   Sheffield •

Kidsgrove •
Stoke-on-Trent   Derby •   • Nottingham

On 28 November 1992 the Department of the Environment announced that it would make available £577 million to buy up 16,000 homes to house the homeless. The main provider of these homes are 2,326 registered Housing Associations. By 8 December 1992, one of these, the Bedfordshire Pilgrims Housing Association, had spent its total allocation (£3.7million) on the purchase of 110 properties

• Tamworth   • Leicester
Birmingham •

In 1993 Bedford Borough Council appointed a Senior Homelessness and Housing Advice Officer, responsible for "a high volume of homelessness cases"

• Rugby

• Bedford
Milton Keynes •
• Luton
Hemel Hempstead •   Chelmsford •

London

• Bristol

Bristol Channel

London Rough Sleepers Initiative (a Government subsidy)
1992   £38 million
1993   £33 million

• Leatherhead

A voluntary organisation, the Cyrenians, funded by local government and private charity, provides supportive housing. Outreach workers are provided for those sleeping rough, for health care, mental health care, and a day centre

Hove • • Brighton

Nightline, a freephone out-of-hours telephone advice service for people with housing problems in London, was established by the charity Shelter in November 1991; it answered 23,000 calls in its first year

• Plymouth   English Channel

0   kilometres   100
0   miles   60

© Martin Gilbert, 1993

133

PRIVATE CHARITY AND PUBLIC WELFARE

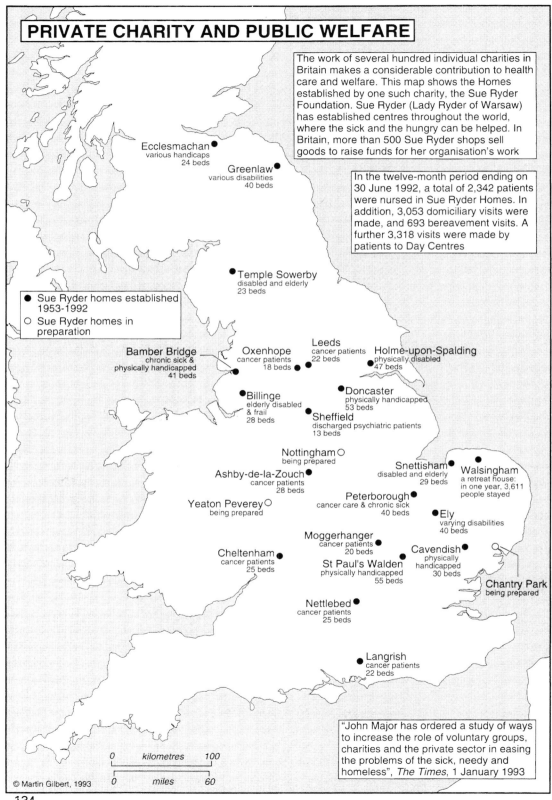

The work of several hundred individual charities in Britain makes a considerable contribution to health care and welfare. This map shows the Homes established by one such charity, the Sue Ryder Foundation. Sue Ryder (Lady Ryder of Warsaw) has established centres throughout the world, where the sick and the hungry can be helped. In Britain, more than 500 Sue Ryder shops sell goods to raise funds for her organisation's work

In the twelve-month period ending on 30 June 1992, a total of 2,342 patients were nursed in Sue Ryder Homes. In addition, 3,053 domiciliary visits were made, and 693 bereavement visits. A further 3,318 visits were made by patients to Day Centres

Ecclesmachan
various handicaps
24 beds

Greenlaw
various disabilities
40 beds

Temple Sowerby
disabled and elderly
23 beds

● Sue Ryder homes established 1953–1992
○ Sue Ryder homes in preparation

Bamber Bridge
chronic sick & physically handicapped
41 beds

Oxenhope
cancer patients
18 beds

Leeds
cancer patients
22 beds

Holme-upon-Spalding
physically disabled
47 beds

Billinge
elderly disabled & frail
28 beds

Doncaster
physically handicapped
53 beds

Sheffield
discharged psychiatric patients
13 beds

Nottingham ○
being prepared

Ashby-de-la-Zouch
cancer patients
28 beds

Snettisham
disabled and elderly
29 beds

Walsingham
a retreat house:
in one year, 3,611
people stayed

Yeaton Peverey ○
being prepared

Peterborough
cancer care & chronic sick
40 beds

Ely
varying disabilities
40 beds

Moggerhanger
cancer patients
20 beds

Cavendish
physically handicapped
30 beds

Cheltenham
cancer patients
25 beds

St Paul's Walden
physically handicapped
55 beds

Chantry Park
being prepared

Nettlebed
cancer patients
25 beds

Langrish
cancer patients
22 beds

"John Major has ordered a study of ways to increase the role of voluntary groups, charities and the private sector in easing the problems of the sick, needy and homeless", *The Times*, 1 January 1993

0   kilometres   100

0   miles   60

© Martin Gilbert, 1993

134

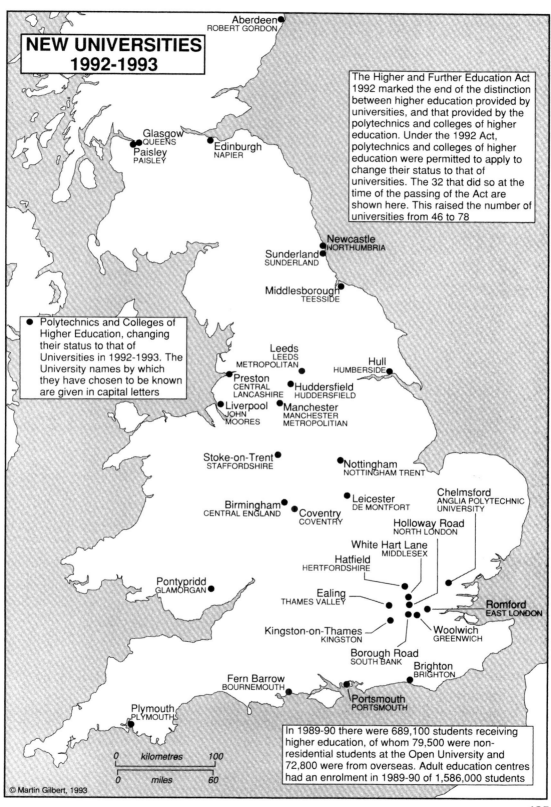

NEW UNIVERSITIES 1992-1993

Aberdeen
ROBERT GORDON

The Higher and Further Education Act 1992 marked the end of the distinction between higher education provided by universities, and that provided by the polytechnics and colleges of higher education. Under the 1992 Act, polytechnics and colleges of higher education were permitted to apply to change their status to that of universities. The 32 that did so at the time of the passing of the Act are shown here. This raised the number of universities from 46 to 78

Glasgow
QUEENS
Paisley
PAISLEY

Edinburgh
NAPIER

Newcastle
NORTHUMBRIA
Sunderland
SUNDERLAND

Middlesborough
TEESSIDE

● Polytechnics and Colleges of Higher Education, changing their status to that of Universities in 1992-1993. The University names by which they have chosen to be known are given in capital letters

Leeds
LEEDS METROPOLITAN

Hull
HUMBERSIDE

Preston
CENTRAL LANCASHIRE

Huddersfield
HUDDERSFIELD

Liverpool
JOHN MOORES

Manchester
MANCHESTER METROPOLITIAN

Stoke-on-Trent
STAFFORDSHIRE

Nottingham
NOTTINGHAM TRENT

Chelmsford
ANGLIA POLYTECHNIC UNIVERSITY

Birmingham
CENTRAL ENGLAND

Coventry
COVENTRY

Leicester
DE MONTFORT

Holloway Road
NORTH LONDON

White Hart Lane
MIDDLESEX

Hatfield
HERTFORDSHIRE

Pontypridd
GLAMORGAN

Ealing
THAMES VALLEY

Romford
EAST LONDON

Kingston-on-Thames
KINGSTON

Woolwich
GREENWICH

Borough Road
SOUTH BANK

Brighton
BRIGHTON

Fern Barrow
BOURNEMOUTH

Portsmouth
PORTSMOUTH

Plymouth
PLYMOUTH

0   kilometres   100

0   miles   60

© Martin Gilbert, 1993

In 1989-90 there were 689,100 students receiving higher education, of whom 79,500 were non-residential students at the Open University and 72,800 were from overseas. Adult education centres had an enrolment in 1989-90 of 1,586,000 students

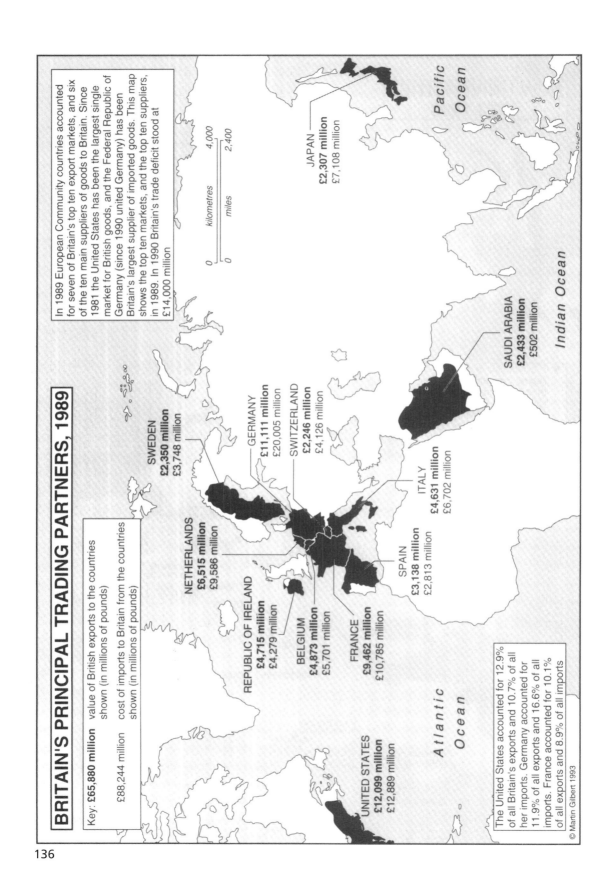

BRITAIN'S PRINCIPAL TRADING PARTNERS, 1989

Key: **£65,880 million** value of British exports to the countries shown (in millions of pounds)

£88,244 million cost of imports to Britain from the countries shown (in millions of pounds)

In 1989 European Community countries accounted for seven of Britain's top ten export markets, and six of the ten main suppliers of goods to Britain. Since 1981 the United States has been the largest single market for British goods, and the Federal Republic of Germany (since 1990 united Germany) has been Britain's largest supplier of imported goods. This map shows the top ten markets, and the top ten suppliers, in 1989. In 1990 Britain's trade deficit stood at £14,000 million

The United States accounted for 12.9% of all Britain's exports and 10.7% of all her imports. Germany accounted for 11.9% of all exports and 16.6% of all imports. France accounted for 10.1% of all exports and 8.9% of all imports

© Martin Gilbert 1993

UNITED STATES
£12,099 million
£12,889 million

SWEDEN
£2,350 million
£3,748 million

GERMANY
£11,111 million
£20,005 million

SWITZERLAND
£2,246 million
£4,126 million

NETHERLANDS
£6,515 million
£9,586 million

REPUBLIC OF IRELAND
£4,715 million
£4,279 million

BELGIUM
£4,873 million
£5,701 million

FRANCE
£9,462 million
£10,785 million

SPAIN
£3,138 million
£2,813 million

ITALY
£4,631 million
£6,702 million

SAUDI ARABIA
£2,433 million
£502 million

JAPAN
£2,307 million
£7,108 million

Atlantic Ocean

Pacific Ocean

Indian Ocean

kilometres 0 — 4,000
miles 0 — 2,400

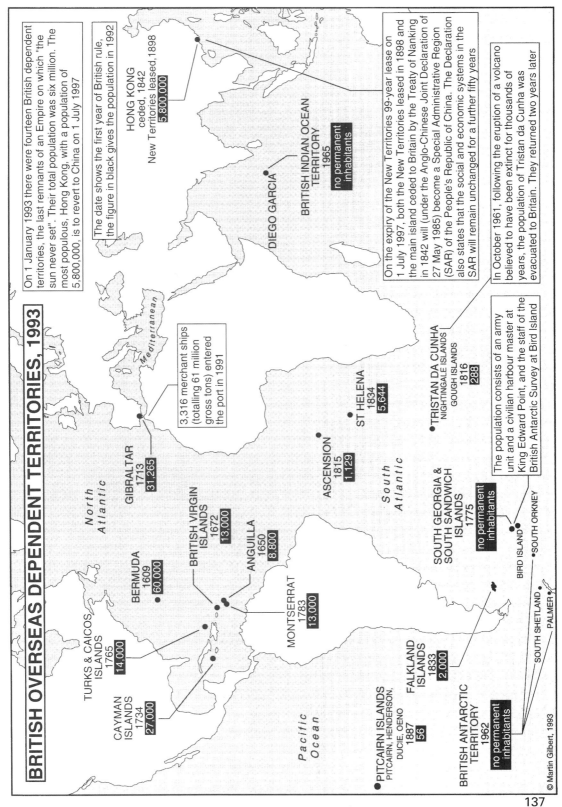

BRITISH OVERSEAS DEPENDENT TERRITORIES, 1993

On 1 January 1993 there were fourteen British dependent territories, the last remnants of an Empire on which "the sun never set". Their total population was six million. The most populous, Hong Kong, with a population of 5,800,000, is to revert to China on 1 July 1997

The date shows the first year of British rule, the figure in black gives the population in 1992

HONG KONG
ceded, 1842
New Territories leased, 1898
5,800,000

DIEGO GARCIA

BRITISH INDIAN OCEAN TERRITORY
1965
no permanent inhabitants

On the expiry of the New Territories 99-year lease on 1 July 1997, both the New Territories leased in 1898 and the main island ceded to Britain by the Treaty of Nanking in 1842 will (under the Anglo-Chinese Joint Declaration of 27 May 1985) become a Special Administrative Region (SAR) of the People's Republic of China. The Declaration also states that the social and economic systems in the SAR will remain unchanged for a further fifty years

In October 1961, following the eruption of a volcano believed to have been extinct for thousands of years, the population of Tristan da Cunha was evacuated to Britain. They returned two years later

3,316 merchant ships (totalling 61 million gross tons) entered the port in 1991

Mediterranean

GIBRALTAR
1713
31,265

ST HELENA
1834
5,644

TRISTAN DA CUNHA
1816
NIGHTINGALE ISLANDS
GOUGH ISLANDS
288

ASCENSION
1815
1,129

North Atlantic

South Atlantic

The population consists of an army unit and a civilian harbour master at King Edward Point, and the staff of the British Antarctic Survey at Bird Island

BRITISH VIRGIN ISLANDS
1672
13,000

ANGUILLA
1650
8,800

BERMUDA
1609
60,000

MONTSERRAT
1783
13,000

SOUTH GEORGIA & SOUTH SANDWICH ISLANDS
1775
no permanent inhabitants

BIRD ISLAND
SOUTH ORKNEY

TURKS & CAICOS ISLANDS
1765
14,000

CAYMAN ISLANDS
1734
27,000

FALKLAND ISLANDS
1833
2,000

SOUTH SHETLAND
PALMER

PITCAIRN ISLANDS
PITCAIRN, HENDERSON, DUCIE, OENO
1887
56

BRITISH ANTARCTIC TERRITORY
1962
no permanent inhabitants

Pacific Ocean

© Martin Gilbert, 1993

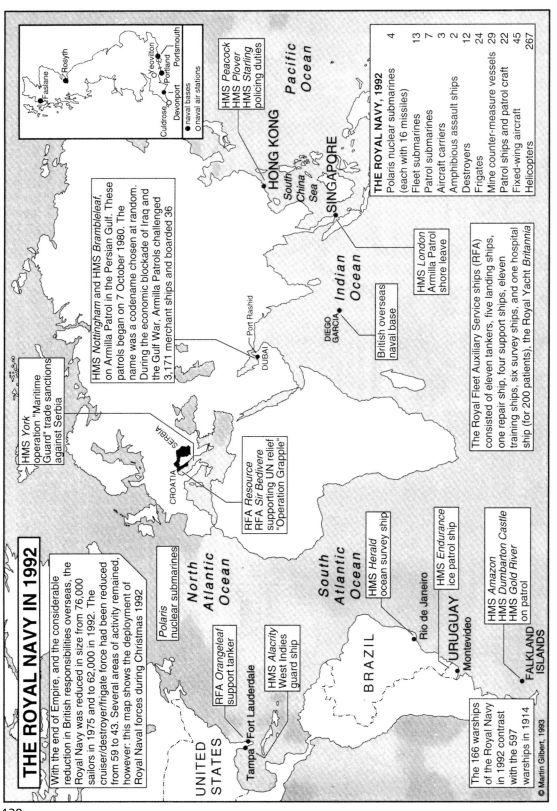

THE ROYAL NAVY IN 1992

With the end of Empire, and the considerable reduction in British responsibilities overseas, the Royal Navy was reduced in size from 76,000 sailors in 1975 and to 62,000 in 1992. The cruiser/destroyer/frigate force had been reduced from 59 to 43. Several areas of activity remained, however: this map shows the deployment of Royal Naval forces during Christmas 1992

Polaris nuclear submarines

RFA *Orangeleaf* support tanker

HMS *Alacrity* West Indies guard ship

The 166 warships of the Royal Navy in 1992 contrast with the 597 warships in 1914

UNITED STATES

Tampa • Fort Lauderdale

North Atlantic Ocean

BRAZIL

South Atlantic Ocean

Rio de Janeiro

URUGUAY
Montevideo

HMS *Herald* ocean survey ship

HMS *Endurance* ice patrol ship

HMS *Amazon*
HMS *Dumbarton Castle*
HMS *Gold River* on patrol

FALKLAND ISLANDS

HMS *York* operation "Maritime Guard" trade sanctions against Serbia

SERBIA

CROATIA

RFA *Resource*
RFA *Sir Bedivere* supporting UN relief "Operation Grapple"

HMS *Nottingham* and HMS *Brambleleaf*, on Armilla Patrol in the Persian Gulf. These patrols began on 7 October 1980. The name was a codename chosen at random. During the economic blockade of Iraq and the Gulf War, Armilla Patrols challenged 3,171 merchant ships and boarded 36

Port Rashid

DUBAI

HMS *London* Armilla Patrol shore leave

DIEGO GARCIA •   *Indian Ocean*

British overseas naval base

HMS *Peacock*
HMS *Plover*
HMS *Starling* policing duties

HONG KONG

South China Sea

SINGAPORE

Pacific Ocean

The Royal Fleet Auxiliary Service ships (RFA) consisted of eleven tankers, five landing ships, one repair ship, four support ships, eleven training ships, six survey ships, and one hospital ship (for 200 patients), the Royal Yacht *Britannia*

THE ROYAL NAVY, 1992

Polaris nuclear submarines (each with 16 missiles)	4
Fleet submarines	13
Patrol submarines	7
Aircraft carriers	3
Amphibious assault ships	2
Destroyers	12
Frigates	24
Mine counter-measure vessels	29
Patrol ships and patrol craft	22
Fixed-wing aircraft	45
Helicopters	267

Faslane
Rosyth
Yeovilton
Culdrose
Portland
Devonport
Portsmouth

● naval bases
○ naval air stations

© Martin Gilbert, 1993

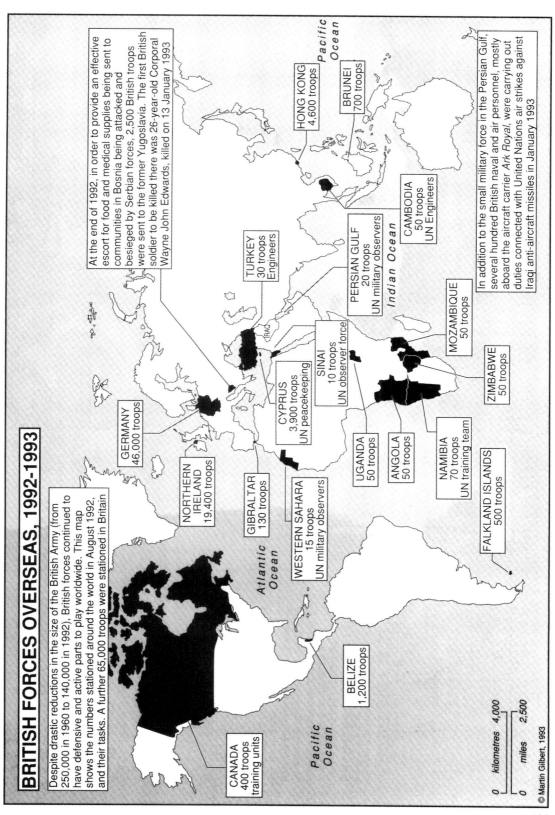

BRITISH FORCES OVERSEAS, 1992-1993

Despite drastic reductions in the size of the British Army (from 250,000 in 1960 to 140,000 in 1992), British forces continued to have defensive and active parts to play worldwide. This map shows the numbers stationed around the world in August 1992, and their tasks. A further 65,000 troops were stationed in Britain

At the end of 1992, in order to provide an effective escort for food and medical supplies being sent to communities in Bosnia being attacked and besieged by Serbian forces, 2,500 British troops were sent to the former Yugoslavia. The first British soldier to be killed there was 26-year-old Corporal Wayne John Edwards, killed on 13 January 1993

In addition to the small military force in the Persian Gulf, several hundred British naval and air personnel, mostly aboard the aircraft carrier *Ark Royal*, were carrying out duties connected with United Nations air strikes against Iraqi anti-aircraft missiles in January 1993

HONG KONG
4,600 troops

BRUNEI
700 troops

CAMBODIA
50 troops
UN Engineers

TURKEY
30 troops
Engineers

PERSIAN GULF
20 troops
UN military observers

SINAI
10 troops
UN observer force

MOZAMBIQUE
50 troops

GERMANY
46,000 troops

CYPRUS
3,900 troops
UN peacekeeping

ZIMBABWE
50 troops

NORTHERN
IRELAND
19,400 troops

UGANDA
50 troops

ANGOLA
50 troops

GIBRALTAR
130 troops

NAMIBIA
70 troops
UN training team

WESTERN SAHARA
15 troops
UN military observers

FALKLAND ISLANDS
500 troops

BELIZE
1,200 troops

CANADA
400 troops
training units

Pacific Ocean

Atlantic Ocean

Indian Ocean

Pacific Ocean

IRAQ

0   kilometres   4,000

0   miles   2,500

© Martin Gilbert, 1993

139

TOWARDS A SINGLE EUROPEAN MARKET, OCTOBER-DECEMBER 1992

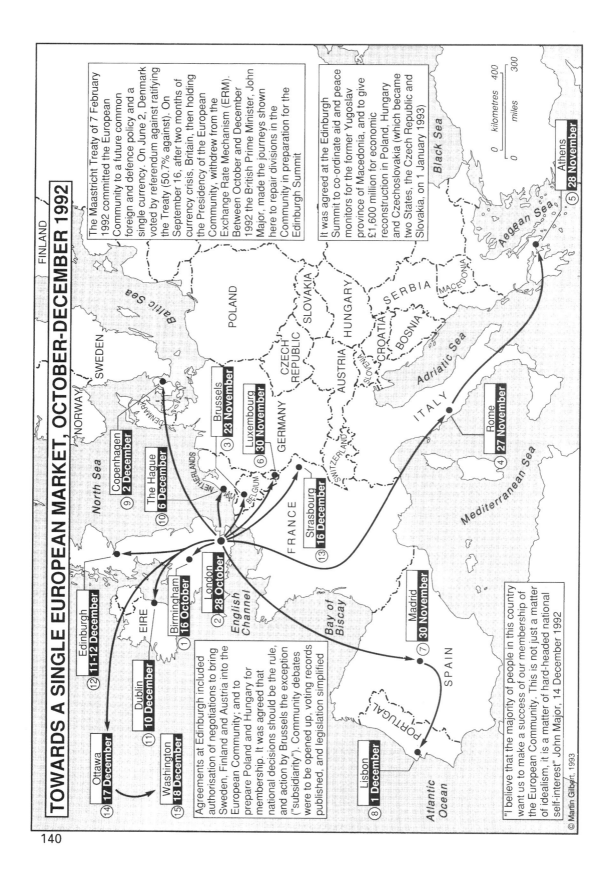

The Maastricht Treaty of 7 February 1992 committed the European Community to a future common foreign and defence policy and a single currency. On June 2, Denmark voted by referendum against ratifying the Treaty (50.7% against). On September 16, after two months of currency crisis, Britain, then holding the Presidency of the European Community, withdrew from the Exchange Rate Mechanism (ERM). Between October and December 1992 the British Prime Minister, John Major, made the journeys shown here to repair divisions in the Community in preparation for the Edinburgh Summit

It was agreed at the Edinburgh Summit to co-ordinate aid and peace monitors for the former Yugoslav province of Macedonia, and to give £1,600 million for economic reconstruction in Poland, Hungary and Czechoslovakia (which became two States, the Czech Republic and Slovakia, on 1 January 1993)

Agreements at Edinburgh included authorisation of negotiations to bring Sweden, Finland and Austria into the European Community; and to prepare Poland and Hungary for membership. It was agreed that national decisions should be the rule, and action by Brussels the exception ("subsidiarity"). Community debates were to be opened up, voting records published, and legislation simplified

"I believe that the majority of people in this country want us to make a success of our membership of the European Community. This is not just a matter of idealism, it is a matter of hard-headed national self-interest" John Major, 14 December 1992

① Birmingham 16 October
② London 28 October
③ Brussels 23 November
④ Rome 27 November
⑤ Athens 28 November
⑥ Luxembourg 30 November
⑦ Madrid 30 November
⑧ Lisbon 1 December
⑨ Copenhagen 2 December
⑩ The Hague 6 December
⑪ Dublin 10 December
⑫ Edinburgh 11-12 December
⑬ Strasbourg 16 December
⑭ Ottawa 17 December
⑮ Washington 18 December

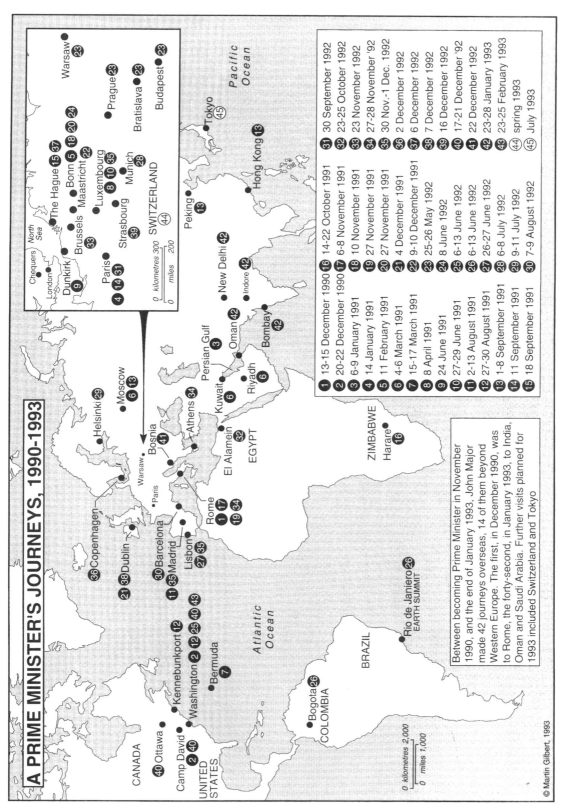

A PRIME MINISTER'S JOURNEYS, 1990–1993

Between becoming Prime Minister in November 1990, and the end of January 1993, John Major made 42 journeys overseas, 14 of them beyond Western Europe. The first, in December 1990, was to Rome, the forty-second, in January 1993, to India, Oman and Saudi Arabia. Further visits planned for 1993 included Switzerland and Tokyo

1	13-15 December 1990	16	14-22 October 1991
2	20-22 December 1990	17	6-8 November 1991
3	6-9 January 1991	18	10 November 1991
4	14 January 1991	19	27 November 1991
5	11 February 1991	20	27 November 1991
6	4-6 March 1991	21	4 December 1991
7	15-17 March 1991	22	9-10 December 1991
8	8 April 1991	23	25-26 May 1992
9	24 June 1991	24	8 June 1992
10	27-29 June 1991	25	6-13 June 1992
11	2-13 August 1991	26	6-13 June 1992
12	27-30 August 1991	27	26-27 June 1992
13	1-8 September 1991	28	6-8 July 1992
14	11 September 1991	29	9-11 July 1992
15	18 September 1991	30	7-9 August 1992
		31	30 September 1992
		32	23-25 October 1992
		33	23 November 1992
		34	27-28 November '92
		35	30 Nov.-1 Dec. 1992
		36	2 December 1992
		37	6 December 1992
		38	7 December 1992
		39	16 December 1992
		40	17-21 December '92
		41	22 December 1992
		42	23-28 January 1993
		43	23-25 February 1993
		44	spring 1993
		45	July 1993

© Martin Gilbert, 1993

THE LONG-TERM UNEMPLOYED, 1993

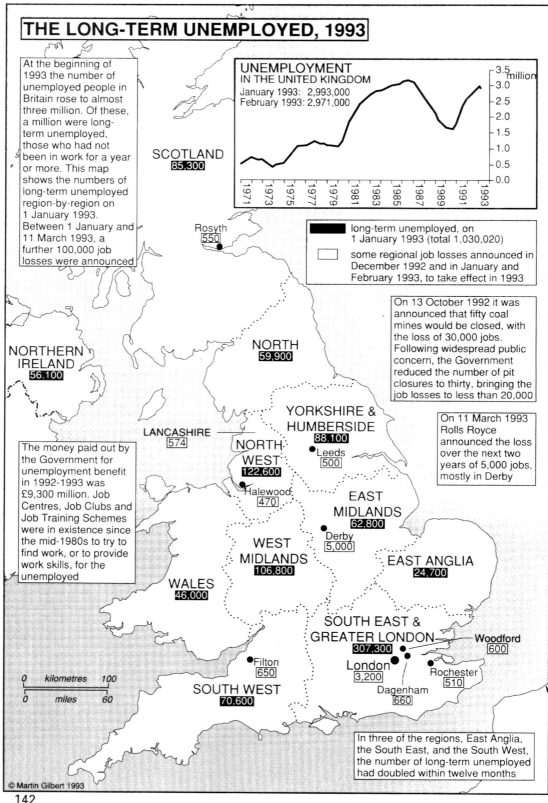

At the beginning of 1993 the number of unemployed people in Britain rose to almost three million. Of these, a million were long-term unemployed, those who had not been in work for a year or more. This map shows the numbers of long-term unemployed region-by-region on 1 January 1993. Between 1 January and 11 March 1993, a further 100,000 job losses were announced

UNEMPLOYMENT
IN THE UNITED KINGDOM
January 1993: 2,993,000
February 1993: 2,971,000

3.5 million
3.0
2.5
2.0
1.5
1.0
0.5
0.0

1971 1973 1975 1977 1979 1981 1983 1985 1987 1989 1991 1993

SCOTLAND
85,300

Rosyth
550

▮ long-term unemployed, on 1 January 1993 (total 1,030,020)

☐ some regional job losses announced in December 1992 and in January and February 1993, to take effect in 1993

NORTHERN IRELAND
56,100

NORTH
59,900

On 13 October 1992 it was announced that fifty coal mines would be closed, with the loss of 30,000 jobs. Following widespread public concern, the Government reduced the number of pit closures to thirty, bringing the job losses to less than 20,000

YORKSHIRE & HUMBERSIDE
88,100

LANCASHIRE
574

NORTH WEST
122,600

Leeds
500

On 11 March 1993 Rolls Royce announced the loss over the next two years of 5,000 jobs, mostly in Derby

The money paid out by the Government for unemployment benefit in 1992-1993 was £9,300 million. Job Centres, Job Clubs and Job Training Schemes were in existence since the mid-1980s to try to find work, or to provide work skills, for the unemployed

Halewood
470

EAST MIDLANDS
62,800

Derby
5,000

WEST MIDLANDS
106,800

EAST ANGLIA
24,700

WALES
46,000

SOUTH EAST & GREATER LONDON
307,300

Woodford
600

Filton
650

London
3,200

Rochester
510

SOUTH WEST
70,600

Dagenham
660

0 kilometres 100
0 miles 60

In three of the regions, East Anglia, the South East, and the South West, the number of long-term unemployed had doubled within twelve months

© Martin Gilbert 1993

MUSLIMS, SIKHS, HINDUS, JEWS AND BUDDHISTS, 1993

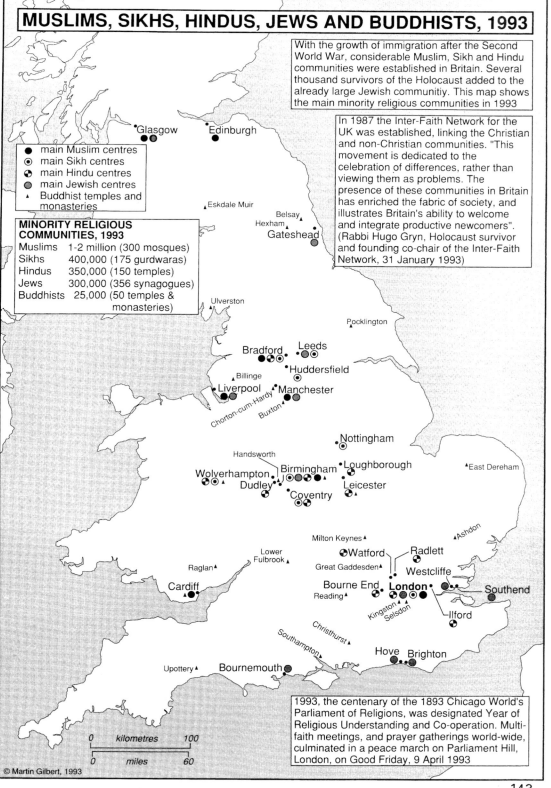

With the growth of immigration after the Second World War, considerable Muslim, Sikh and Hindu communities were established in Britain. Several thousand survivors of the Holocaust added to the already large Jewish communitiy. This map shows the main minority religious communities in 1993

In 1987 the Inter-Faith Network for the UK was established, linking the Christian and non-Christian communities. "This movement is dedicated to the celebration of differences, rather than viewing them as problems. The presence of these communities in Britain has enriched the fabric of society, and illustrates Britain's ability to welcome and integrate productive newcomers". (Rabbi Hugo Gryn, Holocaust survivor and founding co-chair of the Inter-Faith Network, 31 January 1993)

- ● main Muslim centres
- ◉ main Sikh centres
- ◓ main Hindu centres
- ● main Jewish centres
- ▲ Buddhist temples and monasteries

MINORITY RELIGIOUS COMMUNITIES, 1993

Muslims	1-2 million (300 mosques)
Sikhs	400,000 (175 gurdwaras)
Hindus	350,000 (150 temples)
Jews	300,000 (356 synagogues)
Buddhists	25,000 (50 temples & monasteries)

Glasgow
Edinburgh
▲Eskdale Muir
Belsay▲
Hexham▲
Gateshead
▲Ulverston
Pocklington
Bradford Leeds
▲Billinge Huddersfield
Liverpool ▲Manchester
Chorlton-cum-Hardy
Buxton▲
Nottingham
Handsworth
Birmingham Loughborough ▲East Dereham
Wolverhampton
Dudley Leicester
Coventry
Milton Keynes▲
Lower Fulbrook▲ ▲Ashdon
Raglan▲ Watford Radlett
Great Gaddesden▲ Westcliffe
Cardiff Bourne End London Southend
Reading▲ Kingston Ilford
Selsdon
Christhurst▲
Southampton▲ Hove Brighton
Upottery▲ Bournemouth

1993, the centenary of the 1893 Chicago World's Parliament of Religions, was designated Year of Religious Understanding and Co-operation. Multi-faith meetings, and prayer gatherings world-wide, culminated in a peace march on Parliament Hill, London, on Good Friday, 9 April 1993

0 kilometres 100
0 miles 60

© Martin Gilbert, 1993

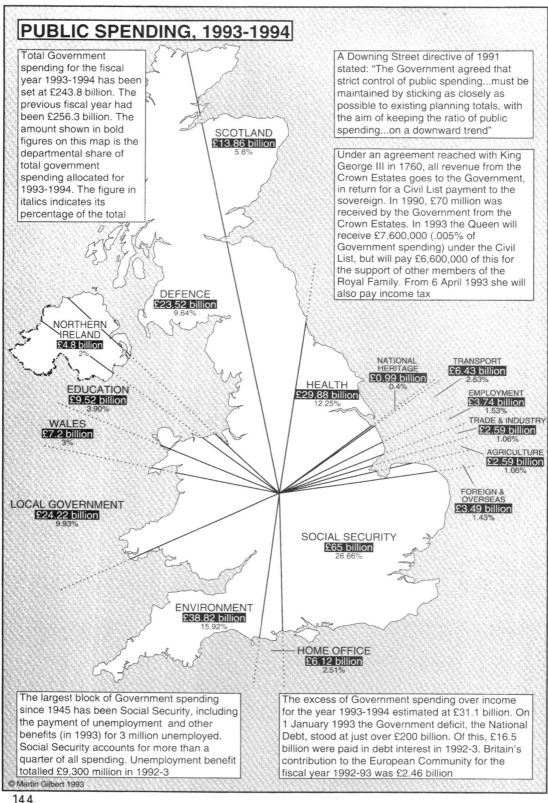

PUBLIC SPENDING, 1993-1994

Total Government spending for the fiscal year 1993-1994 has been set at £243.8 billion. The previous fiscal year had been £256.3 billion. The amount shown in bold figures on this map is the departmental share of total government spending allocated for 1993-1994. The figure in italics indicates its percentage of the total

A Downing Street directive of 1991 stated: "The Government agreed that strict control of public spending...must be maintained by sticking as closely as possible to existing planning totals, with the aim of keeping the ratio of public spending...on a downward trend"

Under an agreement reached with King George III in 1760, all revenue from the Crown Estates goes to the Government, in return for a Civil List payment to the sovereign. In 1990, £70 million was received by the Government from the Crown Estates. In 1993 the Queen will receive £7,600,000 (.005% of Government spending) under the Civil List, but will pay £6,600,000 of this for the support of other members of the Royal Family. From 6 April 1993 she will also pay income tax

SCOTLAND
£13.86 billion
5.6%

DEFENCE
£23.52 billion
9.64%

NORTHERN IRELAND
£4.8 billion
2%

EDUCATION
£9.52 billion
3.90%

WALES
£7.2 billion
3%

NATIONAL HERITAGE
£0.99 billion
0.4%

TRANSPORT
£6.43 billion
2.63%

HEALTH
£29.88 billion
12.25%

EMPLOYMENT
£3.74 billion
1.53%

TRADE & INDUSTRY
£2.59 billion
1.06%

AGRICULTURE
£2.59 billion
1.06%

LOCAL GOVERNMENT
£24.22 billion
9.93%

FOREIGN & OVERSEAS
£3.49 billion
1.43%

SOCIAL SECURITY
£65 billion
26.66%

ENVIRONMENT
£38.82 billion
15.92%

HOME OFFICE
£6.12 billion
2.51%

The largest block of Government spending since 1945 has been Social Security, including the payment of unemployment and other benefits (in 1993) for 3 million unemployed. Social Security accounts for more than a quarter of all spending. Unemployment benefit totalled £9,300 million in 1992-3

The excess of Government spending over income for the year 1993-1994 estimated at £31.1 billion. On 1 January 1993 the Government deficit, the National Debt, stood at just over £200 billion. Of this, £16.5 billion were paid in debt interest in 1992-3. Britain's contribution to the European Community for the fiscal year 1992-93 was £2.46 billion

© Martin Gilbert 1993

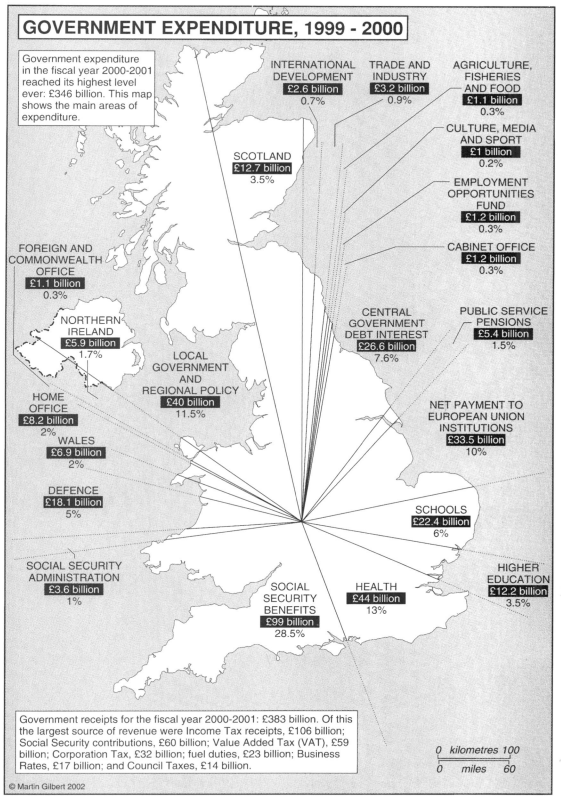

GOVERNMENT EXPENDITURE, 1999 - 2000

Government expenditure in the fiscal year 2000-2001 reached its highest level ever: £346 billion. This map shows the main areas of expenditure.

INTERNATIONAL DEVELOPMENT
£2.6 billion
0.7%

TRADE AND INDUSTRY
£3.2 billion
0.9%

AGRICULTURE, FISHERIES AND FOOD
£1.1 billion
0.3%

CULTURE, MEDIA AND SPORT
£1 billion
0.2%

SCOTLAND
£12.7 billion
3.5%

EMPLOYMENT OPPORTUNITIES FUND
£1.2 billion
0.3%

CABINET OFFICE
£1.2 billion
0.3%

FOREIGN AND COMMONWEALTH OFFICE
£1.1 billion
0.3%

CENTRAL GOVERNMENT DEBT INTEREST
£26.6 billion
7.6%

PUBLIC SERVICE PENSIONS
£5.4 billion
1.5%

NORTHERN IRELAND
£5.9 billion
1.7%

LOCAL GOVERNMENT AND REGIONAL POLICY
£40 billion
11.5%

NET PAYMENT TO EUROPEAN UNION INSTITUTIONS
£33.5 billion
10%

HOME OFFICE
£8.2 billion
2%

WALES
£6.9 billion
2%

DEFENCE
£18.1 billion
5%

SCHOOLS
£22.4 billion
6%

SOCIAL SECURITY ADMINISTRATION
£3.6 billion
1%

SOCIAL SECURITY BENEFITS
£99 billion
28.5%

HEALTH
£44 billion
13%

HIGHER EDUCATION
£12.2 billion
3.5%

Government receipts for the fiscal year 2000-2001: £383 billion. Of this the largest source of revenue were Income Tax receipts, £106 billion; Social Security contributions, £60 billion; Value Added Tax (VAT), £59 billion; Corporation Tax, £32 billion; fuel duties, £23 billion; Business Rates, £17 billion; and Council Taxes, £14 billion.

0 kilometres 100

0 miles 60

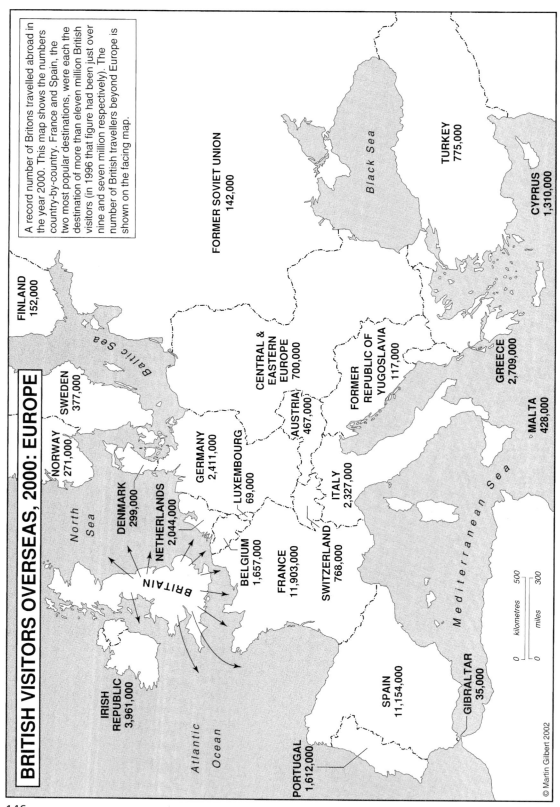

BRITISH VISITORS OVERSEAS, 2000: EUROPE

A record number of Britons travelled abroad in the year 2000. This map shows the numbers country-by-country. France and Spain, the two most popular destinations, were each the destination of more than eleven million British visitors (in 1996 that figure had been just over nine and seven million respectively). The number of British travellers beyond Europe is shown on the facing map.

FINLAND
152,000

FORMER SOVIET UNION
142,000

TURKEY
775,000

CYPRUS
1,310,000

Black Sea

NORWAY
271,000

SWEDEN
377,000

Baltic Sea

GERMANY
2,411,000

CENTRAL &
EASTERN
EUROPE
700,000

AUSTRIA
467,000

FORMER
REPUBLIC OF
YUGOSLAVIA
117,000

GREECE
2,709,000

MALTA
428,000

DENMARK
299,000

NETHERLANDS
2,044,000

LUXEMBOURG
69,000

BELGIUM
1,657,000

North Sea

BRITAIN

ITALY
2,327,000

SWITZERLAND
768,000

FRANCE
11,903,000

Mediterranean Sea

IRISH
REPUBLIC
3,961,000

Atlantic Ocean

SPAIN
11,154,000

GIBRALTAR
35,000

PORTUGAL
1,612,000

0   500
kilometres
0   300
miles

© Martin Gilbert 2002

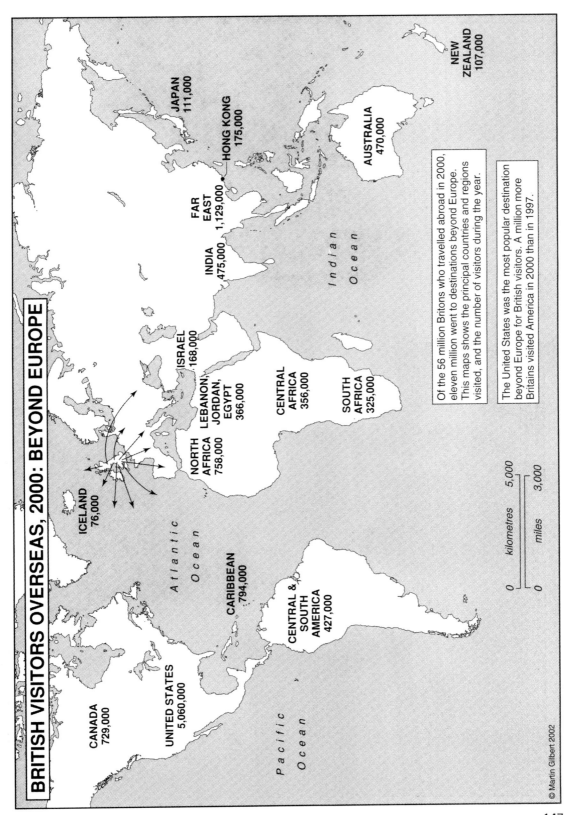

BRITISH VISITORS OVERSEAS, 2000: BEYOND EUROPE

NEW ZEALAND
107,000

JAPAN
111,000

HONG KONG
175,000

AUSTRALIA
470,000

FAR EAST
1,129,000

INDIA
475,000

Indian Ocean

ISRAEL
168,000

LEBANON,
JORDAN,
EGYPT
366,000

CENTRAL
AFRICA
356,000

SOUTH
AFRICA
325,000

NORTH
AFRICA
758,000

Of the 56 million Britons who travelled abroad in 2000, eleven million went to destinations beyond Europe. This maps shows the principal countries and regions visited, and the number of visitors during the year.

The United States was the most popular destination beyond Europe for British visitors. A million more Britains visited America in 2000 than in 1997.

ICELAND
76,000

Atlantic Ocean

CARIBBEAN
794,000

CENTRAL &
SOUTH
AMERICA
427,000

kilometres   5,000

0

miles   3,000

0

CANADA
729,000

UNITED STATES
5,060,000

Pacific Ocean

© Martin Gilbert 2002

147

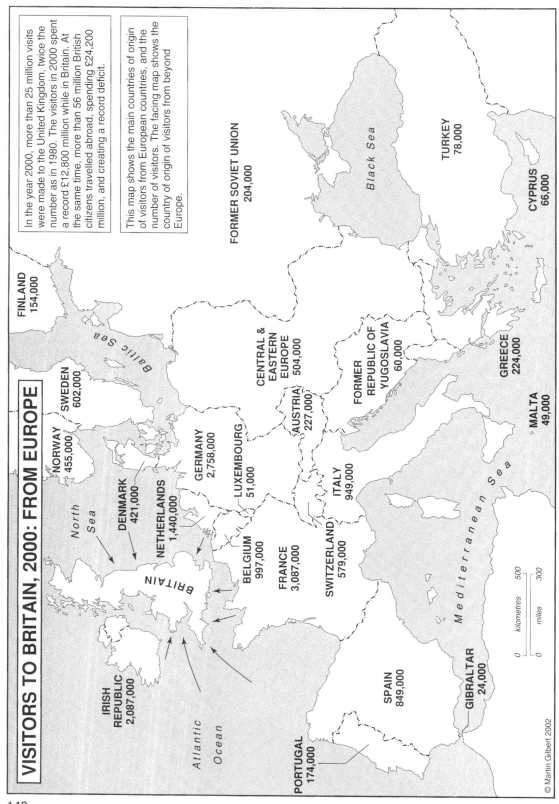

VISITORS TO BRITAIN, 2000: FROM EUROPE

In the year 2000, more than 25 million visits were made to the United Kingdom, twice the number as in 1980. The visitors in 2000 spent a record £12,800 million while in Britain. At the same time, more than 56 million British citizens travelled abroad, spending £24,200 million, and creating a record deficit.

This map shows the main countries of origin of visitors from European countries, and the number of visitors. The facing map shows the country of origin of visitors from beyond Europe.

FINLAND 154,000

FORMER SOVIET UNION 204,000

SWEDEN 602,000

NORWAY 455,000

Baltic Sea

North Sea

DENMARK 421,000

GERMANY 2,758,000

NETHERLANDS 1,440,000

LUXEMBOURG 51,000

CENTRAL & EASTERN EUROPE 504,000

AUSTRIA 227,000

Black Sea

TURKEY 78,000

FORMER REPUBLIC OF YUGOSLAVIA 60,000

GREECE 224,000

CYPRUS 66,000

BELGIUM 997,000

FRANCE 3,087,000

ITALY 949,000

SWITZERLAND 579,000

BRITAIN

IRISH REPUBLIC 2,087,000

Atlantic Ocean

MALTA 49,000

Mediterranean Sea

PORTUGAL 174,000

SPAIN 849,000

GIBRALTAR 24,000

kilometres 0 — 500

miles 0 — 300

© Martin Gilbert 2002

148

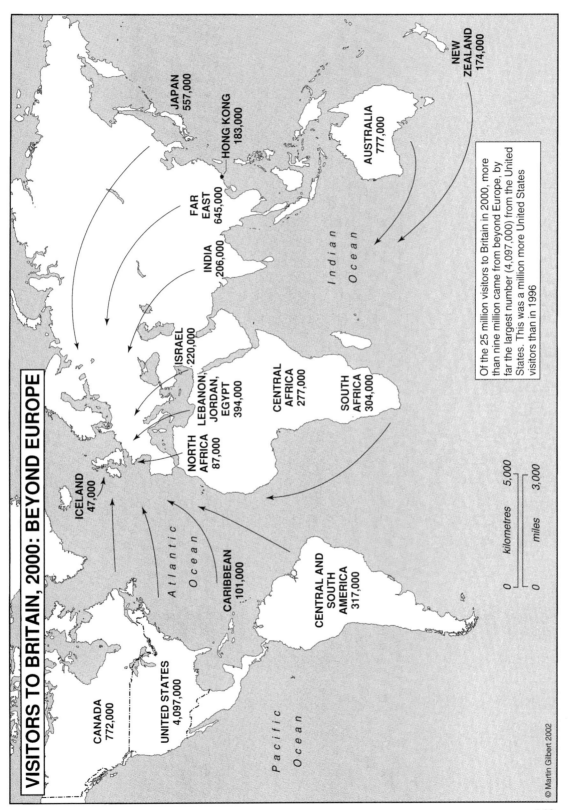

VISITORS TO BRITAIN, 2000: BEYOND EUROPE

JAPAN
557,000

HONG KONG
183,000

FAR
EAST
645,000

INDIA
206,000

ISRAEL
220,000

LEBANON,
JORDAN,
EGYPT
394,000

NORTH
AFRICA
87,000

CENTRAL
AFRICA
277,000

SOUTH
AFRICA
304,000

NEW
ZEALAND
174,000

AUSTRALIA
777,000

*Indian
Ocean*

Of the 25 million visitors to Britain in 2000, more than nine million came from beyond Europe, by far the largest number (4,097,000) from the United States. This was a million more United States visitors than in 1996

*Atlantic
Ocean*

ICELAND
47,000

CARIBBEAN
101,000

CANADA
772,000

UNITED STATES
4,097,000

CENTRAL AND
SOUTH
AMERICA
317,000

*Pacific
Ocean*

5,000
3,000
kilometres
miles
0
0

© Martin Gilbert 2002

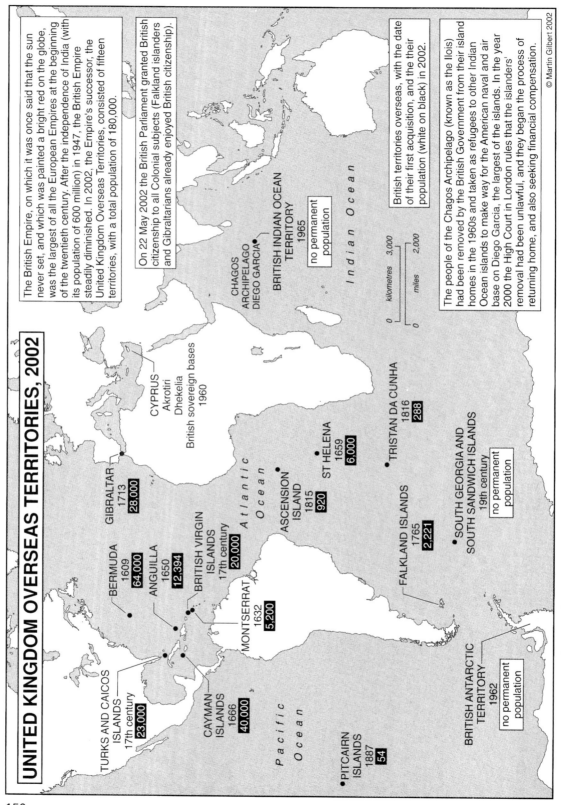

BRITISH ARMED FORCES OVERSEAS, 2002

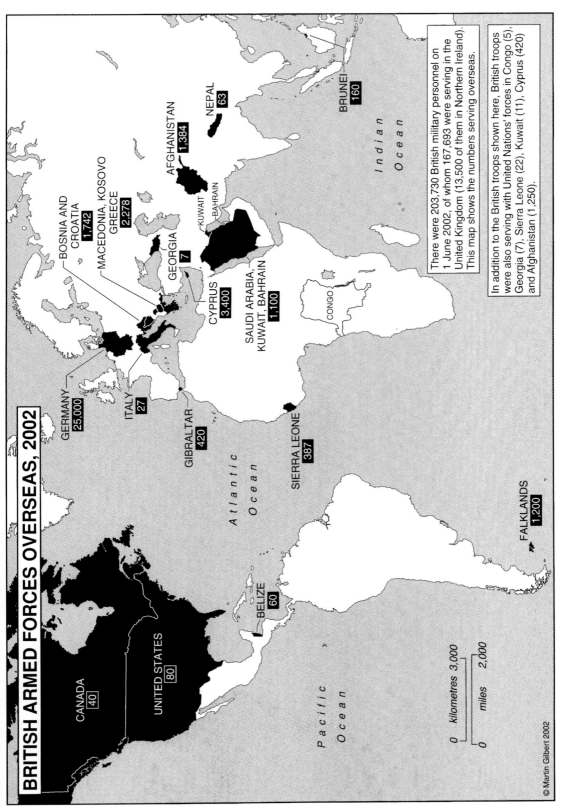

There were 203,730 British military personnel on 1 June 2002, of whom 167,693 were serving in the United Kingdom (13,500 of them in Northern Ireland). This map shows the numbers serving overseas.

In addition to the British troops shown here, British troops were also serving with United Nations' forces in Congo (5), Georgia (7), Sierra Leone (22), Kuwait (11), Cyprus (420) and Afghanistan (1,250).

NEPAL 63

BRUNEI 160

AFGHANISTAN 1,384

Indian Ocean

KUWAIT

BAHRAIN

BOSNIA AND CROATIA 1,742

MACEDONIA, KOSOVO

GREECE 2,278

GEORGIA 7

CYPRUS 3,400

SAUDI ARABIA, KUWAIT, BAHRAIN 1,100

CONGO

GERMANY 25,000

ITALY 27

GIBRALTAR 420

Atlantic Ocean

SIERRA LEONE 387

FALKLANDS 1,200

BELIZE 60

CANADA 40

UNITED STATES 80

Pacific Ocean

0 kilometres 3,000

0 miles 2,000

© Martin Gilbert 2002

151

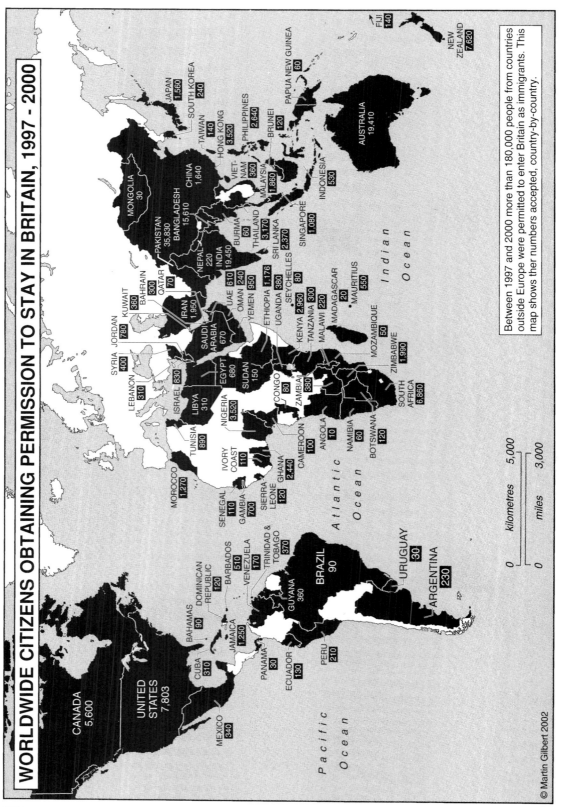

WORLDWIDE CITIZENS OBTAINING PERMISSION TO STAY IN BRITAIN, 1997 - 2000

Between 1997 and 2000 more than 180,000 people from countries outside Europe were permitted to enter Britain as immigrants. This map shows their numbers accepted, country-by-country.

CANADA 5,600

UNITED STATES 7,803

MEXICO 340

BAHAMAS 90

DOMINICAN REPUBLIC 120

CUBA 310

JAMAICA 1,250

PANAMA 30

ECUADOR 130

PERU 210

BARBADOS 510

VENEZUELA 170

TRINIDAD & TOBAGO 370

GUYANA 360

BRAZIL 90

URUGUAY 30

ARGENTINA 230

MOROCCO 1,270

TUNISIA 890

SENEGAL 110

GAMBIA 700

SIERRA LEONE 120

IVORY COAST 110

GHANA 2,440

LIBYA 310

NIGERIA 3,520

CAMEROON 100

EGYPT 680

SUDAN 150

CONGO 80

ZAMBIA 380

ANGOLA 10

NAMIBIA 60

BOTSWANA 120

SOUTH AFRICA 6,860

ZIMBABWE 1,990

MOZAMBIQUE 50

MALAWI 220

TANZANIA 300

MADAGASCAR 20

MAURITIUS 550

SEYCHELLES 80

KENYA 2,960

UGANDA 380

ETHIOPIA 1,176

YEMEN 950

OMAN 240

UAE 610

SAUDI ARABIA 670

ISRAEL 830

LEBANON 310

SYRIA 400

JORDAN 780

IRAN 1,950

KUWAIT 360

BAHRAIN 300

QATAR 70

PAKISTAN 35,830

BANGLADESH 15,610

NEPAL 220

INDIA 19,450

SRI LANKA 2,370

MONGOLIA 30

CHINA 1,640

BURMA 60

THAILAND 3,170

VIET-NAM 360

MALAYSIA 1,860

SINGAPORE 1,080

INDONESIA 530

BRUNEI 120

PHILIPPINES 2,640

HONG KONG 3,520

TAIWAN 140

SOUTH KOREA 240

JAPAN 1,560

PAPUA NEW GUINEA 60

AUSTRALIA 19,410

FIJI 140

NEW ZEALAND 7,620

Pacific Ocean

Atlantic Ocean

Indian Ocean

0   kilometres   5,000

0   miles   3,000

© Martin Gilbert 2002

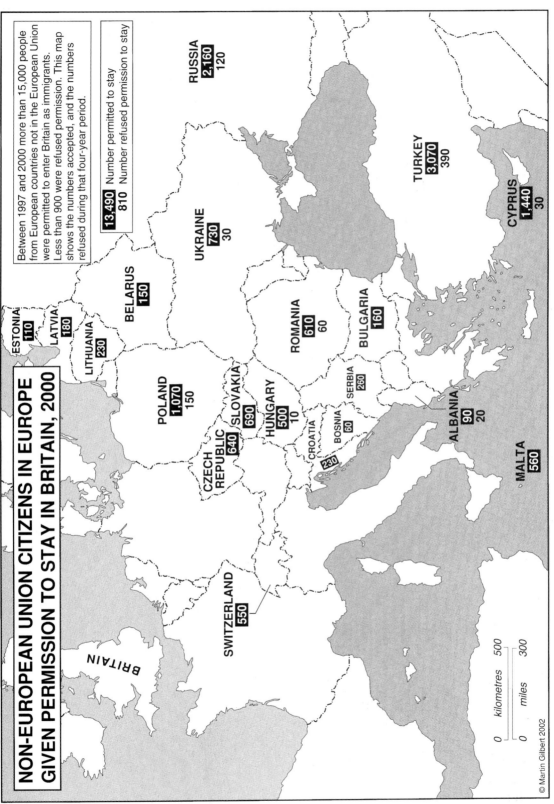

NON-EUROPEAN UNION CITIZENS IN EUROPE GIVEN PERMISSION TO STAY IN BRITAIN, 2000

Between 1997 and 2000 more than 15,000 people from European countries not in the European Union were permitted to enter Britain as immigrants. Less than 900 were refused permission. This map shows the numbers accepted, and the numbers refused during that four-year period.

13,490 Number permitted to stay
810 Number refused permission to stay

RUSSIA **2,160** 120

TURKEY **3,070** 390

CYPRUS **1,440** 30

UKRAINE **730** 30

BELARUS **150**

ESTONIA **110**
LATVIA **180**
LITHUANIA **230**

POLAND **1,070** 150

CZECH REPUBLIC **640**
SLOVAKIA **690**
HUNGARY **500** 10

ROMANIA **610** 60

BULGARIA **160**

SERBIA **260**
CROATIA **230**
BOSNIA **60**

ALBANIA **90** 20

MALTA **560**

SWITZERLAND **550**

BRITAIN

0 kilometres 500
0 miles 300

© Martin Gilbert 2002

BRITISH HUMANITARIAN AID OVERSEAS, 2000-2001

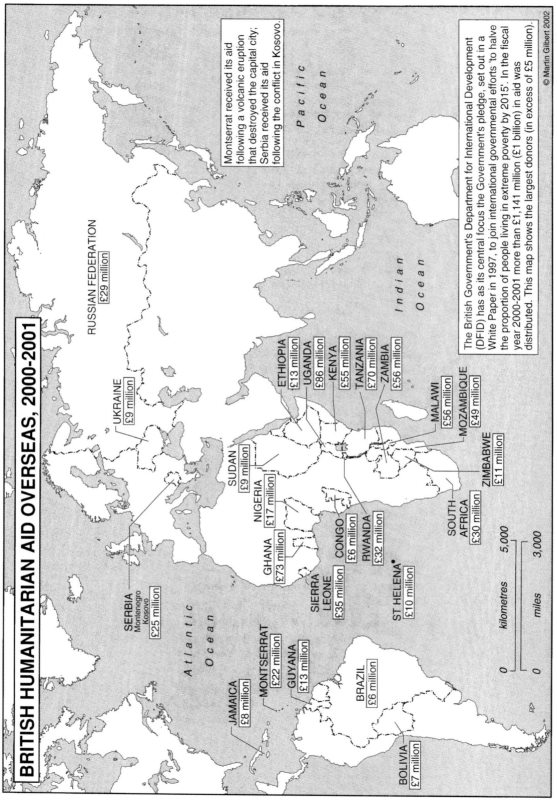

RUSSIAN FEDERATION
£29 million

UKRAINE
£9 million

Montserrat received its aid following a volcanic eruption that destroyed the capital city; Serbia received its aid following the conflict in Kosovo.

Pacific Ocean

Indian Ocean

ETHIOPIA
£13 million

UGANDA
£86 million

KENYA
£55 million

TANZANIA
£70 million

ZAMBIA
£56 million

MALAWI
£56 million

MOZAMBIQUE
£49 million

ZIMBABWE
£11 million

SOUTH AFRICA
£30 million

SUDAN
£9 million

NIGERIA
£17 million

GHANA
£73 million

CONGO
£6 million

RWANDA
£32 million

SIERRA LEONE
£35 million

ST HELENA
£10 million

SERBIA
Montenegro
Kosovo
£25 million

Atlantic Ocean

JAMAICA
£8 million

MONTSERRAT
£22 million

GUYANA
£13 million

BRAZIL
£6 million

BOLIVIA
£7 million

kilometres
0   5,000

miles
0   3,000

The British Government's Department for International Development (DFID) has as its central focus the Government's pledge, set out in a White Paper in 1997, to join international governmental efforts 'to halve the proportion of people living in extreme poverty by 2015'. In the fiscal year 2000-2001 more than £1,141 million (£1 billion) in aid was distributed. This map shows the largest donors (in excess of £5 million).

© Martin Gilbert 2002

154

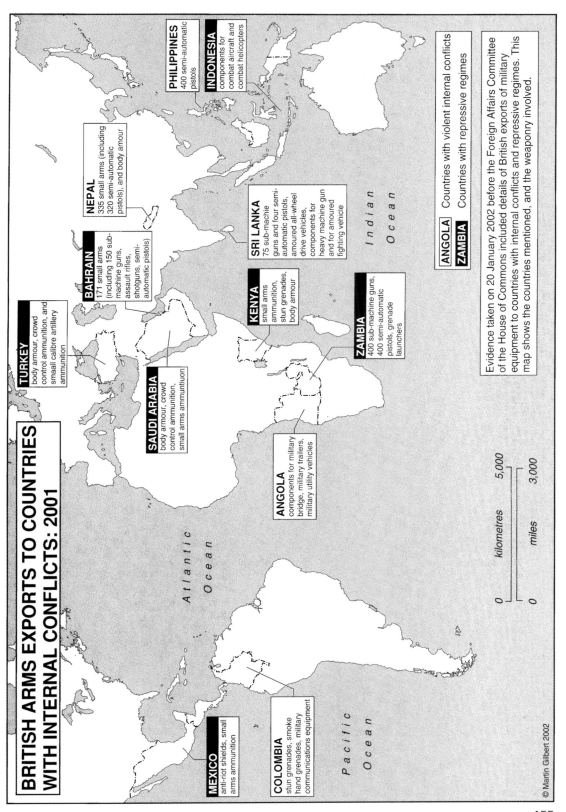

BRITISH ARMS EXPORTS TO COUNTRIES WITH INTERNAL CONFLICTS: 2001

PHILIPPINES
400 semi-automatic pistols

INDONESIA
components for combat aircraft and combat helicopters

NEPAL
335 small arms (including 320 semi-automatic pistols), and body amour

BAHRAIN
171 small arms (including 150 sub-machine guns, assault rifles, shotguns, semi-automatic pistols)

TURKEY
body armour, crowd control ammunition, and smaall calibre artillery ammunition

SAUDI ARABIA
body armour, crowd control ammunition, small arms ammuntiuon

SRI LANKA
75 sub-machie guns and four semi-automatic pistols, amoured all-wheel drive vehicles, components for heavy machine gun and for amoured fighting vehicle

KENYA
small arms ammunition, stun grenades, body armour

ZAMBIA
400 sub-machine guns, 400 semi-automatic pistols, grenade launchers

ANGOLA
components for military bridge, military trailers, military utility vehicles

MEXICO
anti-riot shields, small arms ammunition

COLOMBIA
stun grenades, smoke hand grenades, military communications equipment

Atlantic Ocean

Pacific Ocean

Indian Ocean

ANGOLA Countries with violent internal conflicts
ZAMBIA Countries with repressive regimes

Evidence taken on 20 January 2002 before the Foreign Affairs Committee of the House of Commons included details of British exports of military equipment to countries with internal conflicts and repressive regimes. This map shows the countries mentioned, and the weaponry involved.

0 kilometres	5,000	
0 miles	3,000	

© Martin Gilbert 2002

155

WRITERS IN PRISON, CHAMPIONED BY ENGLISH PEN

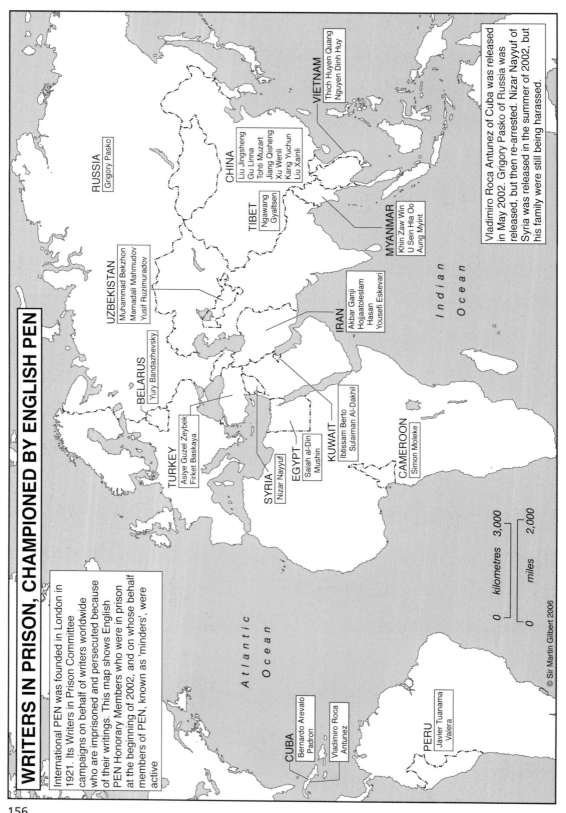

International PEN was founded in London in 1921. Its Writers in Prison Committee campaigns on behalf of writers worldwide who are imprisoned and persecuted because of their writings. This map shows English PEN Honorary Members who were in prison at the beginning of 2002, and on whose behalf members of PEN, known as 'minders', were active

RUSSIA
Grigory Pasko

VIETNAM
Thich Huyen Quang
Nguyen Dinh Huy

CHINA
Liu Jingsheng
Gu Linna
Tohti Muzart
Jiang Qisheng
Xu Wenli
Kang Yuchun
Liu Xainli

TIBET
Ngawang Gyaltsen

MYANMAR
Khin Zaw Win
U Sein Hla Oo
Aung Myint

UZBEKISTAN
Muhammad Bekzhon
Mamadali Mahmudov
Yusif Ruzimuradov

BELARUS
Yury Bandazhevsky

IRAN
Akbar Ganji
Hojjaatoleslam
Hasan
Yousefi Eskevari

TURKEY
Asiye Guzel Zeybek
Firket Baskaya

SYRIA
Nizar Nayyuf

EGYPT
Salah al-Din
Mushin

KUWAIT
Ibtissam Berto
Sulaiman Al-Dakhil

CAMEROON
Simon Moleke

CUBA
Bernardo Arevalo
Padron
Vladimiro Roca
Antunez

PERU
Javier Tuanama
Valera

Vladimiro Roca Antunez of Cuba was released in May 2002. Grigory Pasko of Russia was released, but then re-arrested. Nizar Nayyuf of Syria was released in the summer of 2002, but his family were still being harassed.

Atlantic Ocean

Indian Ocean

0   kilometres   3,000

0   miles   2,000

© Sir Martin Gilbert 2006

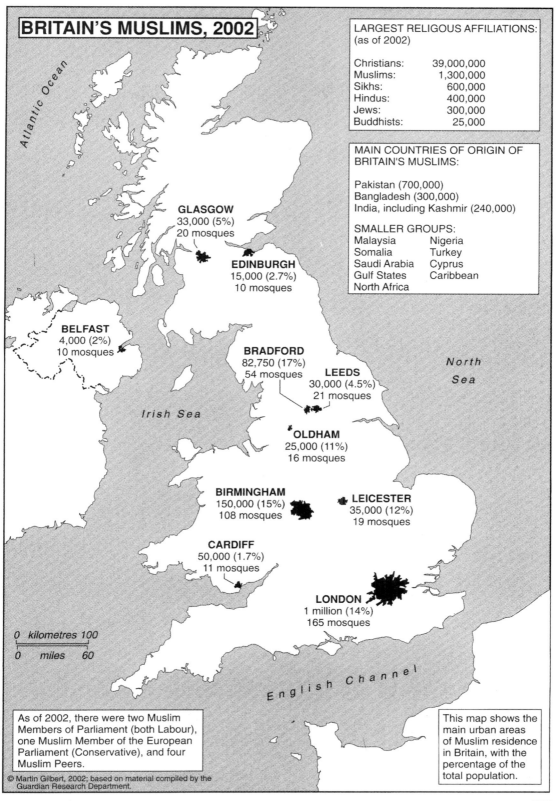

BRITAIN'S MUSLIMS, 2002

Atlantic Ocean

LARGEST RELIGOUS AFFILIATIONS:
(as of 2002)

Christians: 39,000,000
Muslims: 1,300,000
Sikhs: 600,000
Hindus: 400,000
Jews: 300,000
Buddhists: 25,000

MAIN COUNTRIES OF ORIGIN OF BRITAIN'S MUSLIMS:

Pakistan (700,000)
Bangladesh (300,000)
India, including Kashmir (240,000)

SMALLER GROUPS:
Malaysia   Nigeria
Somalia   Turkey
Saudi Arabia   Cyprus
Gulf States   Caribbean
North Africa

GLASGOW
33,000 (5%)
20 mosques

EDINBURGH
15,000 (2.7%)
10 mosques

North Sea

BELFAST
4,000 (2%)
10 mosques

BRADFORD
82,750 (17%)
54 mosques

LEEDS
30,000 (4.5%)
21 mosques

Irish Sea

OLDHAM
25,000 (11%)
16 mosques

BIRMINGHAM
150,000 (15%)
108 mosques

LEICESTER
35,000 (12%)
19 mosques

CARDIFF
50,000 (1.7%)
11 mosques

LONDON
1 million (14%)
165 mosques

0 kilometres 100
0   miles   60

English Channel

As of 2002, there were two Muslim Members of Parliament (both Labour), one Muslim Member of the European Parliament (Conservative), and four Muslim Peers.

© Martin Gilbert, 2002; based on material compiled by the Guardian Research Department.

This map shows the main urban areas of Muslim residence in Britain, with the percentage of the total population.

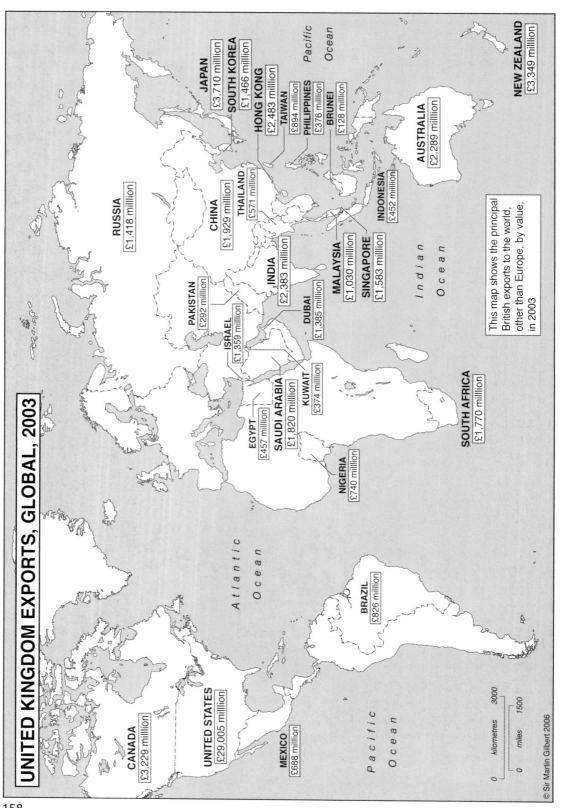

UNITED KINGDOM EXPORTS, GLOBAL, 2003

CANADA £3,229 million

UNITED STATES £29,005 million

MEXICO £688 million

BRAZIL £826 million

RUSSIA £1,418 million

PAKISTAN £292 million

ISRAEL £1,359 million

EGYPT £457 million

SAUDI ARABIA £1,820 million

KUWAIT £374 million

DUBAI £1,385 million

INDIA £2,383 million

CHINA £1,929 million

THAILAND £571 million

JAPAN £3,710 million

SOUTH KOREA £1,466 million

HONG KONG £2,483 million

TAIWAN £894 million

PHILIPPINES £376 million

BRUNEI £128 million

MALAYSIA £1,030 million

SINGAPORE £1,583 million

INDONESIA £452 million

NIGERIA £740 million

SOUTH AFRICA £1,770 million

AUSTRALIA £2,289 million

NEW ZEALAND £3,349 million

This map shows the principal British exports to the world, other than Europe, by value, in 2003

Pacific Ocean

Indian Ocean

Atlantic Ocean

Pacific Ocean

0   kilometres   3000

0   miles   1500

© Sir Martin Gilbert 2006

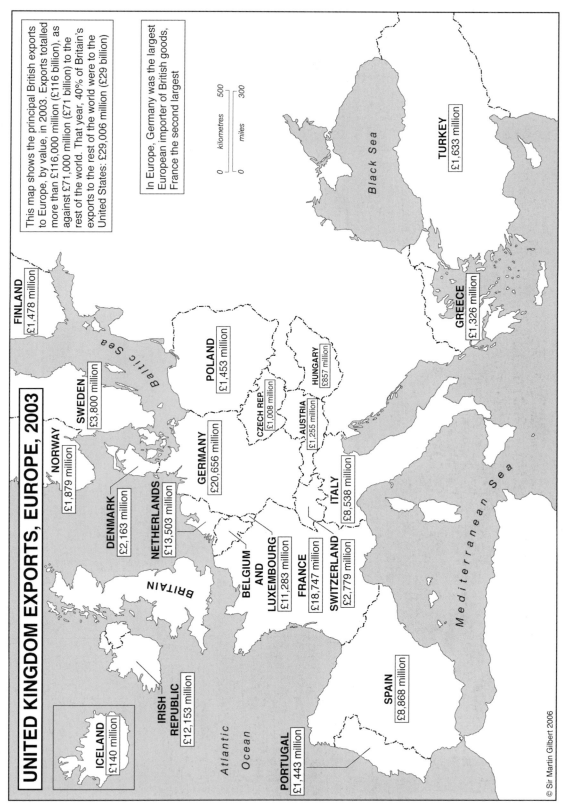

UNITED KINGDOM EXPORTS, EUROPE, 2003

This map shows the principal British exports to Europe, by value, in 2003. Exports totalled more than £116,000 million (£116 billion), as against £71,000 million (£71 billion) to the rest of the world. That year, 40% of Britain's exports to the rest of the world were to the United States: £29,006 million (£29 billion)

In Europe, Germany was the largest European importer of British goods, France the second largest

ICELAND £140 million

IRISH REPUBLIC £12,153 million

FINLAND £1,478 million

NORWAY £1,879 million

SWEDEN £3,800 million

Baltic Sea

DENMARK £2,163 million

NETHERLANDS £13,503 million

GERMANY £20,656 million

POLAND £1,453 million

CZECH REP. £1,008 million

HUNGARY £857 million

AUSTRIA £1,255 million

BELGIUM AND LUXEMBOURG £11,283 million

FRANCE £18,747 million

SWITZERLAND £2,779 million

ITALY £8,538 million

BRITAIN

Atlantic Ocean

PORTUGAL £1,443 million

SPAIN £8,868 million

Mediterranean Sea

GREECE £1,326 million

TURKEY £1,633 million

Black Sea

0 — 500 kilometres
0 — 300 miles

© Sir Martin Gilbert 2006

159

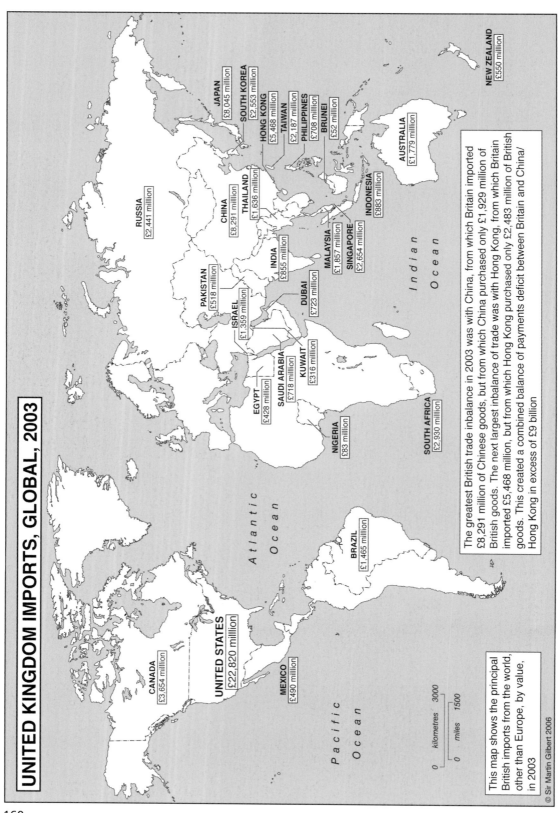

UNITED KINGDOM IMPORTS, GLOBAL, 2003

RUSSIA
£2,441 million

JAPAN
£8,045 million

SOUTH KOREA
£2,553 million

HONG KONG
£5,468 million

TAIWAN
£2,187 million

PHILIPPINES
£708 million

BRUNEI
£52 million

AUSTRALIA
£1,779 million

NEW ZEALAND
£550 million

CHINA
£8,291 million

THAILAND
£1,636 million

INDONESIA
£883 million

PAKISTAN
£518 million

INDIA
£855 million

MALAYSIA
£1,857 million

SINGAPORE
£2,654 million

ISRAEL
£1,359 million

DUBAI
£723 million

EGYPT
£428 million

SAUDI ARABIA
£718 million

KUWAIT
£316 million

NIGERIA
£83 million

SOUTH AFRICA
£2,930 million

Indian Ocean

Atlantic Ocean

BRAZIL
£1,465 million

CANADA
£3,654 million

UNITED STATES
£22,820 million

MEXICO
£490 million

Pacific Ocean

The greatest British trade inbalance in 2003 was with China, from which Britain imported £8,291 million of Chinese goods, but from which China purchased only £1,929 million of British goods. The next largest inbalance of trade was with Hong Kong, from which Britain imported £5,468 million, but from which Hong Kong purchased only £2,483 million of British goods. This created a combined balance of payments deficit between Britain and China/Hong Kong in excess of £9 billion

0   kilometres   3000

0   miles   1500

This map shows the principal British imports from the world, other than Europe, by value, in 2003

© Sir Martin Gilbert 2006

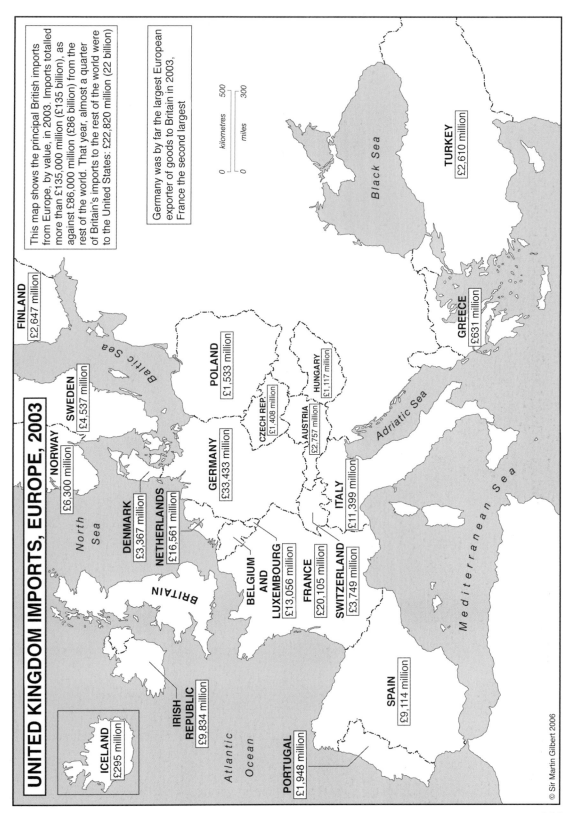

UNITED KINGDOM IMPORTS, EUROPE, 2003

This map shows the principal British imports from Europe, by value, in 2003. Imports totalled more than £135,000 million (£135 billion), as against £86,000 million (£86 billion) from the rest of the world. That year, almost a quarter of Britain's imports to the rest of the world were to the United States: £22,820 million (22 billion)

Germany was by far the largest European exporter of goods to Britain in 2003, France the second largest

ICELAND £295 million

FINLAND £2,647 million

NORWAY £6,300 million

SWEDEN £4,537 million

DENMARK £3,367 million

NETHERLANDS £16,561 million

IRISH REPUBLIC £9,834 million

BELGIUM AND LUXEMBOURG £13,056 million

GERMANY £33,433 million

POLAND £1,533 million

CZECH REP. £1,408 million

AUSTRIA £2,757 million

HUNGARY £1,117 million

FRANCE £20,105 million

SWITZERLAND £3,749 million

ITALY £11,399 million

PORTUGAL £1,948 million

SPAIN £9,114 million

GREECE £631 million

TURKEY £2,610 million

North Sea

Baltic Sea

Atlantic Ocean

BRITAIN

Adriatic Sea

Mediterranean Sea

Black Sea

0   kilometres   500

0   miles   300

© Sir Martin Gilbert 2006

161

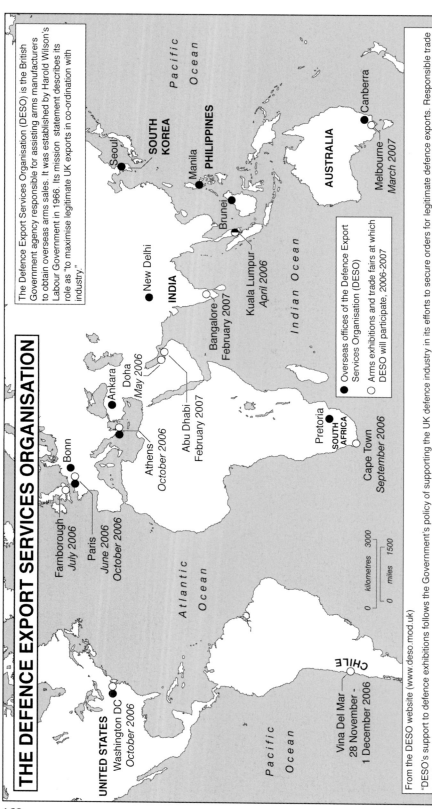

THE DEFENCE EXPORT SERVICES ORGANISATION

The Defence Export Services Organisation (DESO) is the British Government agency responsible for assisting arms manufacturers to obtain overseas arms sales. It was established by Harold Wilson's Labour Government in 1966. Its mission statement describes its role as "to maximise legitimate UK exports in co-ordination with industry."

UNITED STATES
Washington DC
October 2006

Bonn

Farnborough
July 2006

Paris
June 2006

Doha
May 2006

Ankara

Athens
October 2006

Abu Dhabi
February 2007

INDIA
New Delhi

Bangalore
February 2007

Kuala Lumpur
April 2006

Brunei

SOUTH KOREA
Seoul

Manila
PHILIPPINES

AUSTRALIA

Canberra

Melbourne
March 2007

SOUTH AFRICA
Pretoria

Cape Town
September 2006

CHILE

Vina Del Mar
28 November - 1 December 2006

Pacific Ocean

Atlantic Ocean

Indian Ocean

Pacific Ocean

● Overseas offices of the Defence Export Services Organisation (DESO)
○ Arms exhibitions and trade fairs at which DESO will participate, 2006-2007

0   kilometres   3000
0   miles   1500

© Sir Martin Gilbert 2006

From the DESO website (www.deso.mod.uk)

"DESO's support to defence exhibitions follows the Government's policy of supporting the UK defence industry in its efforts to secure orders for legitimate defence exports. Responsible trade in defence exports, together with our own defence efforts, can help ensure security and peace around the world, by providing the UK's friends and allies with equipment necessary for self-defence"

"Defence exhibitions enable prospective purchasers and manufacturers of equipment to come together at a central point. They provide a very effective facility for the UK defence industry to demonstrate its product range to potential overseas customers. They also enable those responsible for providing equipment for our own armed forces to see the capabilities and products of other nations' defence industries"

"To assist companies exhibiting at any legitimate exhibition, DESO can provide help from an Army Equipment Support Team (EST). The EST is a special unit formed with specifically selected soldiers with operational experience to demonstrate UK manufactured equipment. When deployed, the associated cost is met by UK industry."

"Ministers and Government Officials attend legitimate exhibitions and trade fairs in line with their official duties in support of the Government's defence export policy."

PRINCIPAL BRITISH ARMS SALES OVERSEAS, 2004

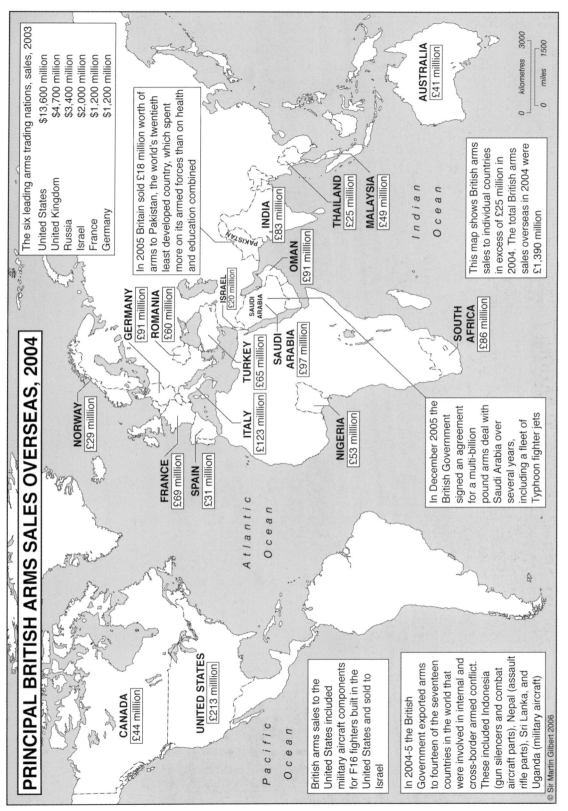

The six leading arms trading nations, sales, 2003

United States	$13,600 million
United Kingdom	$4,700 million
Russia	$3,400 million
Israel	$2,000 million
France	$1,200 million
Germany	$1,200 million

In 2005 Britain sold £18 million worth of arms to Pakistan, the world's twentieth least developed country, which spent more on its armed forces than on health and education combined

AUSTRALIA £41 million

THAILAND £25 million

MALAYSIA £49 million

Indian Ocean

INDIA £83 million

PAKISTAN

OMAN £91 million

This map shows British arms sales to individual countries in excess of £25 million in 2004. The total British arms sales overseas in 2004 were £1,390 million

GERMANY £91 million

ROMANIA £60 million

ISRAEL £20 million

SAUDI ARABIA

SOUTH AFRICA £86 million

NORWAY £29 million

TURKEY £65 million

SAUDI ARABIA £97 million

FRANCE £69 million

SPAIN £31 million

ITALY £123 million

NIGERIA £53 million

Atlantic Ocean

In December 2005 the British Government signed an agreement for a multi-billion pound arms deal with Saudi Arabia over several years, including a fleet of Typhoon fighter jets

CANADA £44 million

UNITED STATES £213 million

Pacific Ocean

British arms sales to the United States included military aircraft components for F-16 fighters built in the United States and sold to Israel

In 2004-5 the British Government exported arms to fourteen of the seventeen countries in the world that were involved in internal and cross-border armed conflict. These included Indonesia (gun silencers and combat aircraft parts), Nepal (assault rifle parts), Sri Lanka, and Uganda (military aircraft)

0   kilometres   3000
0   miles   1500

© Sir Martin Gilbert 2006

UNITED KINGDOM CITIZENSHIP APPLICATIONS GRANTED, 2004: EUROPE

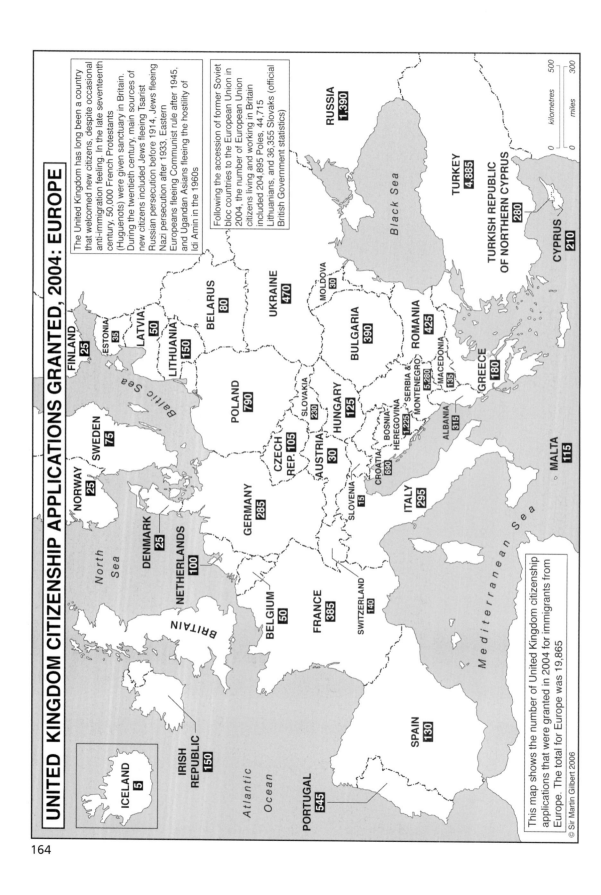

The United Kingdom has long been a country that welcomed new citizens, despite occasional anti-immigration feeling. In the late seventeenth century, 50,000 French Protestants (Huguenots) were given sanctuary in Britain. During the twentieth century, main sources of new citizens included Jews fleeing Tsarist Russian persecution before 1914, Jews fleeing Nazi persecution after 1933, Eastern Europeans fleeing Communist rule after 1945, and Ugandan Asians fleeing the hostility of Idi Amin in the 1960s

Following the accession of former Soviet bloc countries to the European Union in 2004, the number of European Union citizens living and working in Britain included 204,895 Poles, 44,715 Lithuanians, and 36,355 Slovaks (official British Government statistics)

ICELAND 5

IRISH REPUBLIC 150

PORTUGAL 545

SPAIN 130

FRANCE 385

BELGIUM 50

NETHERLANDS 100

DENMARK 25

NORWAY 25

SWEDEN 75

FINLAND 25

ESTONIA 35

LATVIA 50

LITHUANIA 150

BELARUS 80

UKRAINE 470

MOLDOVA 30

RUSSIA 1,390

GERMANY 285

SWITZERLAND 140

CZECH REP. 105

AUSTRIA 30

POLAND 790

SLOVAKIA 280

HUNGARY 125

SLOVENIA 15

CROATIA 690

BOSNIA HERCEGOVINA 1,225

SERBIA & MONTENEGRO 5,280

ITALY 295

MALTA 115

ALBANIA 315

MACEDONIA 185

BULGARIA 390

ROMANIA 425

GREECE 180

TURKEY 4,885

TURKISH REPUBLIC OF NORTHERN CYPRUS 280

CYPRUS 210

Black Sea

North Sea

Baltic Sea

Atlantic Ocean

Mediterranean Sea

BRITAIN

0   kilometres   500

0   miles   300

This map shows the number of United Kingdom citizenship applications that were granted in 2004 for immigrants from Europe. The total for Europe was 19,865

© Sir Martin Gilbert 2006

164

UNITED KINGDOM CITIZENSHIP APPLICATIONS GRANTED, 2004: ASIA

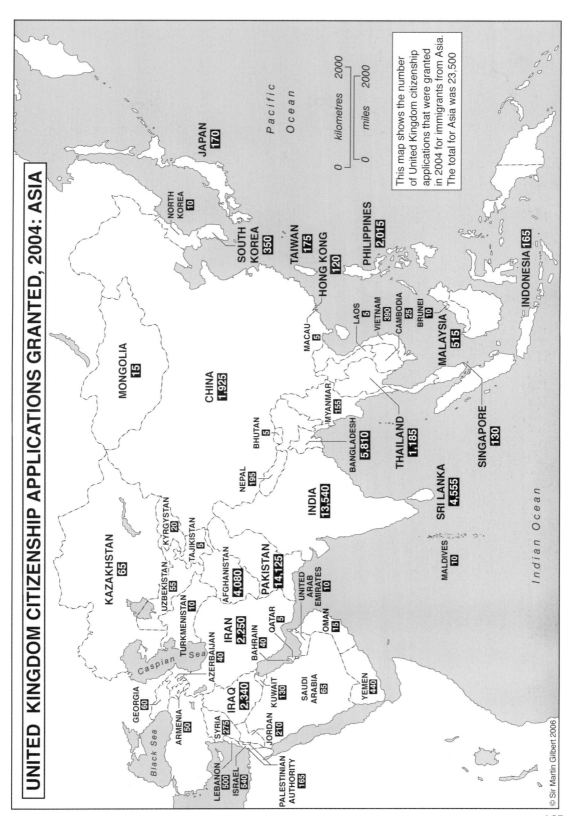

This map shows the number of United Kingdom citizenship applications that were granted in 2004 for immigrants from Asia. The total for Asia was 23,500.

JAPAN 170

NORTH KOREA 10

SOUTH KOREA 350

TAIWAN 175

HONG KONG 120

PHILIPPINES 2,015

INDONESIA 165

Pacific Ocean

MONGOLIA 15

CHINA 1,925

MACAU 5

LAOS 5

VIETNAM 390

CAMBODIA 25

BRUNEI 10

MALAYSIA 515

SINGAPORE 130

MYANMAR 155

BHUTAN 5

BANGLADESH 5,810

THAILAND 1,185

SRI LANKA 4,555

NEPAL 195

INDIA 13,540

MALDIVES 10

Indian Ocean

KAZAKHSTAN 65

KYRGYSTAN 20

TAJIKISTAN 5

UZBEKISTAN 55

TURKMENISTAN 10

AFGHANISTAN 4,080

PAKISTAN 14,125

UNITED ARAB EMIRATES 10

OMAN 15

IRAN 2,250

QATAR 5

AZERBAIJAN 40

BAHRAIN 40

KUWAIT 130

SAUDI ARABIA 65

YEMEN 440

GEORGIA 60

ARMENIA 50

IRAQ 2,340

SYRIA 275

JORDAN 210

LEBANON 500

ISRAEL 540

PALESTINIAN AUTHORITY 165

Caspian Sea

Black Sea

© Sir Martin Gilbert 2006

kilometres 0 2000

miles 0 2000

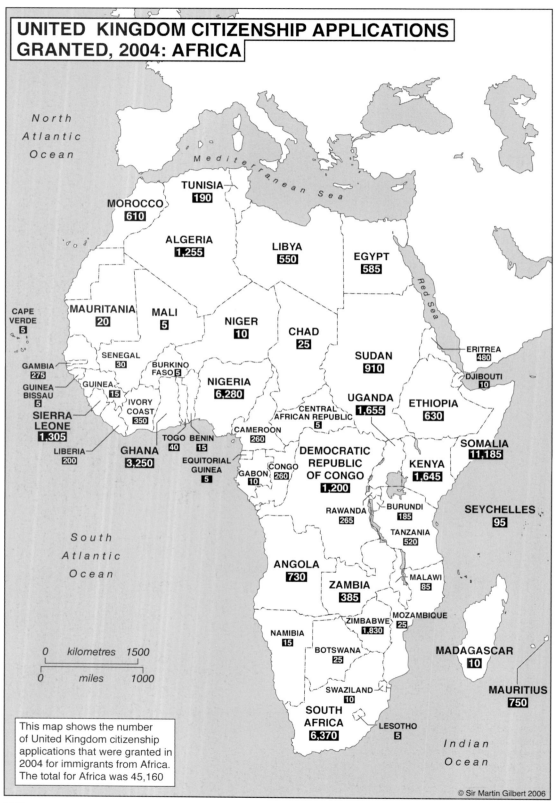

UNITED KINGDOM CITIZENSHIP APPLICATIONS GRANTED, 2004: AFRICA

North Atlantic Ocean

Mediterranean Sea

TUNISIA 190

MOROCCO 610

ALGERIA 1,255

LIBYA 550

EGYPT 585

Red Sea

CAPE VERDE 5

MAURITANIA 20

MALI 5

NIGER 10

CHAD 25

SUDAN 910

ERITREA 480

DJIBOUTI 10

GAMBIA 275

SENEGAL 30

BURKINO FASO 5

NIGERIA 6,280

UGANDA 1,655

ETHIOPIA 630

GUINEA BISSAU 5

GUINEA 15

SIERRA LEONE 1,305

IVORY COAST 350

CENTRAL AFRICAN REPUBLIC 5

SOMALIA 11,185

LIBERIA 200

GHANA 3,250

TOGO 40 BENIN 15

CAMEROON 260

DEMOCRATIC REPUBLIC OF CONGO 1,200

KENYA 1,645

EQUITORIAL GUINEA 5

GABON 10 CONGO 260

RAWANDA 265

BURUNDI 185

SEYCHELLES 95

TANZANIA 520

South Atlantic Ocean

ANGOLA 730

ZAMBIA 385

MALAWI 85

MOZAMBIQUE 25

NAMIBIA 15

ZIMBABWE 1,830

MADAGASCAR 10

BOTSWANA 25

SWAZILAND 10

MAURITIUS 750

0 kilometres 1500

0 miles 1000

SOUTH AFRICA 6,370

LESOTHO 5

Indian Ocean

This map shows the number of United Kingdom citizenship applications that were granted in 2004 for immigrants from Africa. The total for Africa was 45,160

© Sir Martin Gilbert 2006

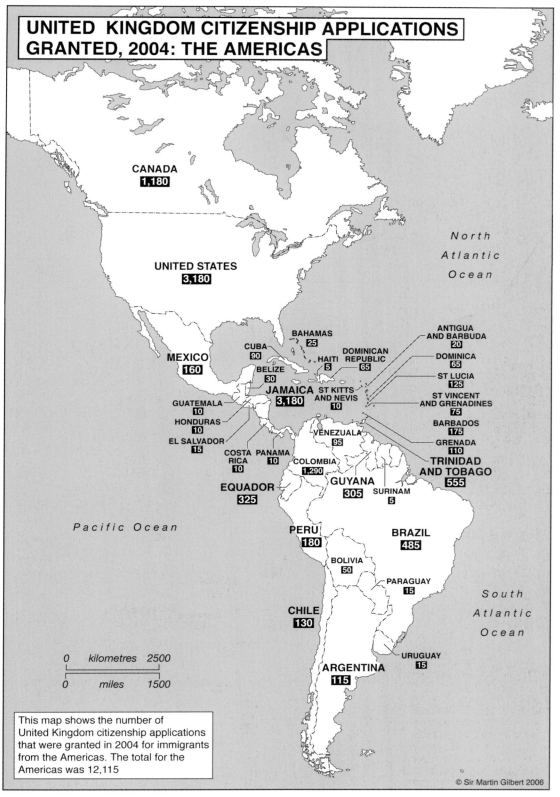

UNITED KINGDOM CITIZENSHIP APPLICATIONS GRANTED, 2004: THE AMERICAS

CANADA
1,180

North Atlantic Ocean

UNITED STATES
3,180

BAHAMAS **25**

ANTIGUA AND BARBUDA **20**

CUBA **90**

HAITI **5**

DOMINICAN REPUBLIC **65**

DOMINICA **65**

MEXICO **160**

BELIZE **30**

ST LUCIA **125**

JAMAICA **3,180**

ST KITTS AND NEVIS **10**

ST VINCENT AND GRENADINES **75**

GUATEMALA **10**

BARBADOS **175**

HONDURAS **10**

VENEZUALA **95**

GRENADA **110**

EL SALVADOR **15**

COSTA RICA **10**

PANAMA **10**

COLOMBIA **1,290**

TRINIDAD AND TOBAGO **555**

EQUADOR **325**

GUYANA **305**

SURINAM **5**

Pacific Ocean

PERU **180**

BRAZIL **485**

BOLIVIA **50**

PARAGUAY **15**

South Atlantic Ocean

CHILE **130**

URUGUAY **15**

ARGENTINA **115**

| 0 | kilometres | 2500 |
| 0 | miles | 1500 |

This map shows the number of
United Kingdom citizenship applications
that were granted in 2004 for immigrants
from the Americas. The total for the
Americas was 12,115

© Sir Martin Gilbert 2006

167

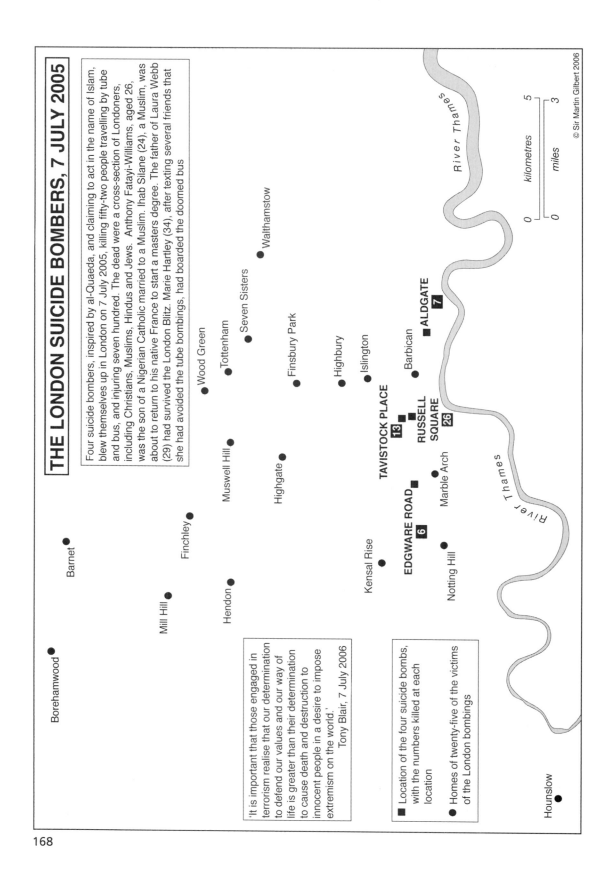

THE LONDON SUICIDE BOMBERS, 7 JULY 2005

Four suicide bombers, inspired by al-Quaeda, and claiming to act in the name of Islam, blew themselves up in London on 7 July 2005, killing fifty-two people travelling by tube and bus, and injuring seven hundred. The dead were a cross-section of Londoners, including Christians, Muslims, Hindus and Jews. Anthony Fatayi-Williams, aged 26, was the son of a Nigerian Catholic married to a Muslim. Ihab Silane (24), a Muslim, was about to return to his native France to start a masters degree. The father of Laura Webb (29) had survived the London Blitz. Marie Hartley (34), after texting several friends that she had avoided the tube bombings, had boarded the doomed bus

'It is important that those engaged in terrorism realise that our determination to defend our values and our way of life is greater than their determination to cause death and destruction to innocent people in a desire to impose extremism on the world.'
Tony Blair, 7 July 2006

■ Location of the four suicide bombs, with the numbers killed at each location

● Homes of twenty-five of the victims of the London bombings

Borehamwood

Barnet

Mill Hill

Finchley

Hendon

Muswell Hill

Highgate

Kensal Rise

Notting Hill

Hounslow

EDGWARE ROAD **6**

Marble Arch

TAVISTOCK PLACE **13**

RUSSELL SQUARE **26**

Wood Green

Tottenham

Seven Sisters

Walthamstow

Finsbury Park

Highbury

Islington

Barbican

ALDGATE **7**

River Thames

River Thames

0   kilometres   5
0   miles   3

© Sir Martin Gilbert 2006

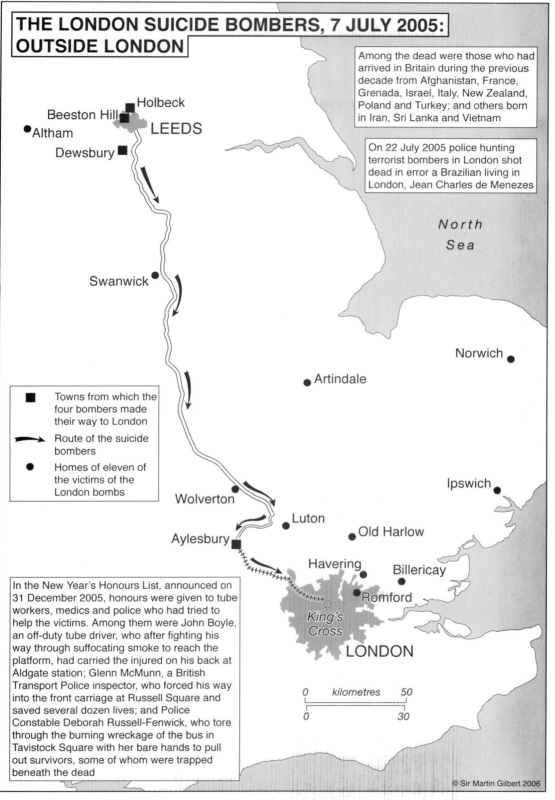

THE LONDON SUICIDE BOMBERS, 7 JULY 2005: OUTSIDE LONDON

Among the dead were those who had arrived in Britain during the previous decade from Afghanistan, France, Grenada, Israel, Italy, New Zealand, Poland and Turkey; and others born in Iran, Sri Lanka and Vietnam

On 22 July 2005 police hunting terrorist bombers in London shot dead in error a Brazilian living in London, Jean Charles de Menezes

Holbeck

Beeston Hill

Altham

LEEDS

Dewsbury

North Sea

Swanwick

Norwich

Artindale

■ Towns from which the four bombers made their way to London

➤ Route of the suicide bombers

● Homes of eleven of the victims of the London bombs

Ipswich

Wolverton

Luton

Old Harlow

Aylesbury

Havering

Billericay

Romford

King's Cross

LONDON

In the New Year's Honours List, announced on 31 December 2005, honours were given to tube workers, medics and police who had tried to help the victims. Among them were John Boyle, an off-duty tube driver, who after fighting his way through suffocating smoke to reach the platform, had carried the injured on his back at Aldgate station; Glenn McMunn, a British Transport Police inspector, who forced his way into the front carriage at Russell Square and saved several dozen lives; and Police Constable Deborah Russell-Fenwick, who tore through the burning wreckage of the bus in Tavistock Square with her bare hands to pull out survivors, some of whom were trapped beneath the dead

0 kilometres 50

0 30

© Sir Martin Gilbert 2006

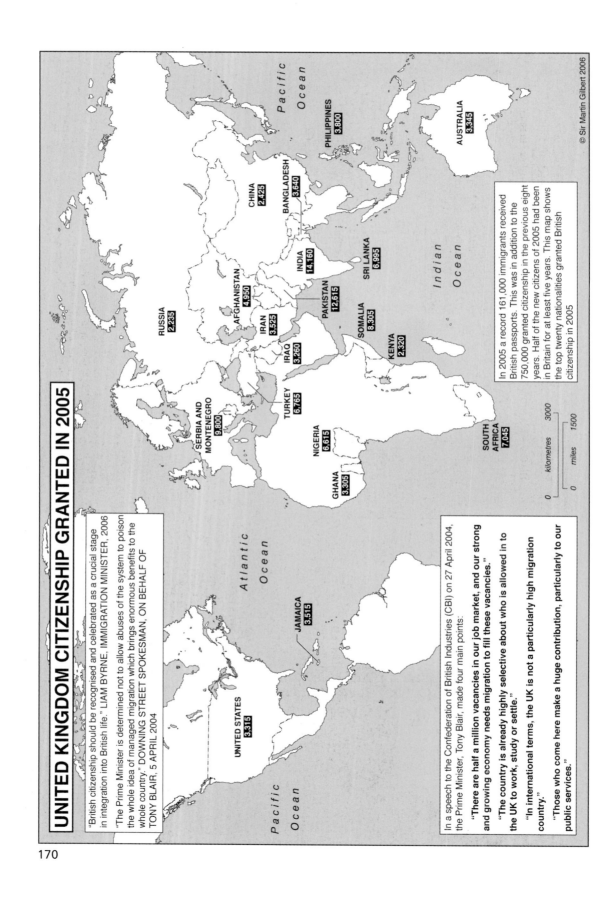

UNITED KINGDOM CITIZENSHIP GRANTED IN 2005

"British citizenship should be recognised and celebrated as a crucial stage in integration into British life." LIAM BYRNE, IMMIGRATION MINISTER, 2006

"The Prime Minister is determined not to allow abuses of the system to poison the whole idea of managed migration which brings enormous benefits to the whole country." DOWNING STREET SPOKESMAN, ON BEHALF OF TONY BLAIR, 5 APRIL 2004

In 2005 a record 161,000 immigrants received British passports. This was in addition to the 750,000 granted citizenship in the previous eight years. Half of the new citizens of 2005 had been in Britain for at least five years. This map shows the top twenty nationalities granted British citizenship in 2005

In a speech to the Confederation of British Industries (CBI) on 27 April 2004, the Prime Minister, Tony Blair, made four main points:

"There are half a million vacancies in our job market, and our strong and growing economy needs migration to fill these vacancies."

"The country is already highly selective about who is allowed in to the UK to work, study or settle."

"In international terms, the UK is not a particularly high migration country."

"Those who come here make a huge contribution, particularly to our public services."

© Sir Martin Gilbert 2006

UNITED STATES 3,315

JAMAICA 3,515

RUSSIA 2,235

SERBIA AND MONTENEGRO 9,800

TURKEY 6,765

GHANA 3,305

NIGERIA 6,615

IRAQ 3,260

IRAN 3,525

AFGHANISTAN 4,950

SOUTH AFRICA 7,045

KENYA 2,320

SOMALIA 8,305

PAKISTAN 12,615

INDIA 14,160

SRI LANKA 6,995

CHINA 2,425

BANGLADESH 3,640

PHILIPPINES 3,800

AUSTRALIA 3,345

Pacific Ocean

Atlantic Ocean

Pacific Ocean

Indian Ocean

0   kilometres   3000
0   miles   1500

170

GLOBAL IMPORTS: FRESH FRUIT AND VEGETABLES ON SALE IN LONDON

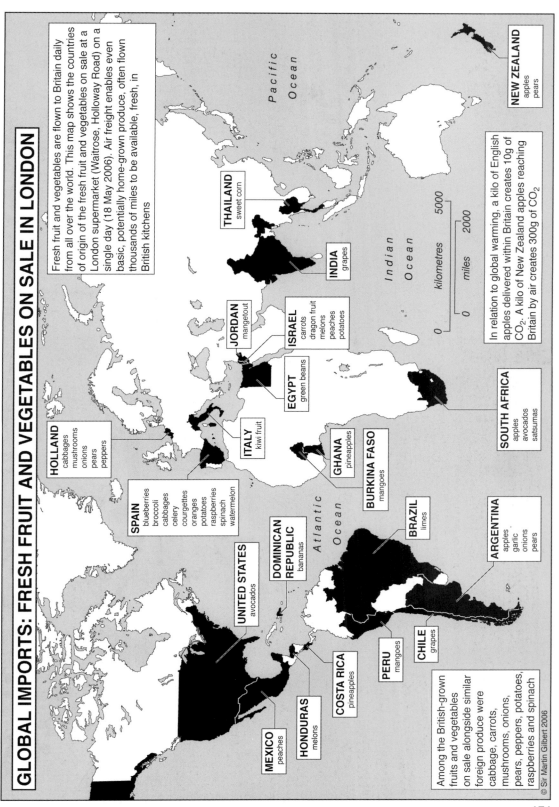

Fresh fruit and vegetables are flown to Britain daily from all over the world. This map shows the countries of origin of the fresh fruit and vegetables on sale at a London supermarket (Waitrose, Holloway Road) on a single day (18 May 2006). Air freight enables even basic, potentially home-grown produce, often flown thousands of miles to be available, fresh, in British kitchens

In relation to global warming, a kilo of English apples delivered within Britain creates 10g of CO₂. A kilo of New Zealand apples reaching Britain by air creates 300g of CO₂

Among the British-grown fruits and vegetables on sale alongside similar foreign produce were cabbage, carrots, mushrooms, onions, pears, peppers, potatoes, raspberries and spinach

Pacific Ocean

Indian Ocean

Atlantic Ocean

kilometres   5000

0   miles   2000

0

NEW ZEALAND
apples
pears

THAILAND
sweet corn

INDIA
grapes

JORDAN
mangetout

ISRAEL
carrots
dragon fruit
melons
peaches
potatoes

EGYPT
green beans

ITALY
kiwi fruit

GHANA
pineapples

BURKINA FASO
mangoes

SOUTH AFRICA
apples
avocados
satsumas

HOLLAND
cabbages
mushrooms
onions
pears
peppers

SPAIN
blueberries
broccoli
cabbages
celery
courgettes
oranges
potatoes
raspberries
spinach
watermelon

BRAZIL
limes

ARGENTINA
apples
garlic
onions
pears

CHILE
grapes

PERU
mangoes

COSTA RICA
pineapples

DOMINICAN REPUBLIC
bananas

UNITED STATES
avocados

HONDURAS
melons

MEXICO
peaches

171

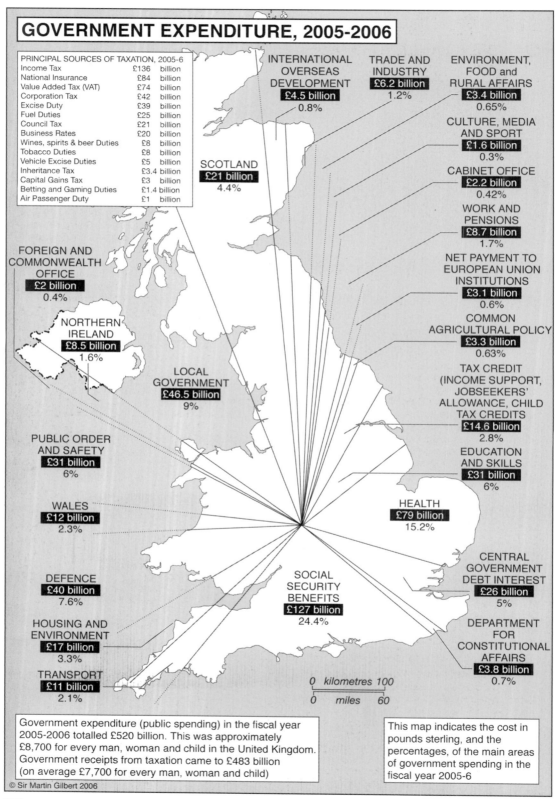

GOVERNMENT EXPENDITURE, 2005-2006

PRINCIPAL SOURCES OF TAXATION, 2005-6

Income Tax	£136	billion
National Insurance	£84	billion
Value Added Tax (VAT)	£74	billion
Corporation Tax	£42	billion
Excise Duty	£39	billion
Fuel Duties	£25	billion
Council Tax	£21	billion
Business Rates	£20	billion
Wines, spirits & beer Duties	£8	billion
Tobacco Duties	£8	billion
Vehicle Excise Duties	£5	billion
Inheritance Tax	£3.4 billion	
Capital Gains Tax	£3	billion
Betting and Gaming Duties	£1.4 billion	
Air Passenger Duty	£1	billion

INTERNATIONAL OVERSEAS DEVELOPMENT
£4.5 billion
0.8%

TRADE AND INDUSTRY
£6.2 billion
1.2%

ENVIRONMENT, FOOD and RURAL AFFAIRS
£3.4 billion
0.65%

CULTURE, MEDIA AND SPORT
£1.6 billion
0.3%

CABINET OFFICE
£2.2 billion
0.42%

WORK AND PENSIONS
£8.7 billion
1.7%

NET PAYMENT TO EUROPEAN UNION INSTITUTIONS
£3.1 billion
0.6%

COMMON AGRICULTURAL POLICY
£3.3 billion
0.63%

TAX CREDIT (INCOME SUPPORT, JOBSEEKERS' ALLOWANCE, CHILD TAX CREDITS
£14.6 billion
2.8%

EDUCATION AND SKILLS
£31 billion
6%

SCOTLAND
£21 billion
4.4%

FOREIGN AND COMMONWEALTH OFFICE
£2 billion
0.4%

NORTHERN IRELAND
£8.5 billion
1.6%

LOCAL GOVERNMENT
£46.5 billion
9%

PUBLIC ORDER AND SAFETY
£31 billion
6%

WALES
£12 billion
2.3%

HEALTH
£79 billion
15.2%

CENTRAL GOVERNMENT DEBT INTEREST
£26 billion
5%

DEFENCE
£40 billion
7.6%

SOCIAL SECURITY BENEFITS
£127 billion
24.4%

HOUSING AND ENVIRONMENT
£17 billion
3.3%

DEPARTMENT FOR CONSTITUTIONAL AFFAIRS
£3.8 billion
0.7%

TRANSPORT
£11 billion
2.1%

0   kilometres 100
0   miles   60

Government expenditure (public spending) in the fiscal year 2005-2006 totalled £520 billion. This was approximately £8,700 for every man, woman and child in the United Kingdom. Government receipts from taxation came to £483 billion (on average £7,700 for every man, woman and child)

This map indicates the cost in pounds sterling, and the percentages, of the main areas of government spending in the fiscal year 2005-6

© Sir Martin Gilbert 2006

HOME TOWNS OF BRITISH SOLDIERS KILLED IN IRAQ, MARCH 2003 - MAY 2006

With the outbreak of hostilities on 20 March 2003, Britain, under the premiership of Tony Blair, was the principal ally of the United States, led by President George W. Bush, in the war to overthrow Saddam Hussein and establish a democratic regime in Iraq. Following the fall of Baghdad on 9 April 2003, British troops were principally based in southern Iraq, centred on the port city of Basra, where their task was to maintain and support the local Iraqi administration, while under repeated attack from Iraqi insurgents

Between 21 March 2003 and 19 May 2006, a total of 111 British service personnel died in Iraq. Of these, 87 were killed in action, the rest in accidents, of natural causes or illness. This map shows the home towns of more than fifty of them

The first British servicewoman to die in action was Flight Lieutenant Sarah-Jane Mulvihill, aged 32, from Canterbury, a Flight Operations Officer. Among those killed were six men who were engaged to be married. Many of those killed were the fathers of young children

Atlantic Ocean

Irish Sea

North Sea

English Channel

Lochgelly • Glenrothes
Perth •
Goven • Dunfermline
• Glasgow
Paisley • Edinburgh
• Irvine
Hawick •
Newcastle-upon-Tyne •
Washington •
Crawleyside •
Northallerton •
Bishopdale • Scarborough
Skipton • • York
East Brierley • • Leeds
Horse Matty
Southport •
Hoylake • Liverpool • Doncaster
Llandudno • • Wythenshawe
Denbigh • • Louth
• Ellesmere Port
Llanuwchllyn • Stoke-on-Trent
Littleworth • Swadlincote
Welshpool • • Tamworth
Walsall • North Walsham
Castle Bromwich • Nuneaton
• Haslingfield
• Colchester
Resolven • Ware •
Swindon • London • Plumstead
Warminster • • Westgate-on-Sea
Chessington • Erith
Salisbury • • Canterbury
Romsey • Winchester Crawley
Exeter • • Fareham
Tavistock • Hamworthy Poole •
• Plymouth
Helston • Falmouth
Budock Water

0 kilometres 100
0 miles 60

Among the British deaths in Iraq were members of the Argyll and Sutherland Highlanders, Black Watch, Cheshire Regiment, Coldstream Guards, Defence Fire Service, Engineer Regiment (Explosive Ordnance Disposal), Household Cavalry Regiment, Intelligence Corps, Irish Guards, King's Own Scottish Borderers, King's Royal Hussar's, Light Infantry, Lowland Regiment, Parachute Regiment, Princess of Wales' Royal Regiment, Queen's Lancashire Regiment, Royal Air Force, Royal Artillery, Royal Electrical and Mechanical Engineers (REME), Royal Green Jackets, Royal Highland Fusiliers, Royal Logistic Corps, Royal Marines, Royal Military Police, Royal Navy, Royal Regiment of Fusiliers, Royal Regiment of Wales, Royal Signals, Royal Tank Regiment, Royal Welch Fusiliers, Signal Regiment (Air Support), Staffordshire Regiment, Transport Squadron, Tyne-Tees Regiment, and Welsh Guards

© Sir Martin Gilbert 2006

173

Routledge History

The Routledge Atlas of Russian History, 4th Edition

Martin Gilbert

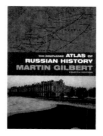

The complex and often turbulent history of Russia over the course of 2000 years is brought to life in a series of 177 maps by one of the most prolific and successful historian authors today.

This new edition of *The Routledge Atlas of Russian History* covers not simply the wars and expansion of Russia but also a wealth of less conspicuous details of its history from famine and anarchism to the growth of naval strength and the strengths of the river systems.

From 800 BC to the fall of the Soviet Union, this indispensable guide to Russian history covers:

- war and conflict: from the triumph of the Goths between 200 and 400 BC to the defeat of Germany at the end of the Second World War and the end of the Cold War.
- politics: from the rise of Moscow in the Middle Ages to revolution, the fall of the monarchy and the collapse of communism.
- industry, economics and transport: from the Trans-Siberian Railway between 1891 and 1917 to the Virgin Lands Campaign and the growth of heavy industry.
- society, trade and culture: from the growth of monasticism to peasant discontent, Labour Camps and the geographical distribution of ethnic Russians.

Now bringing new material to view, and including eight new maps, this popular atlas will more than readily gain a place on the bookshelves of anyone interested in the history of Russia.

978–0–415–39483–3 (HB)
978–0–415–39484–0 (PB)

Routledge Atlas of the Arab-Israeli Conflict, 8th Edition

Martin Gilbert

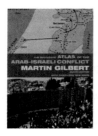

The Routledge Atlas of the Arab-Israeli Conflict traces not only the tangled and bitter history of the Arab-Jewish struggle from the early twentieth century to the present, it also illustrates the move towards finding peace and the efforts to bring the horrors of the fighting to an end through negotiation and proposals for agreed boundaries. In 155 maps, the complete history of the conflict is revealed including:

- the Prelude and Background to the Conflict: from the siting of the Palestinian Jews before the Arab Conquest to the attitude of Britain to the Arabs between 1917 and the present.
- the Jewish National Home: from the Zionist plan for Palestine in 1919 to the state of the Arab world from 1945 to 1962
- the Intensification of the Conflict: from the Arab response to the UN partition plan of 1947 to the first steps towards the independence of Israel in 1948
- the State of Israel: from the Israeli War of Independence and the Six Day War to the horrific War of Yom Kippur and the Intifada
- the Moves to find peace: from Camp David to the escalating troubles of the present day

978–0–415–35901–6
978–0–415–35900–9

Atlas of Jewish History, 7th Edition

Martin Gilbert

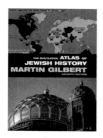

A comprehensive and detailed picture of the Jewish people in maps.
Tracing the world-wide migrations of the Jews from ancient
Mesopotamia to modern Israel, this newly updated edition spans over
four thousand years of history in 140 maps. It presents a vivid picture
of a fascinating people and the trials and tribulations which have
haunted their story. The themes covered include:

- Prejudice and Violence – from the destruction of Jewish independence between 722
  and 586 BC to the Chmielnicki Massacres 1648–1656 and the flight from German
  persecution in the 1930s
- Migrations and Movements – from the entry into the Promised Land to the exodus
  from Ethiopia between 1974 and 1984
- Society and Status – from the geography of the Jews of China between 1000 and 1932
  to the situation of the New York Jewry in 1900 and the position of the Jews of Syria
- Trade and Culture – from Jewish trade routes between 800 and 900 to the use of
  Hebrew printing presses between 1444 and 1860 and communal life in the ghettoes
- Politics, Government and War: from the Court Jews of the fifteenth century to the
  founding, wars and progress of the modern State of Israel

978–0–415–39963–4 (HB)
978–0–415–39966–1 (PB)

The Routledge Atlas of American History, 5th Edition

Martin Gilbert

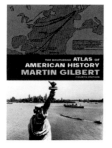

'. . . especially clear and helpful . . . well laid out and useful for quick reference'

The Economist

This new edition of *The Routledge Atlas of American History* presents a series of 157 clear and detailed maps, accompanied by informative captions, facts and figures. Updated with additional maps and text and including significant recent events, the complete history of America is unravelled through vivid representations of all the significant landmarks, including:

- politics — from the annexation of Texas to the battle for black voting rights and the results of the 2004 Presidential election
- military events — from the War of Independence and America's standing in two world wars to the conflicts in Korea, Vietnam and the Gulf, includes new maps covering the war in Iraq, the American campaign in Afghanistan and the War on Terror
- social history — from the abolition of slavery to the growth of female emancipation
- transport — from nineteenth-century railroads and canals to recent ventures into space
- economics — from early farming and industry to the state of America today.

The history of North America from early settlement to the present day is presented to students and enthusiasts of the subject in this fundamental reference book.

978–0–415–35902–3 (HB)
978–0–415–35903–X (PB)

The Routledge Atlas of the Holocaust: The Complete History

Martin Gilbert

'Another historical masterwork . . . the world's first statistical reference book showing the chronological destruction of the main Jewish communities in Europe during the 1939–45 war' – *The Daily Telegraph*

'As vivid as it is harrowing . . . many of these maps show both individual escapes and concerted resistance in a tragically one-sided struggle in which the enemy was often not just the German but the local population' – *The Economist*

The harrowing history of the Nazi attempt to annihilate the Jews of Europe during the Second World War is illustrated in this series of 320 highly detailed maps. The horror of the time is further revealed by shocking photographs. The maps do not concentrate solely on the fate of the Jews; they also set their chronological story in the broader context of the way.

978–0–415–28145–4 (HB)
978–0–415–28146–1 (PB)

Available at all good bookshops
For ordering and further information please visit:
www.routledge.com